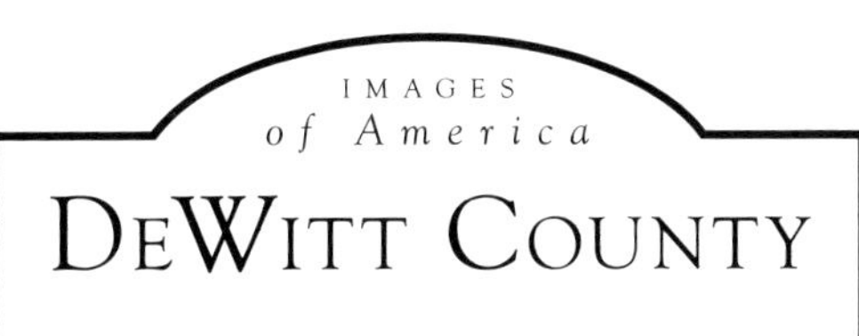
IMAGES
of America
DEWITT COUNTY

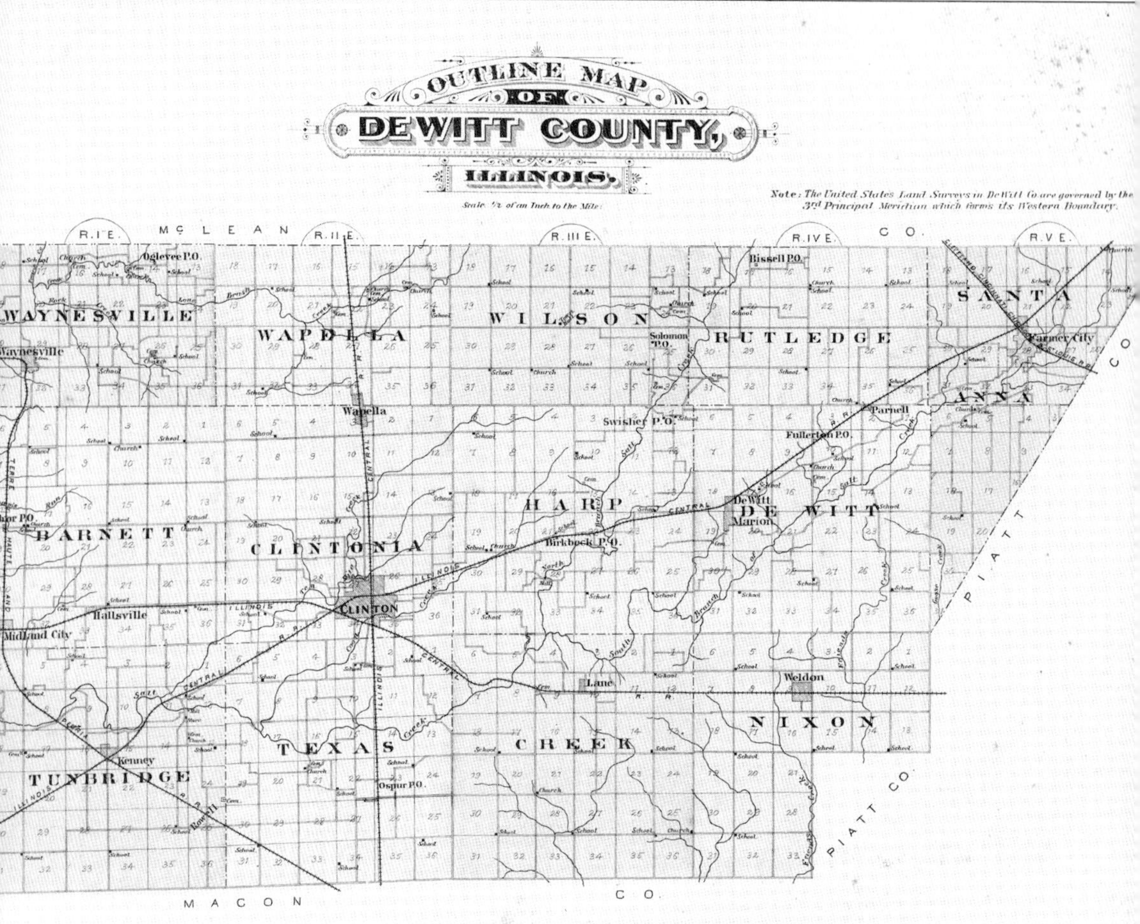

This 1894 plat shows the entire DeWitt County, shaped like an anvil missing the left side angle, by then well established with towns and small communities spread across 13 townships. Fullerton, Swisher, Bissell, Solomon, Birkbeck, Tabor, Olgevee, and Ospur apparently only had a post office. Many of the county sections had a school, usually placed near the boundary with another section. (Courtesy of the Library of Congress, Geography and Map Division.)

On the Cover: Just east of Clinton lies Weldon Springs, created as groundwater escapes from sand and gravel. It was part of an immense river valley that had been buried under glacial sediment after the ice age. This early-1900s photograph shows visitors to the park enjoying the area, purchased prior to the Civil War by Lawrence Weldon. (Courtesy of C.H. Moore Homestead and DeWitt County Museum.)

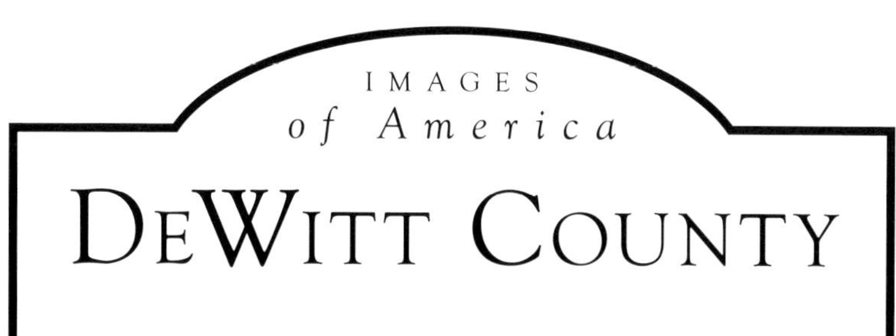

Maureen Holtz

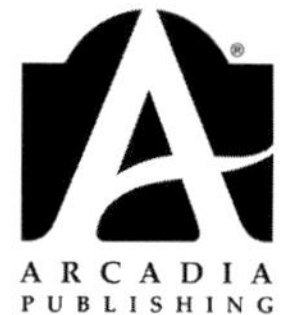

Copyright © 2026 by Maureen Holtz
ISBN 987-1-4671-6305-7

Published by Arcadia Publishing
Charleston, South Carolina

Printed in the United States of America

Library of Congress Control Number: 2025949146

For all general information, please contact Arcadia Publishing:
Telephone 843-853-2070
Fax 843-853-0044
E-mail sales@arcadiapublishing.com

Visit us on the Internet at www.arcadiapublishing.com

This book is dedicated to one source of DeWitt County lore–my husband, Michael–and to my parents, who instilled in me an appreciation for history.

Contents

Acknowledgments 6

Introduction 7

1. Clinton until the Early 1900s 9
2. Clinton into the 2000s 35
3. Farmer City 65
4. From Weldon to Weldon Springs 91
5. Waynesville and Wapella 101
6. Kenney and Hallsville 115

Acknowledgments

I thank the following libraries and staff for helping me with my research: Vespasian Warner Public Library's Bobbi Perryman and Adara Meyen; Weldon Public Library's Lori Rich; Waynesville Township Public Library staff; and Farmer City Public Library's Skye Little.

Thanks also to Steve Woods; Wapella's Jane Buraglio and Kim Donovan; Mike Morse of the Kenney Heritage Association; Joey Long, Schelli Kirby, and Larry Buss of the C.H. Moore Homestead and DeWitt County Museum Association; the DeWitt County Genealogical Society's Terri Lemmel and Joann Manley; and Farmer City Genealogical & Historical Society volunteers Susan Ryan, Bob Tharp, and Bob Scarborough. Also many thanks to collectors Mark Woods, Lynn Almacher, Ken Atchison, the McLean County Museum of History, and several local newspapers.

Using one of the following abbreviations, I have included each image's source at the end of its caption.

Abbreviations
(AC.)—Author's collection
(CJ.)—*Clinton Journal*
(DCGS.)—DeWitt County Genealogical Society, Clinton, Illinois
(DCM.)—C.H. Moore Homestead and DeWitt County Museum, Clinton, Illinois
(DPL.)—Decatur Public Library
(FCGHS.)—Farmer City Genealogical & Historical Society
(FCL.)—Farmer City Library
(GW.)—© Gordon Woods
(H-AMP.)—Harry and Ann Morrison Papers, Boise State University Special Collections and Archives
(H-R.)—Decatur's *Herald-Review* newspaper
(ILDC.)—Illinois Library Digital Collections
(JS.)—Jered Shofner
(KA.)—Clinton's Ken Atchison
(KD.)—Wapella's Kim Donovan
(KHAM.)—Kenney Heritage Association Museum
(LA.)—Lynn Almacher and the Don Scott Collection
(LOCGM.)—Library of Congress, Geography and Map Division
(LOCMD.)—Library of Congress, Manuscript Division
(MWC.)—Mark Woods Collection, Clinton, Illinois
(MCMH.)—Bloomington's McLean County Museum of History
(VWPL.)—Vespasian Warner Public Library, Clinton, Illinois
(WPL.)—Weldon Public Library
(WTL.)—Waynesville Township Library
(WVT.)—Wapella Village Trustees

INTRODUCTION

Founded in 1839, DeWitt County, Illinois, was formed by combining parts of Macon and McLean Counties and includes approximately 398 acres of land and almost 8 acres of water. By 1858, the county had created 13 townships: Clintonia, Barnett, Creek, DeWitt, Harp, Nixon, Rutledge, Santa Anna, Texas, Tunbridge, Wapella, Waynesville, and Wilson.

In 1824, the first pioneers had already gathered in the area north of what eventually became Kenney. Some of these included Elisha Butler Sr. (1802–1848), along with Jacob Coppenbarger (1769–1841) and his wife, Catherine. That same year, Butler married Coppenbarger's daughter Mary Ann. Other arrivals that year included a widow, Lucinda Shugart (1783–1840), and her two sons, Edom (who later taught in the area's first school) and Zion.

In 1828, Jacob Coppenbarger filed the area's first land entry. When the Black Hawk War erupted in 1832, his three sons joined Elisha Butler to fight. Over time, the Coppenbargers and more figured prominently in local history.

Other early pioneers included the Walker family, the Fruit family, the Bowles family, and the Randolph family. After settling there in 1830, William Randolph (1792–1867) traded a horse and wagon to obtain 80 acres of Butler's land. Another prominent settler, Darius Hall (1799–1879), arrived in 1831 in Tunbridge Township.

The township's name was eventually chosen after games with names of the first mill, built in 1838. Two of the builders of Salt Creek's first bridge disputed the strength of the structure after its construction. When a wagon hauled a weight of three tons over the bridge, the name Tonbridge was considered appropriate. Soon it became Tunbridge after the Old English usage of "Tun" for location names. Eventually, the township's first community, Franklin, was renamed Tunbridge.

The next area to be settled was Waynesville, named after Gen. "Mad" Anthony Wayne. Prettyman Marvel Jr. (1801–1842) and his wife, Rebecca (1806–1893), arrived in the area in early 1826 and built a residence just south of an area called Big Grove. Another resident, George Isham, filed a plat for the town in 1832, and soon it flourished, especially with Marvel and his wife's 14 children adding to the population. With more settlers came additional towns. These included Clinton, Kenney, Hallsville, Farmer City (formerly named Mount Pleasant), Wapella, Weldon, Lane, Midland City (formerly Dunham), Birkbeck, Bucks, Carle Springs, DeWitt (formerly Marion), Fullerton, Jenkins, Ospur, Parnell, Rowell, Solomon, Tabor, Craig, and Watkins. Many communities are now home to a handful of residents, while some have none.

Only by looking on old maps or reading old newspapers might one learn of communities such as Shoo Fly, northeast of Weldon in Nixon Township and once home to a store, blacksmith shop, and school. It was supposedly given that name due to the area's prevalence of horseflies. Other towns included Harp Township's Niptight and Wapella Township's Jimtown and Zabriski.

Niptight, southeast of Birkbeck, lay east and north of Charter Oak School. An atlas from 1875 listed the town's businesses as a brickyard, gristmill and sawmill, and store selling groceries and notions. Zabriski (sometimes called Zabriska) lay four miles north of Wapella. It included Long

Point Christian Church and a post office. The post office, however, was discontinued after Wapella's was established in 1852. Located on Rock Creek, in 1897, Jimtown boasted a bank, hotel, tobacco processing service, distillery, basket maker, dance hall, park, and fishing and boating opportunities. In the 1960s, the Jimtown Gun Club lay slightly northwest outside Wapella.

Organized in the 1850s, Nixon Township was one of the last established in the county. The first resident was Cicero Twist (1819–1903), eventual owner of 450 acres of prairie land around Weldon. He and other members of the Twist family are buried in Lane's Lisenby Cemetery.

The county's prairies, climate, rich soil, and water resources made for vast acres of cultivated farmlands in addition to towns and smaller communities. Around the 1880s, the Osage orange tree (a member of the mulberry family and totally unrelated to oranges) began being used for fencing. Also nicknamed "hedge apple tree," it was championed because it was considered horse-high, bull-strong, and pig-tight and widely used until the invention of barbed wire. The thorny tree still thrives in central Illinois and occasionally appears as fencing in older areas.

By the late 1840s, the area became known for its connections to several famous politicians, most notably Abraham Lincoln. While traveling the Eighth Judicial Circuit as a lawyer for 20 years, Lincoln forged relationships with people who featured prominently in his later years. These people included future Civil War general George B. McClellan, future Supreme Court justice David Davis of Bloomington, and Lincoln's later presidential opponent Stephen A. Douglas. Douglas had been Lincoln's cocounsel in 1840 in DeWitt County's first murder trial one year after the circuit court's first session. Another famous DeWitt County resident was C.H. Moore, who had faced off against Lincoln in some cases and partnered with him on others. On September 2, 1858, Moore introduced Lincoln to a crowd of 10,000 people waiting to hear him speak.

Over the next decades, DeWitt County suffered through railroads going broke and depressions in 1857, 1873, 1893, 1907, and the Great Depression commencing in 1929. Natural disasters pummeled it: tornadoes, floods, wind damage, ice storms, and heavy snow. An April 1927 tornado destroyed most of the buildings on the county fairgrounds, north of Clinton. A second tornado in May 1968 killed two people in Wapella and two in Farmer City, injured at least 75, uprooted trees, pulled down power lines, and destroyed many homes and vehicles. But people rallied each time the hits came.

Throughout the decades, even as local businesses closed, DeWitt County farmland continued to feed not just the community but also the wallet. DeWitt County residents can count themselves fortunate that, through many generous donations, the county enhanced what they needed or already had: schools, a hospital, a nursing home, libraries, and parks.

My sources have included many newspapers and books. I hope this collection of images entertains you and enriches your appreciation for DeWitt County's history.

One

Clinton until the Early 1900s

Around 1828–1829, brothers Benjamin and Landers Slatten (1813–1892) settled on land and built a cabin near the current Clinton High School. It was the third settlement in what eventually became DeWitt County. In 1830, after selling their cabin to Joseph Clifton and his brother, the Slattens moved to Coon Creek.

In late 1835, two Bloomington legislators and land speculators made an initial survey of the land midway between Bloomington and Decatur, filing an official plat in October 1836 and naming the town Clinton after DeWitt Clinton, New York's governor in the 1820s. Eventually, through an act pushed through the state legislature in 1839, DeWitt County was formed by combining portions of Macon and McLean Counties. During an election to determine which town should become the county seat, Clinton was pitted against the town of Marion (whose name was later changed to DeWitt). Clinton won with 303 votes against Marion's 180.

The first post office was established west of Clinton Square in 1836 by Miles Gray, a tailor on Quincy Street. By 1845, mostly frame structures filled the square. As the town grew, it brought the railroad, businesses, and schools. Clinton gave one teacher the opportunity to save money for new challenges. Around 1856–1857, John Wesley Powell taught in Clinton before becoming famous through his explorations of the great American West.

With railroads came lawsuits. During the peak years of 1841–1847, when the Eighth Judicial Circuit consisted of 15 counties, Abraham Lincoln and other lawyers and judges traveled the road between courthouses, staying in taverns, inns, farmhouses, or homes of associates. Over years practicing in the area, Lincoln forged relationships with people who grew in importance in state and national history.

Clinton takes pride that it was at the county courthouse, during his campaign for presidency against Stephen A. Douglas, when Lincoln purportedly stated, "You can fool all the people some of the time and some of the people all the time, but you cannot fool all the people all the time."

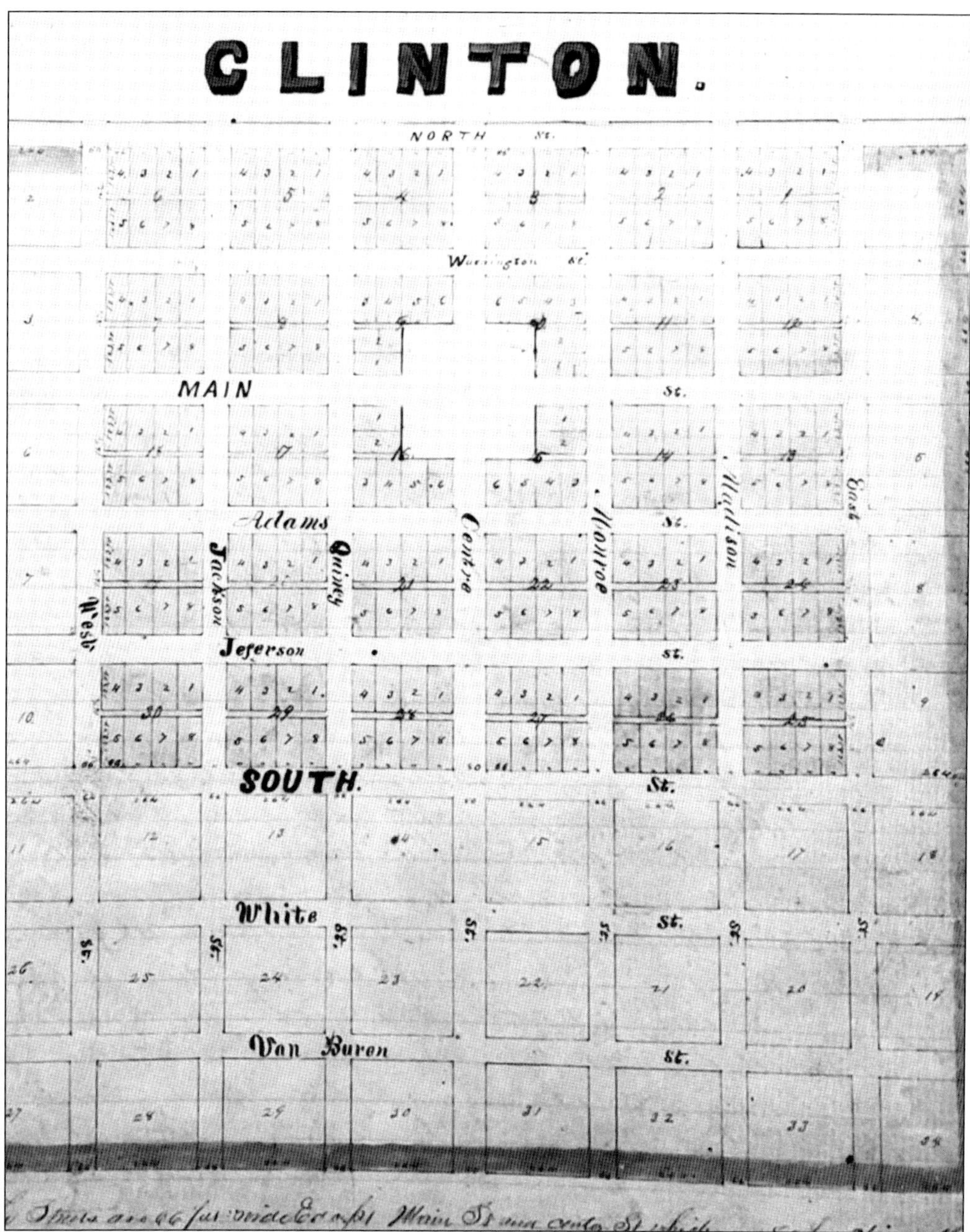

Although land entries had been made for various area settlers in the late 1820s and early 1830s, the town of Clinton only began after 1834. That year, McLean County state legislator James Allen and land speculator and lawyer Jesse Fell (great-grandfather of future Illinois governor Adlai Stevenson) were traveling from Decatur to Bloomington. After pausing near an Indian mound, they decided it was a great place to start a town. At the time, the nearest town, Waynesville, was 15 miles north. On October 3, 1835, they platted the town, with each taking possession of a quarter section of land. They named the village Clinton in honor of DeWitt Clinton, the former governor of New York. At the time, the area belonged to Macon County. Illinois governor Thomas Carlin granted the charter for the formation of DeWitt County in 1839. (DCGS.)

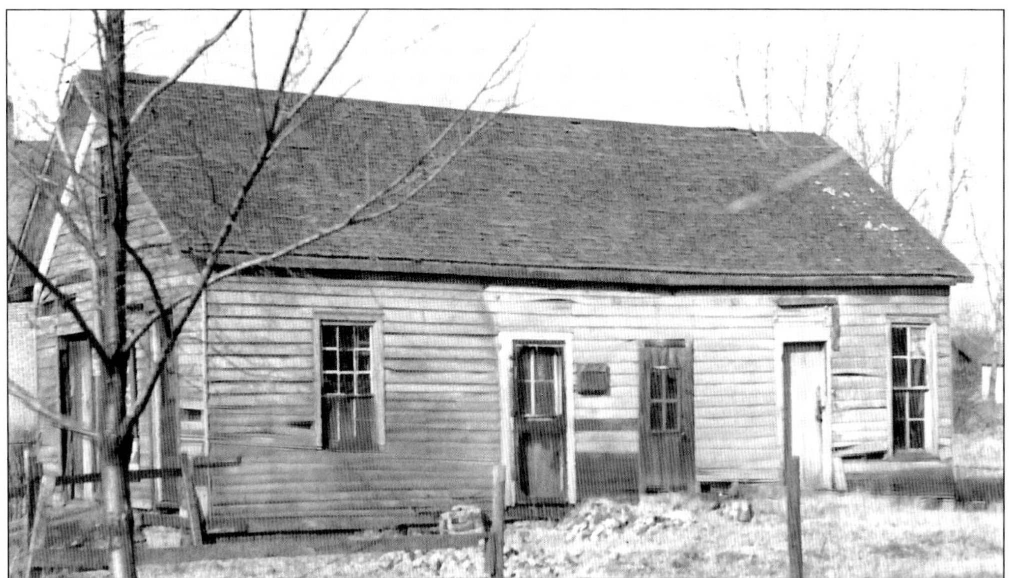

DeWitt County's first courthouse, constructed in 1839 near the current city hall, was used for county, social, religious, and school purposes. After a new courthouse was erected, the first was moved. In 1893, it sat at the corner of Madison and Adams Streets, the residence of a Mrs. Melvin Lowry. It was an auto repair shop in the 800 block of Woodlawn Street in the 1940s and was demolished in 1951. (MWC.)

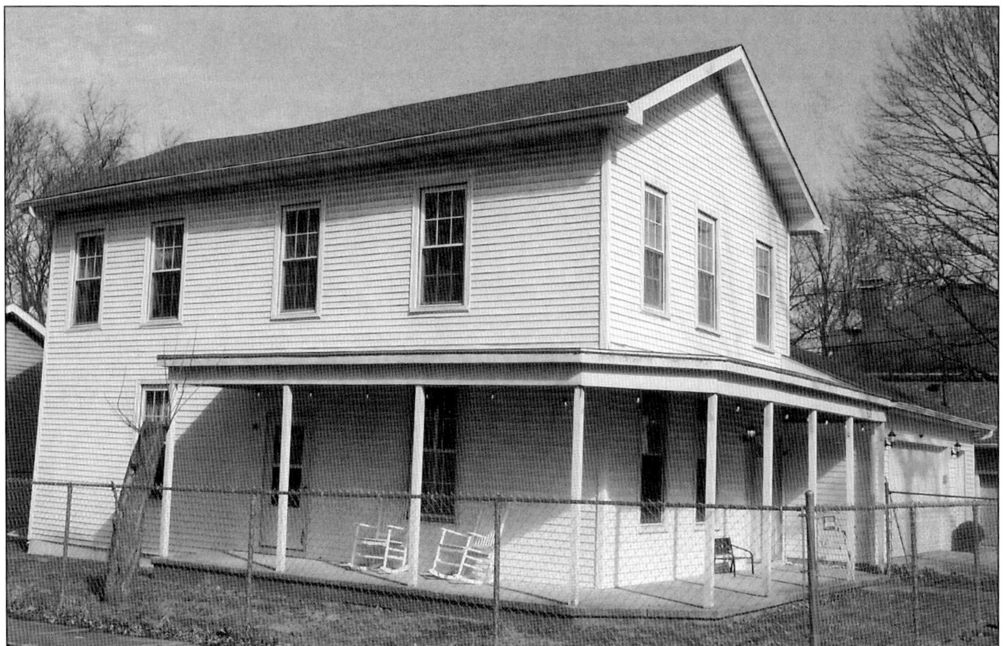

William Anderson built a hotel at Center and Clay Streets around 1839 that was used by Stephen A. Douglas and Abraham Lincoln while traveling the law circuit. In 1900, it was moved to its current location of 121 West Clay Street, where owners rented out apartments. It was referred to as the Brady House after Francis Brady Sr. moved there in 1963. (AC.)

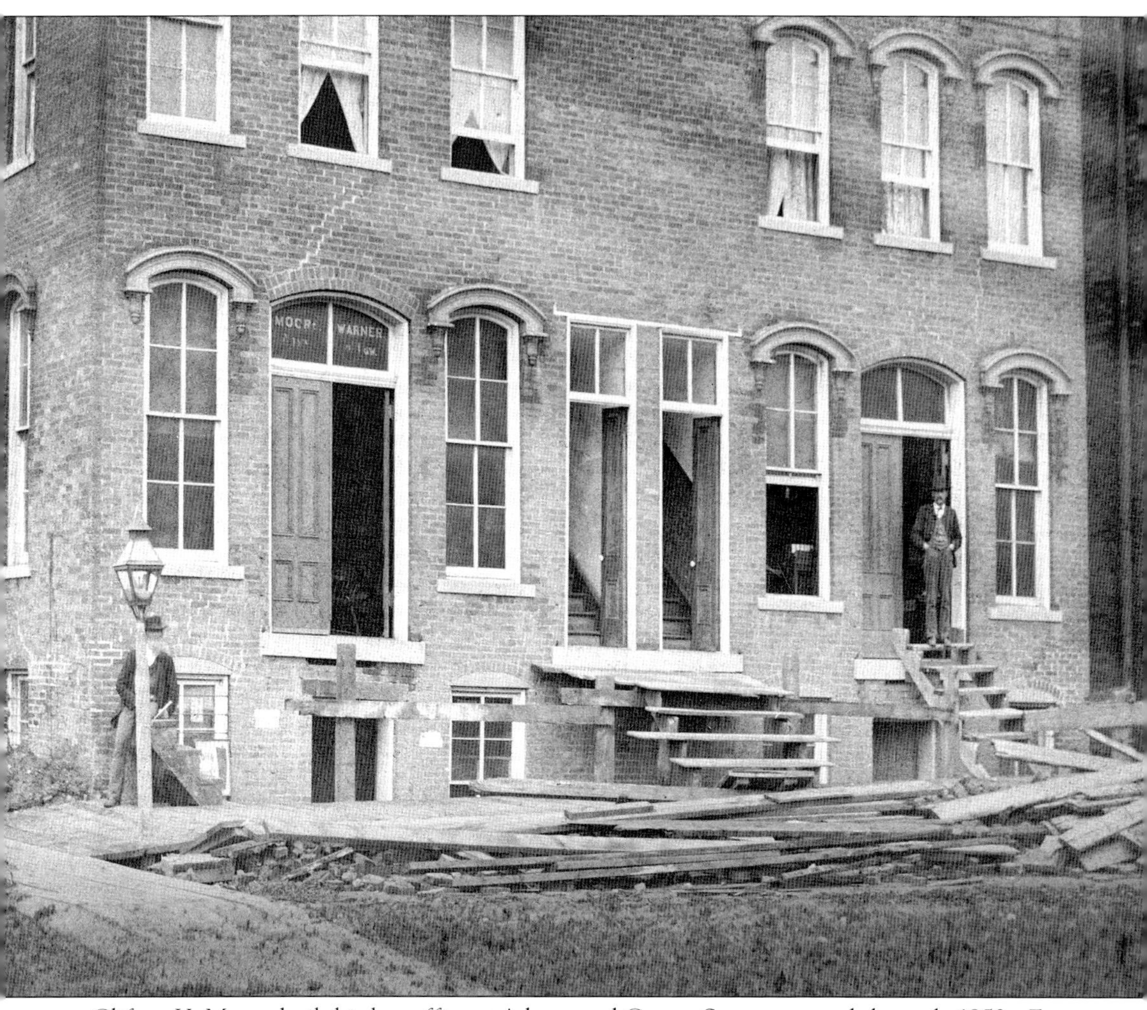

Clifton H. Moore built his law office at Adams and Center Streets around the early 1850s. From 1856 to 1858, Abraham Lincoln joined in Moore's law practice, later the offices of Moore and Vespasian "Pash" Warner. In this c. 1900 photograph, their names appear on the transom above the left doorway. Two unidentified men face the camera above a construction project at the Center Street entrance. Sitting diagonally across the street, Alvin and Rebecca Barnett's two-story Barnett Tavern also served as a boardinghouse. Among other lawyers and judges, Lincoln also sought lodging there. Early Clinton residents remembered evenings sitting in the tavern and listening to Lincoln's stories. The legend is that after one of his comments about Rebecca Barnett's custard, she never served it to him again. Demolished in the 1930s, the location is now a parking lot. (DCM.)

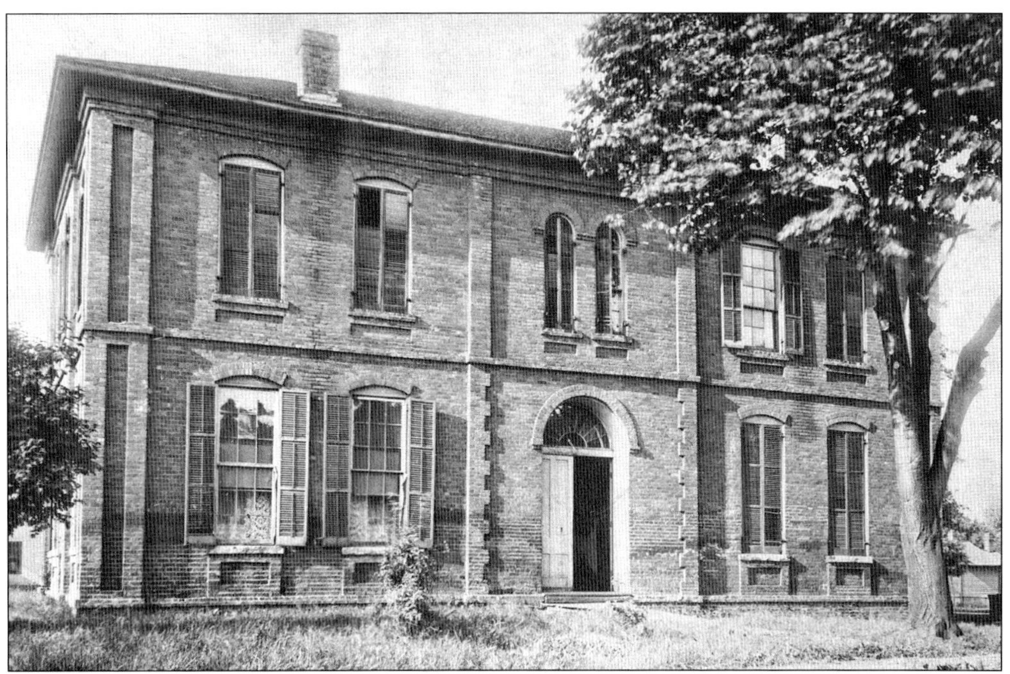

In 1856, C.H. Moore donated property between Quincy and Jackson Streets for a new school to replace a rough frame building used since 1846. The two-story, four-room, brick replacement was soon named after Supt. Thomas McCorkle. McCorkle School was Clinton's only school from 1856 to the late 1860s. (DCM.)

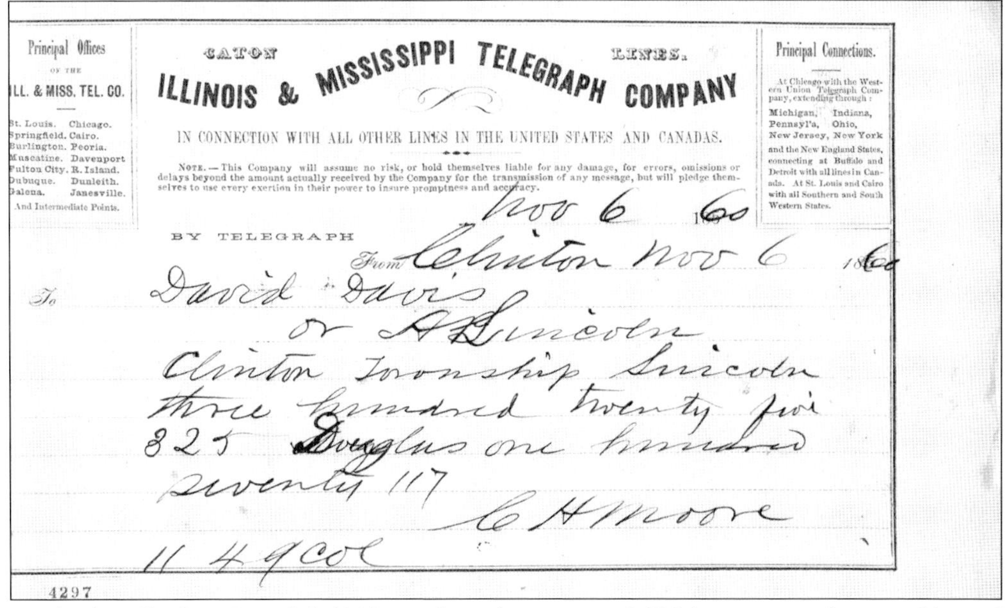

Principal Offices of the ILL. & MISS. TEL. CO.

St. Louis. Chicago. Springfield. Cairo. Burlington. Peoria. Muscatine. Davenport. Fulton City. R. Island. Dubuque. Dunleith. Galena. Janesville. And Intermediate Points.

CATON LINES.

ILLINOIS & MISSISSIPPI TELEGRAPH COMPANY

IN CONNECTION WITH ALL OTHER LINES IN THE UNITED STATES AND CANADAS.

NOTE.—This Company will assume no risk, or hold themselves liable for any damage, for errors, omissions or delays beyond the amount actually received by the Company for the transmission of any message, but will pledge themselves to use every exertion in their power to insure promptness and accuracy.

Principal Connections.

At Chicago with the Western Union Telegraph Company, extending through: Michigan, Indiana, Pennsyl'a, Ohio, New Jersey, New York and the New England States, connecting at Buffalo and Detroit with all lines in Canada. At St. Louis and Cairo with all Southern and South Western States.

Nov 6 1860

BY TELEGRAPH

From Clinton Nov 6 1860

To David Davis
or A Lincoln
Clinton Township Lincoln
three hundred twenty five
325 Douglus one hundred
seventy 117
C H Moore
11 4 9 Col

4297

Involved in Abraham Lincoln's 1860 presidential campaign, C.H. Moore sent a telegram addressed to either recipient, Lincoln or David Davis (Lincoln's campaign manager), announcing election results from Clintonia Township. Lincoln carried the town with 325 votes compared to Stephen Douglas's 117 votes. DeWitt County flipped from Democratic to Republican, giving 1,258 total votes to Lincoln. Douglas garnered 42.15 percent of the county. (LOCMD.)

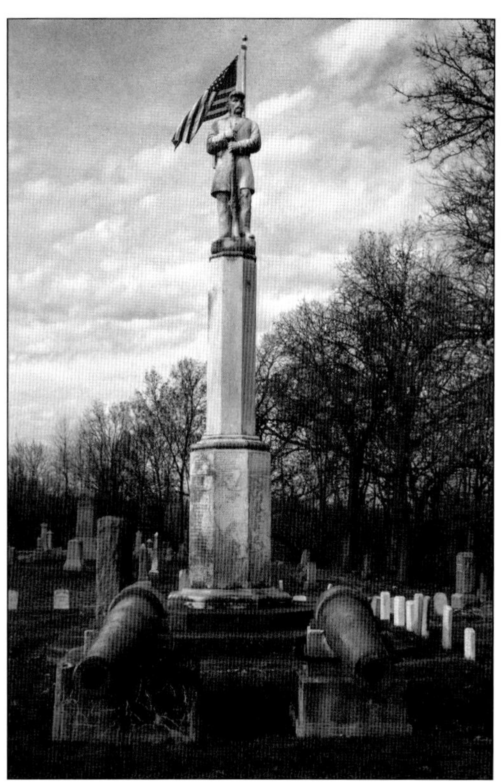

This statue in Woodlawn Cemetery commemorates the death of Civil War Union soldiers from the area. In 1861, upon the death of George Gideon's son Edwin while fighting for the Union, Gideon buried him on family land. Gideon allowed other families to bury over 80 civil war veterans in what became known as the Soldiers' Plot. The city later purchased 65 acres of surrounding land for more burials. (AC.)

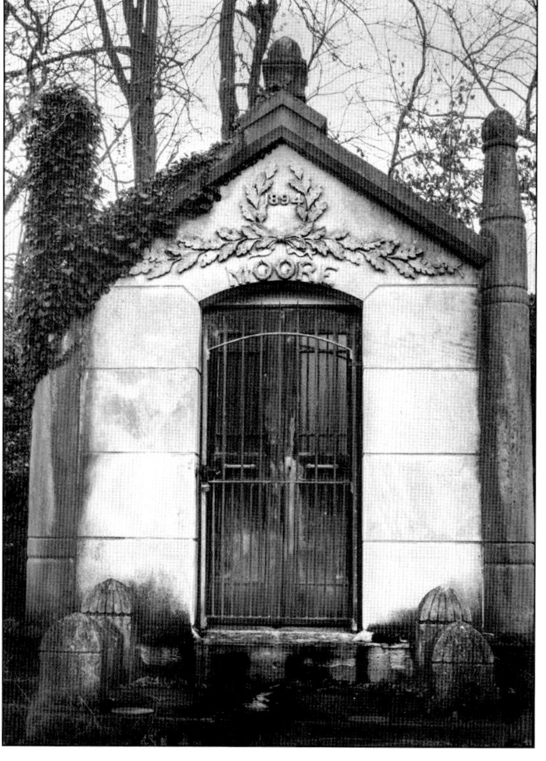

Clifton Haswell Moore (1817–1901) was buried in this mausoleum located across the street from what is now the Moore Homestead. Born in New York and the eldest of eight children, he later taught school. At age 21, he studied law in Pekin, Illinois. After setting up his law practice in Clinton in 1841, he joined with David Davis in the purchase of thousands of acres of Midwest land. (AC.)

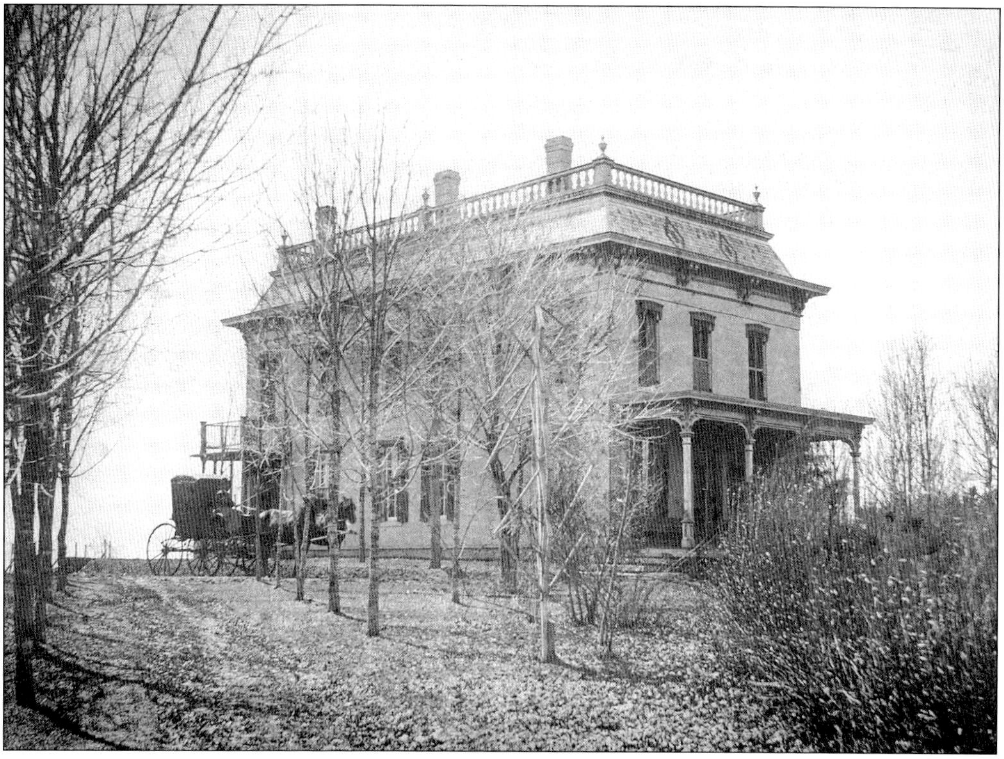

Before moving into Clinton, C.H. Moore lived northeast of town along a road known as 750 North but also called "Trust Road," named after the Moore Trust. Moore had bought land from Bloomington judge David Davis to build an impressive home, one where Abraham Lincoln occasionally stayed. Moore moved into town in 1880 after buying the house of his widowed brother-in-law John Bishop. (DCM.)

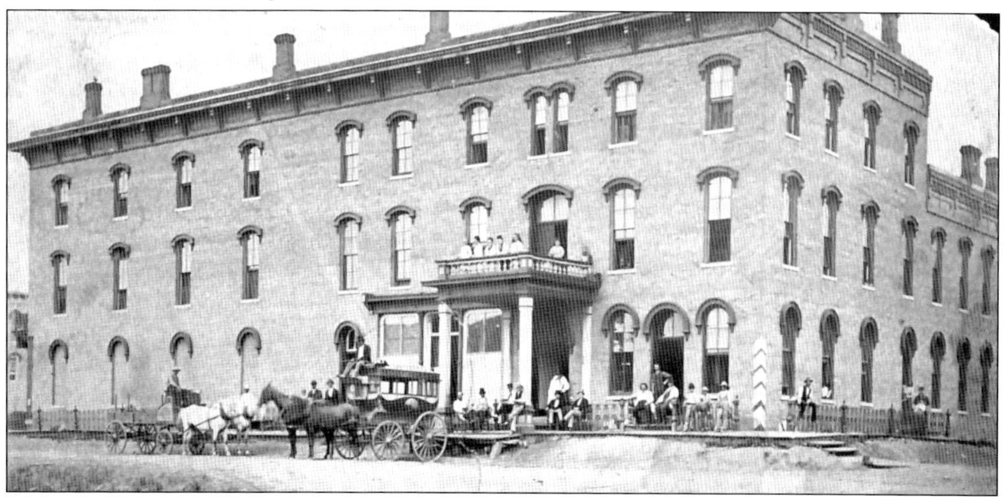

Hoping the Illinois Central Railroad would relocate its Springfield headquarters to Clinton, the Magill brothers raised $10,000 to build the Magill Hotel in 1872 on the site of a burned-down North Center Street store. Over the years, it housed many railroad employees and travelers. In the 1970s, it became an apartment hotel, but it closed in the late 1980s. It is now in the National Register of Historic Places. (VWPL.)

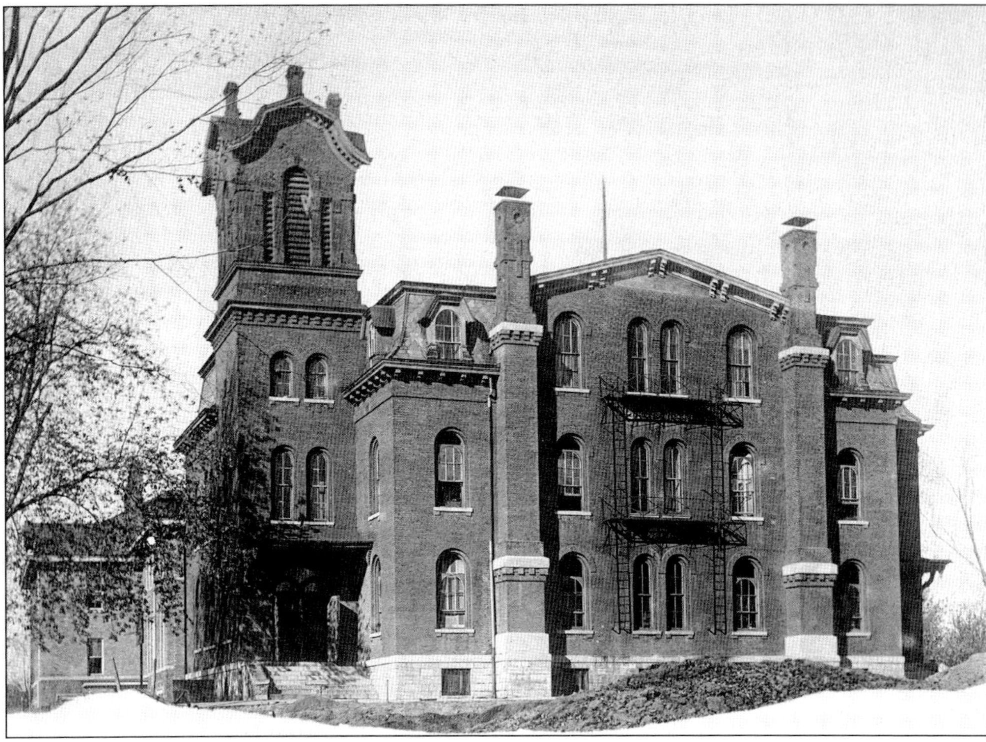

The land called Seminary Hill became the site for Washington Elementary School (later referred to as "Old Washington School"), built around 1869. The three-story brick building, which included a cupola and other adornments, eventually contained 12 classrooms and their teachers. By 1910, there were 300 students. The first three-year high school group graduated in 1872. In 1894, the first four-year class graduated. (DCM.)

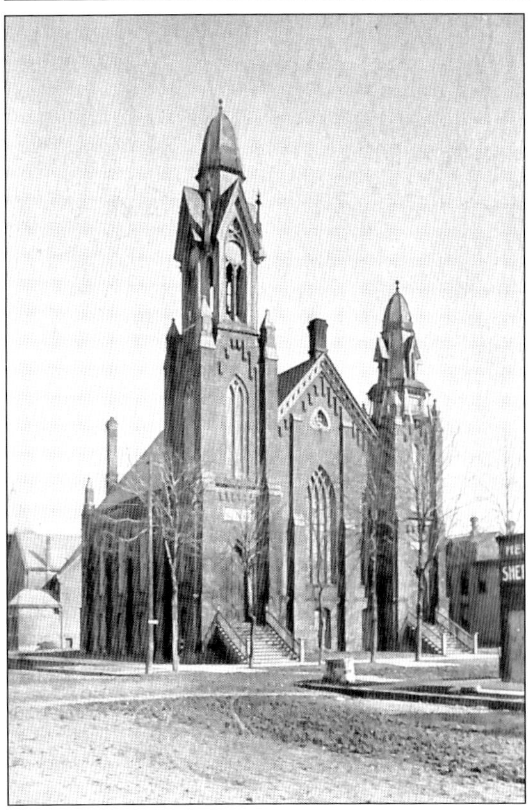

In 1839, ten residents formed a Methodist church organization in Clinton. Soon they moved to the courthouse for services, finally building the Methodist Episcopal church in 1848 at the southeast corner of Adams and Madison Streets. Soon, increased membership required a bigger replacement at Main and Madison Streets, with construction from 1868 through 1871. Yet another new church was built in 1954. (VWPL.)

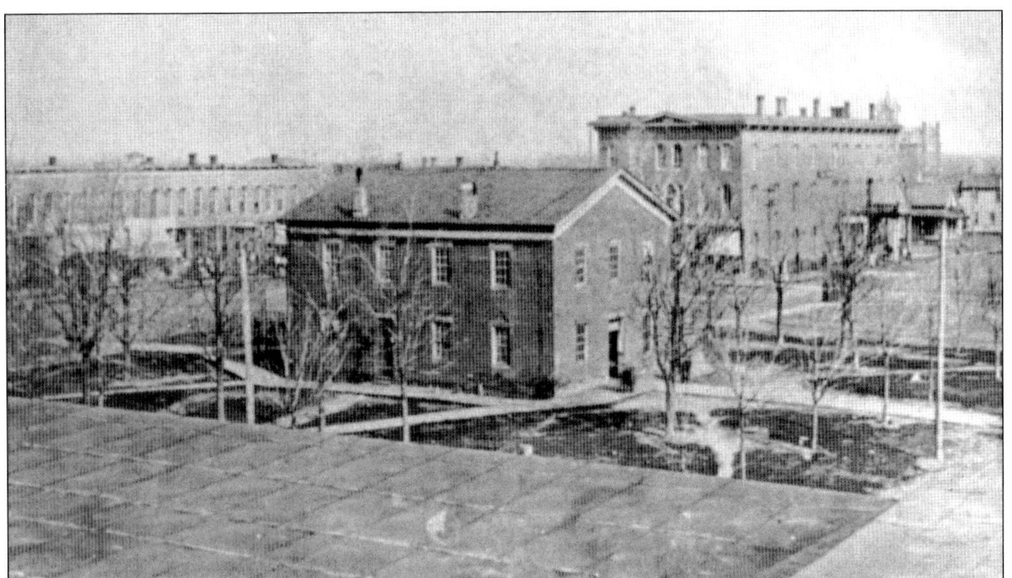

Seen in the 1880s, the second DeWitt County Courthouse (built in 1849 and dedicated in 1850) appears inside Clinton's town square, later called "Mr. Lincoln's Square." The three-story Magill Hotel stands in the background, with Washington School's cupola looming behind it. After the courthouse was deemed unsafe in 1891, court was held in Rennick's Opera House until a new courthouse was ready in 1893. (DCM.)

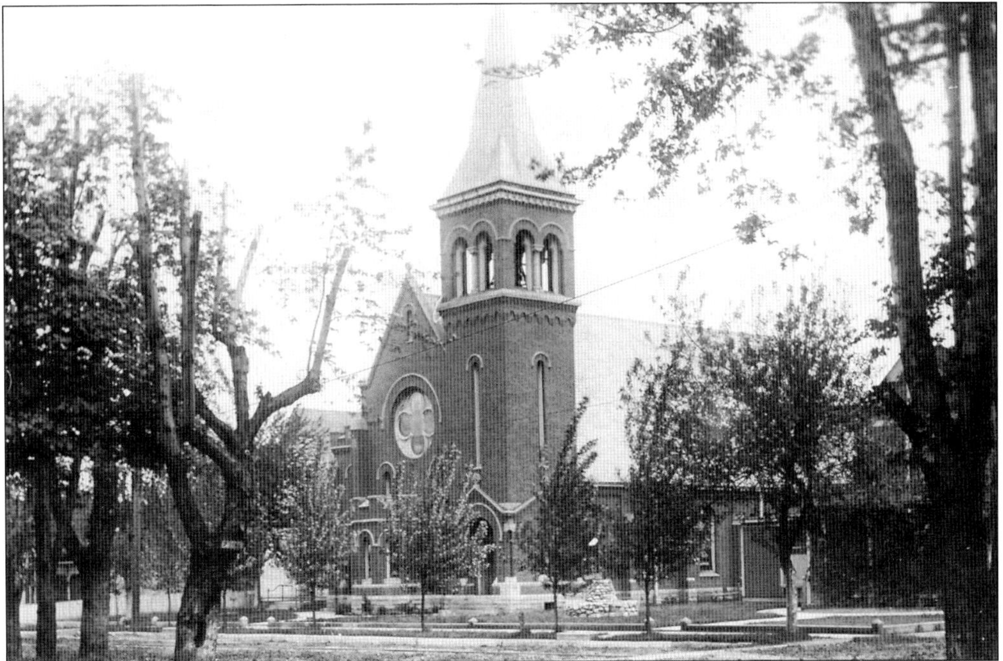

In 1879, a frame Catholic church, St. John the Baptist, and a rectory were built where the current parish hall stands, with the first resident priest arriving in 1893. The church was replaced in 1904, and a grade school was constructed in 1915. Nauvoo's Benedictine Sisters lived on its top floor, teaching until the school closed in 1968 for lack of teachers. It was razed in 1983, leaving a parking lot. (VWPL.)

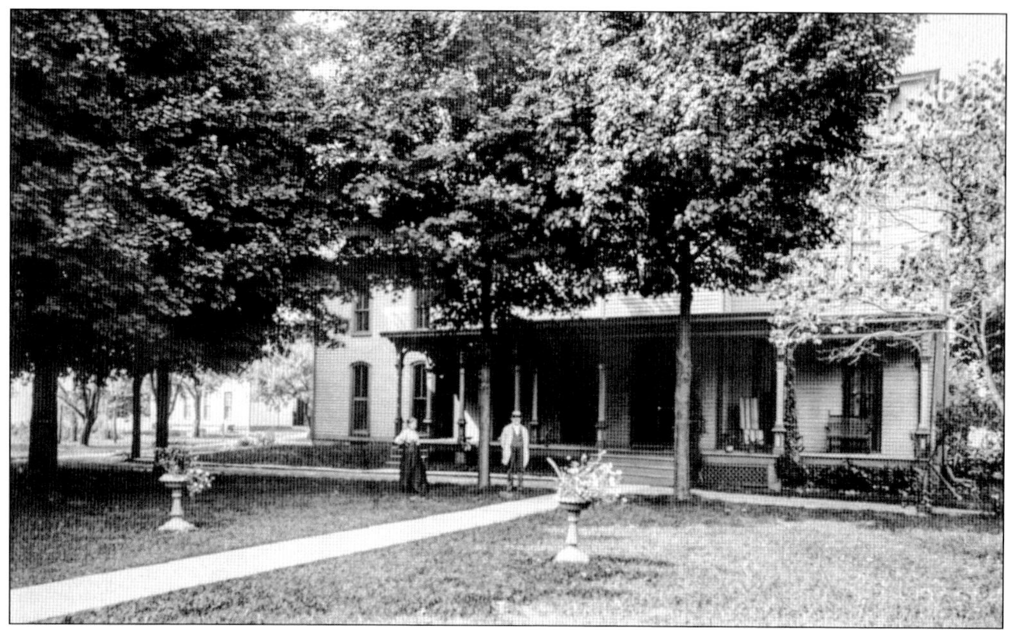

C.H. Moore lived at 219 East Woodlawn Street from 1880 until his 1901 death. The house is now the DeWitt County Museum and home to the popular annual Apple and Pork Festival. Appearing in this photograph are Rose (left), Moore's second wife, and Moore on the lawn, with the estate's still-existing barn in the background. (DCM.)

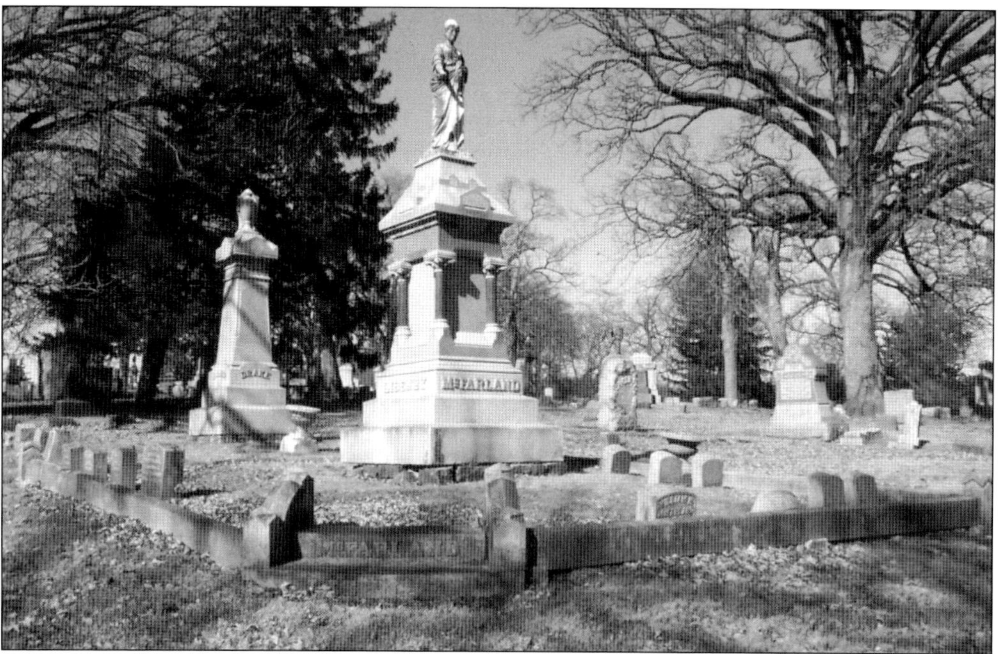

Augustus Lisenby married Sarah "Sallie" McFarland in 1871. In 1874 and again in 1880, her newly born baby boys did not survive long. After giving birth to a stillborn son in October 1885, she died within days. For her Woodlawn Cemetery gravesite, her husband commissioned an Italian marble statue (now missing a hand) that was carved in her likeness. Shortly afterward, he left for a new life in California. (AC.)

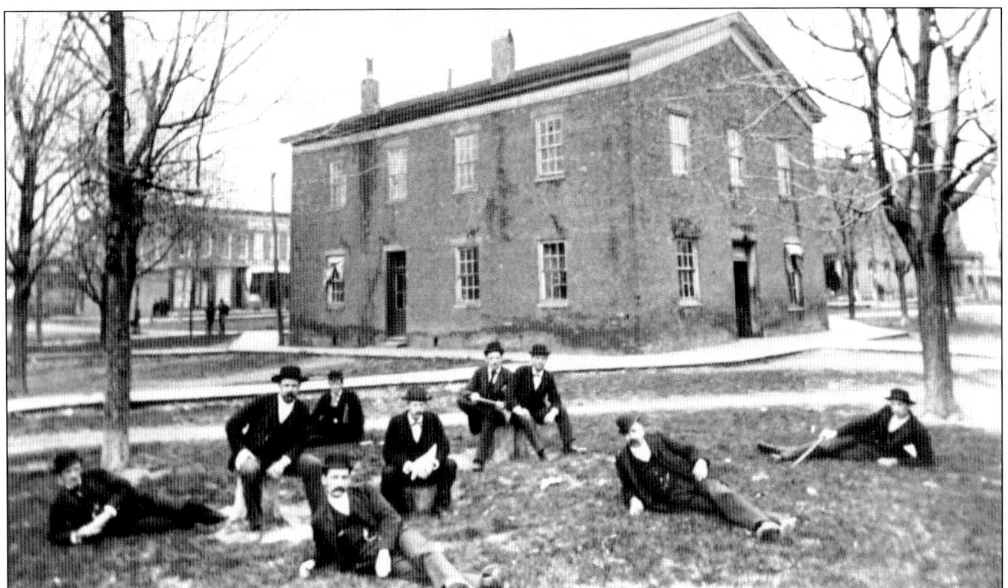

Nine men lounge on the square by DeWitt County's second courthouse in 1890. The Magill Hotel, partly owned by Henry Rennick, peeks to the right behind the courthouse. To the left is the square's west side. In later years, Watkins Jewelers occupied the left corner building at 600 West Side Square. The square was lighted with gasoline lamps in 1872. (VWPL.)

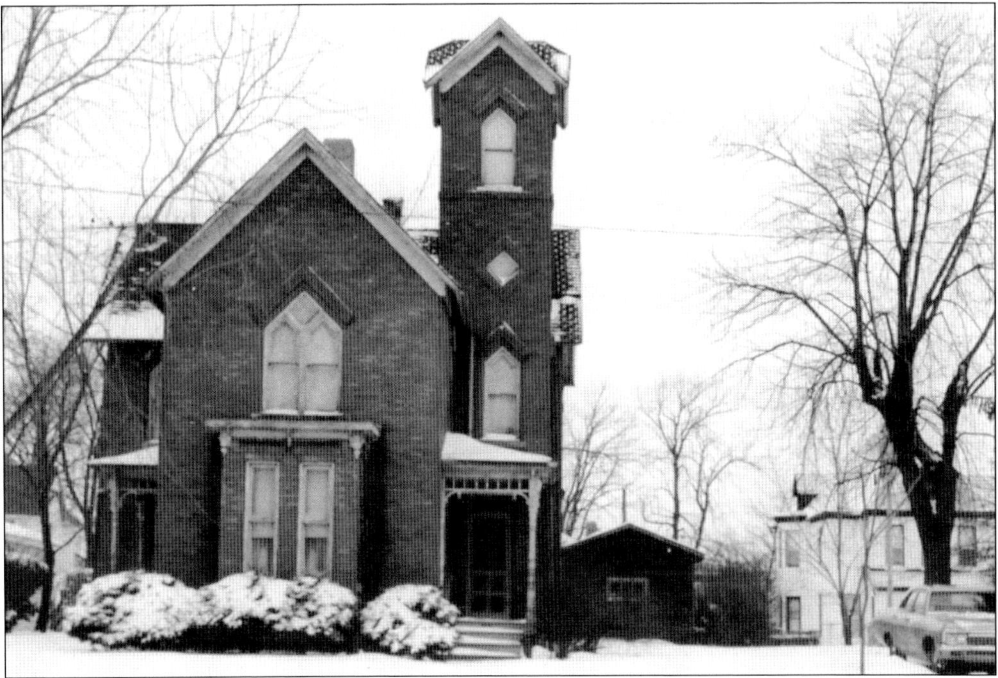

C.S. Meredith's home (photographed in the 1970s) at 315 North Quincy Street was constructed in September 1890. A month later, his young daughter died after a short bout of diphtheritic croup. By 1895, the Meredith family sold the property to John Warner. Other owners were Warner's granddaughter Frances Warner Crist and the former president of Millikin University, Dr. J. Walter Malone. (AC.)

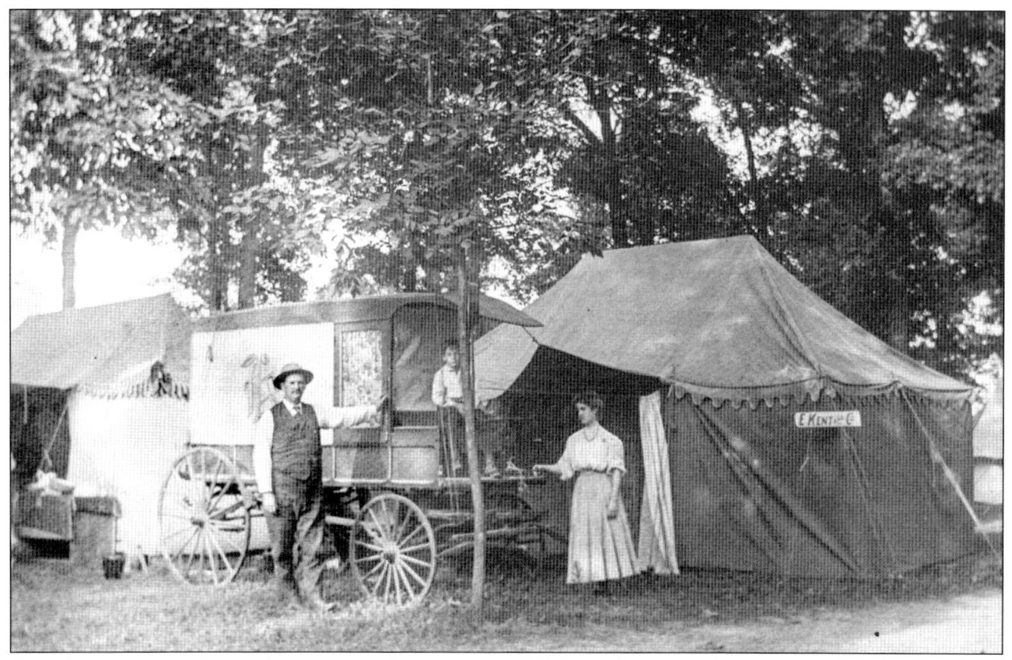

An advertisement for E. Kent and Co. hangs from a Weldon Springs Chautauqua tent around 1910. From left to right are Emmett Kent's son Fred; Fred's son Emmett; and Fred's wife, Rose. During the Civil War, the Kent Lumber Company's warehouse served food to passing Union soldiers. The founder's grandson and namesake Emmett Kent (the boy on the wagon) helped form the DeWitt County Museum Association. (DCM.)

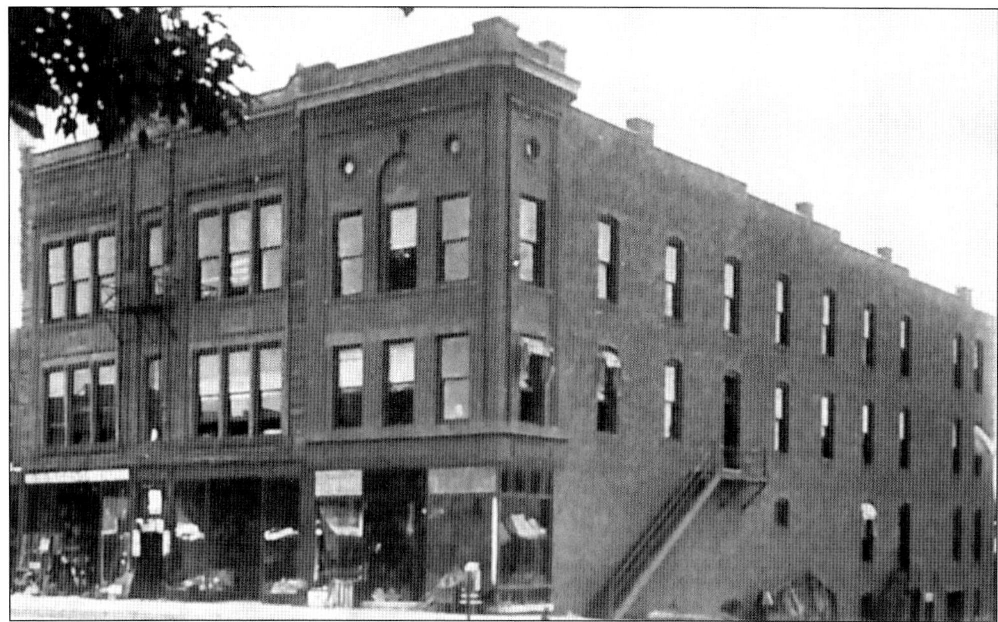

The Rennick-Corder buildings stand at the southeast corner of South Center and Main Streets. Corder's drugstore occupied the building to the right, with Dr. Thomas Cantrell (1864–1936) on the second floor. The building to the left became Rennick's Opera House. Although the facade displays a date of 1893, the opera house actually opened in October 1892. (VWPL.)

A map from 1892 highlights portions of the Illinois Central Railroad. Chartered in 1850 and incorporated in 1851, the line ran north to south from the Great Lakes to the Gulf of Mexico. Over 700 miles of the line opened for traffic in 1856. It was the first railroad to receive lands granted by the passage of the Illinois Central Land Grant Bill. (LOCGM.)

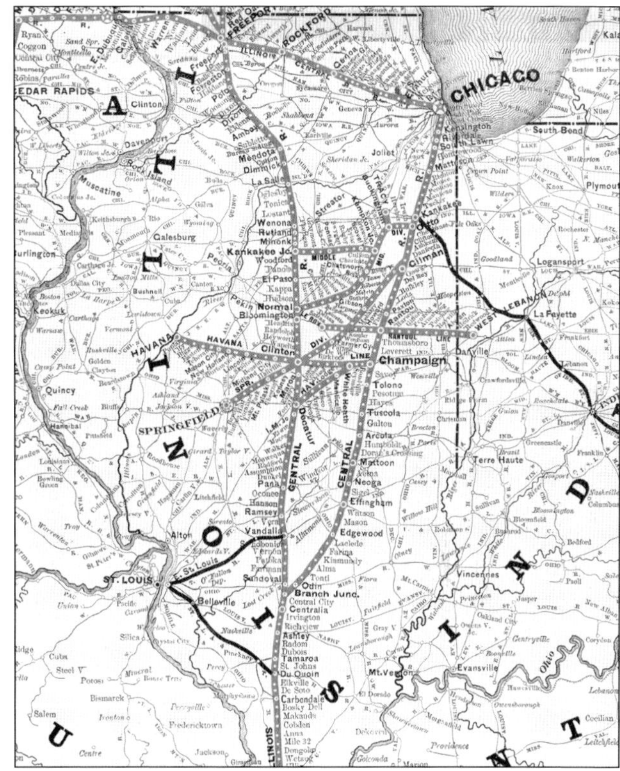

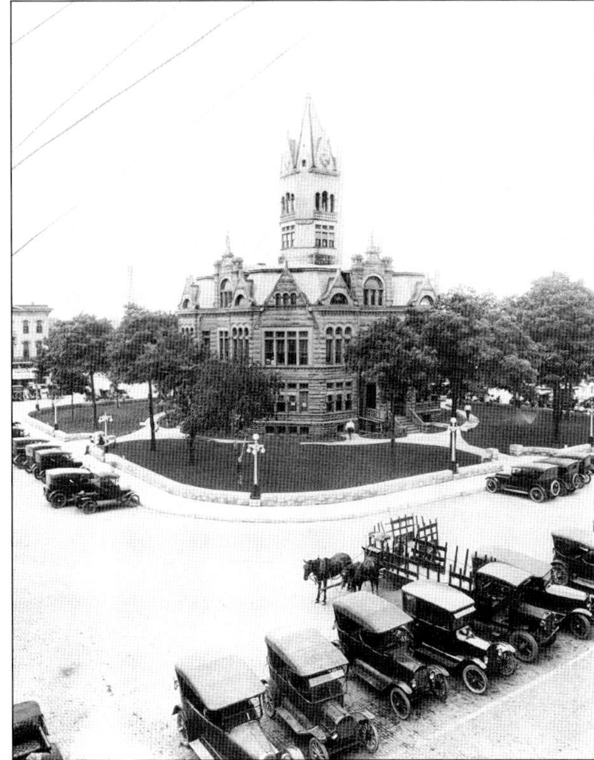

The county's third courthouse, an octagonal 1893 three-story stone structure with cupola and bell, was designed by Henry Elliott of Chicago and constructed by C.F. Schultz & Company. Early on, the courthouse was not always fully used. During the 1904–1905 school year, a kindergarten utilized the jury room. The building was demolished in 1987 after its 1986 replacement was built north of the square. (DCM.)

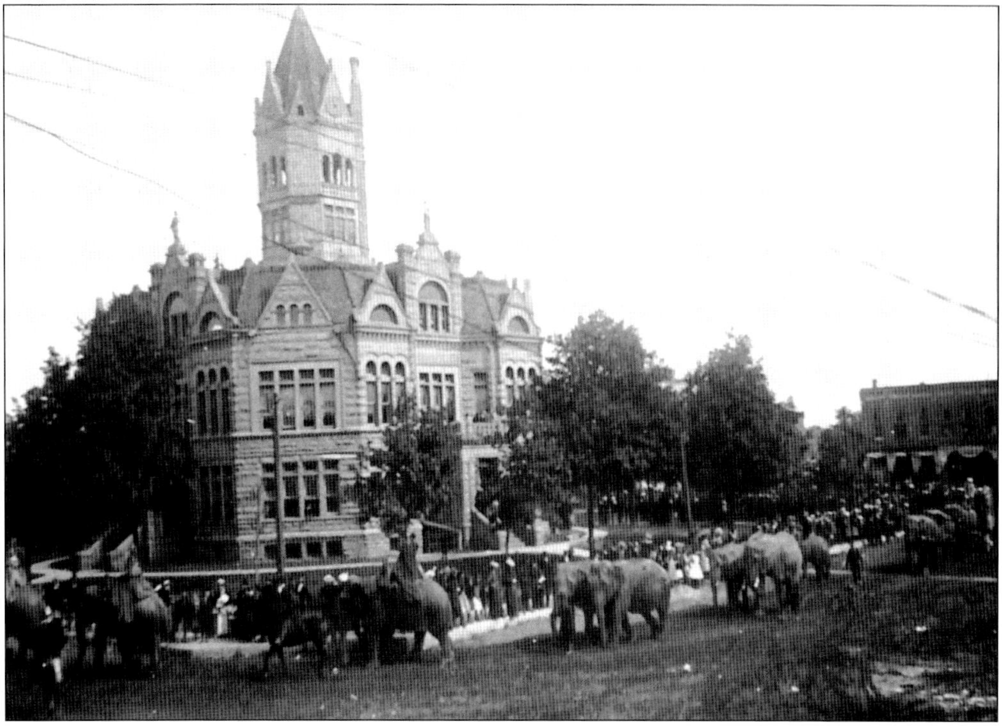

Elephants and camels, along with circus wagons and horses, parade around the third county courthouse around the late 1890s. This may be the three-ring organization Cook & Whitby Colossal English Circus, Museum and Menagerie, Allied with America's Racing Association and Jupiter the Riding Lion, which pitched tents in Clinton in May 1894. (VWPL.)

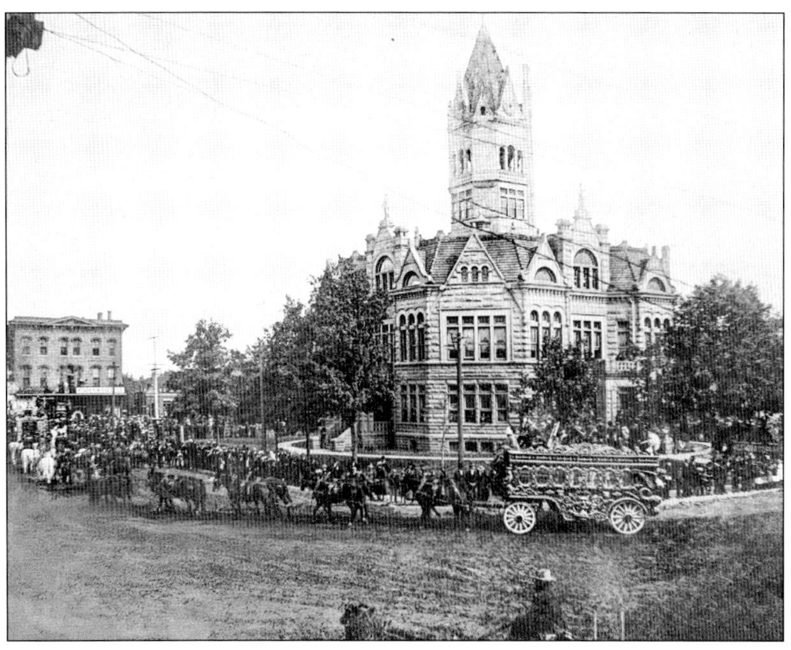

Wagons and horses from the Forepaugh & Sells Brothers Circus parade around Clinton Square in September 1899. Requiring seven acres for its spread, the circus set up on a parcel of land northeast of Clinton. In the left background, a sign appears above the Magill Hotel advertising the Readey Dry Goods Company. (DCM.)

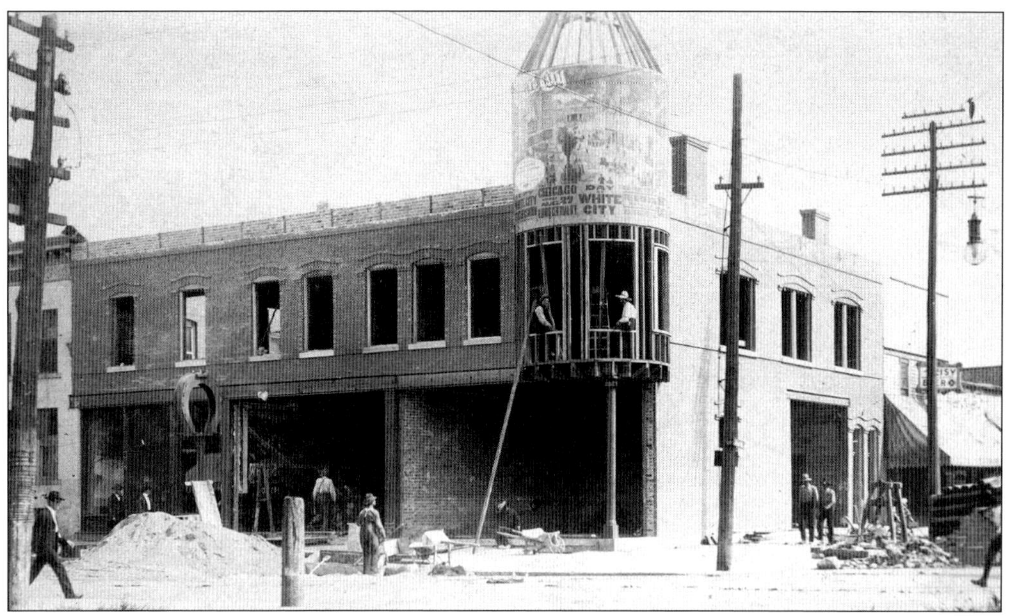

The building at Washington and Monroe Streets is shown undergoing construction. The tower's advertisement offered travel on the Illinois Central Railroad to Chicago's Columbian Exposition on Sunday, August 17, 1893. Other businesses at that location over the years included a Baptist church in the 1950s and a café in the 1960s. The Central Hotel stands to the left. (DCM.)

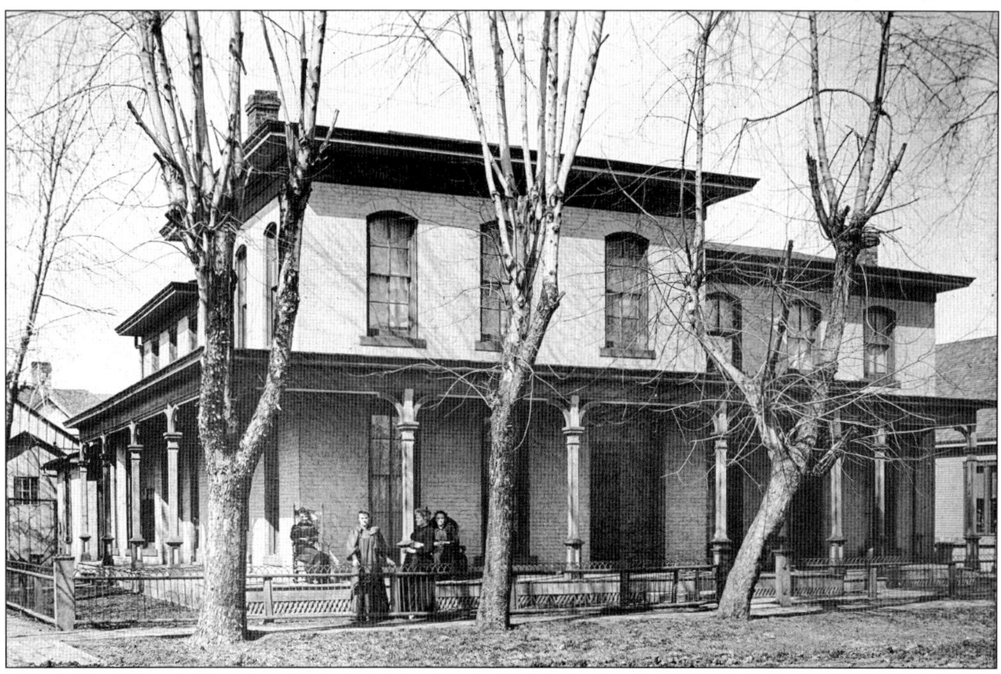

Notes on the back of this photograph read: "Our first house in Clinton. North Madison Street—present St. John's school. 1893—October 14 to 1894 October 3. Clinton, Illinois. The Fred Balls. Southeast lower left corner—our room." Attorney Frederick Ball and his wife, Ivanilla (née Dunham), moved to Madison and Macon Streets after their 1893 marriage. St. John's Elementary School was later located on the property. (DCM.)

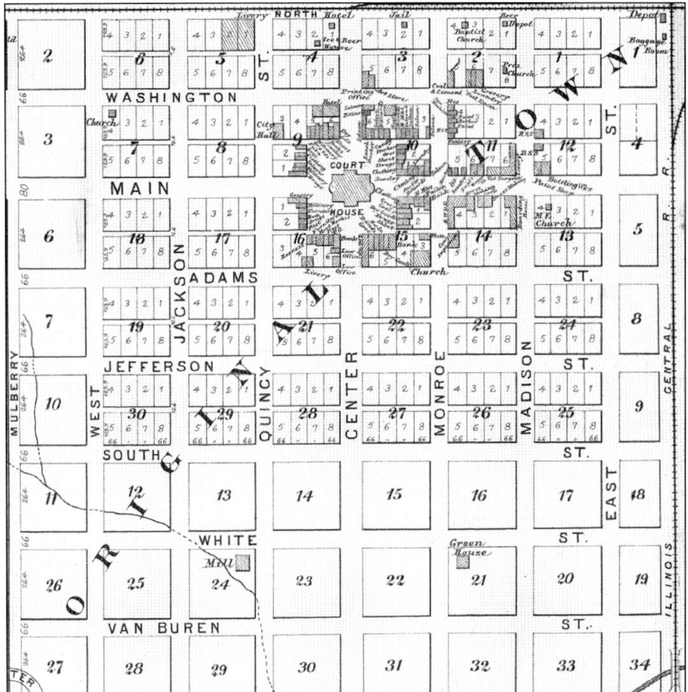

The "Original Town" of Clinton is shown in this 1894 plat. The depot is at the upper right corner. A block north of the Magill Hotel at Washington and Center Streets is another hotel at the corner of North and Center Streets. Many businesses cluster around the square, including, among others, saloons, restaurants, barbers, a meat market, a grocery, a billiard hall, a shoe store, a pharmacy, a clothing store, and a jeweler. (LOCGM.)

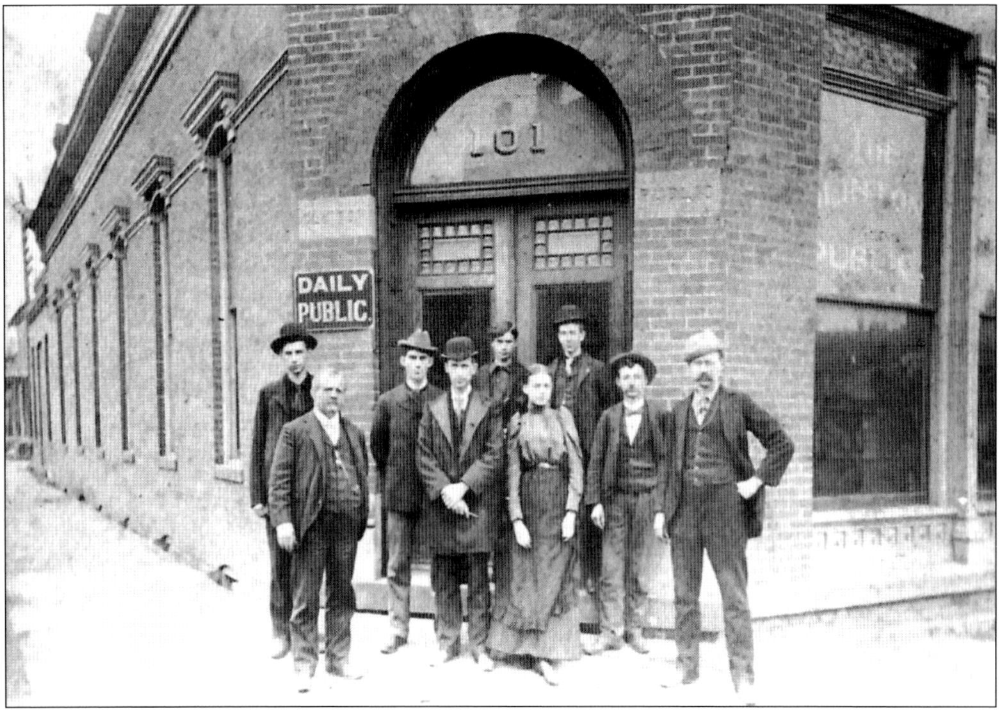

Eight unidentified men and one woman, employees of the *Clinton Daily Public* newspaper, stand outside their office building at 101 East Washington Street. The newspaper, in business since at least 1895, was one of two Clinton newspapers that later merged with the *Clinton Morning Journal*. Sorrento's Pizza currently occupies the building. (VWPL.)

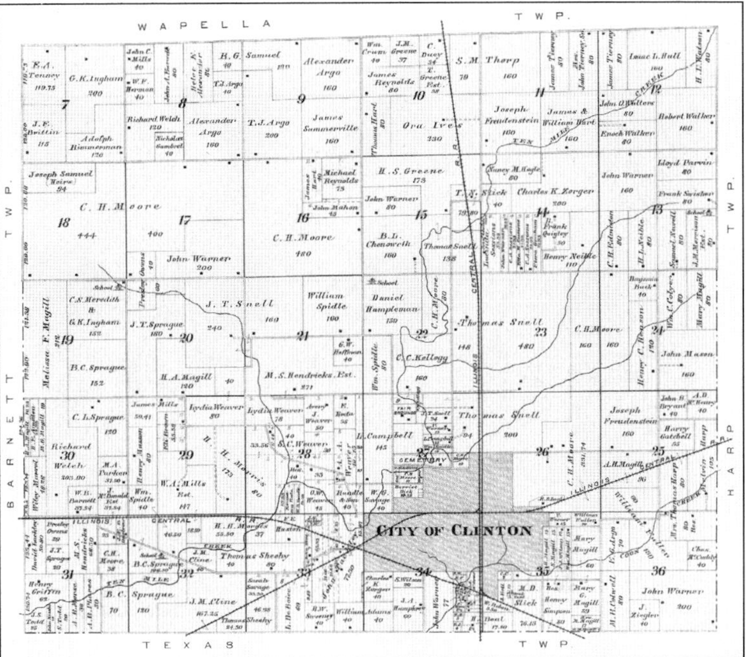

This 1894 plat map shows Clintonia Township, the area outside the city itself. As the eye follows the Illinois Central Railroad line diagonally east out of town, the railroad cuts across land owned by C.H. Moore and A.H. Magill. Besides more Magill family members, other landowners included Thomas Snell, John Warner, and the Argo and Freudenstein families. (LOCGM.)

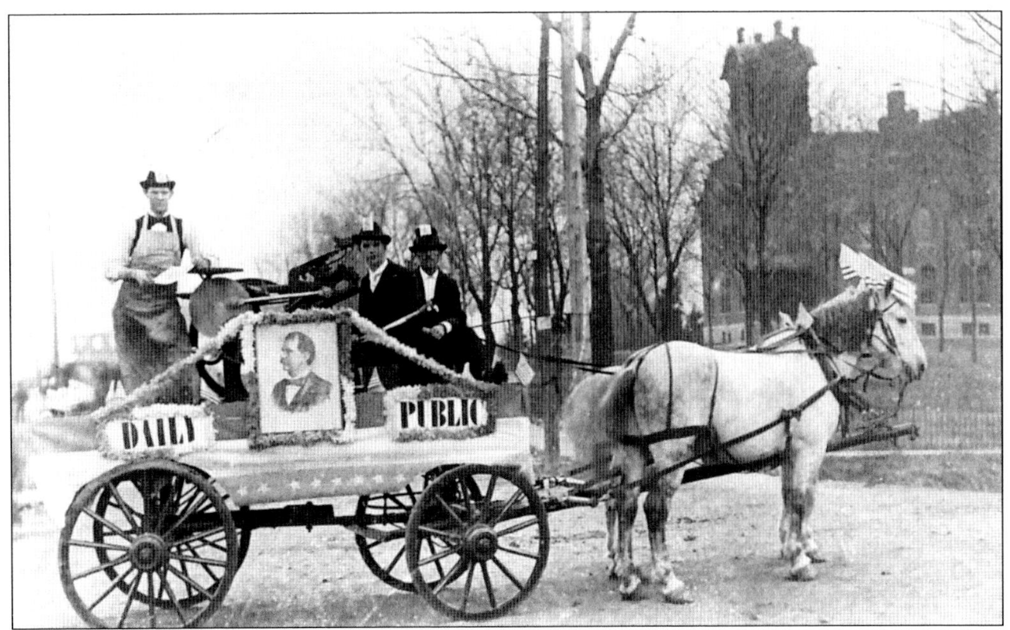

Clinton Daily Public newspaper employees pose in front of Washington School with a buggy carrying printing equipment and decorated for the Tanner Day parade on October 29, 1896. Almost 2,800 people marched past the Magill Hotel's balcony reviewing stand. John Tanner, the Republican candidate for Illinois governor, opposed the Democrat incumbent, Gov. John Peter Altgeld, who had his own parade in Clinton on October 12. Tanner won. (VWPL.)

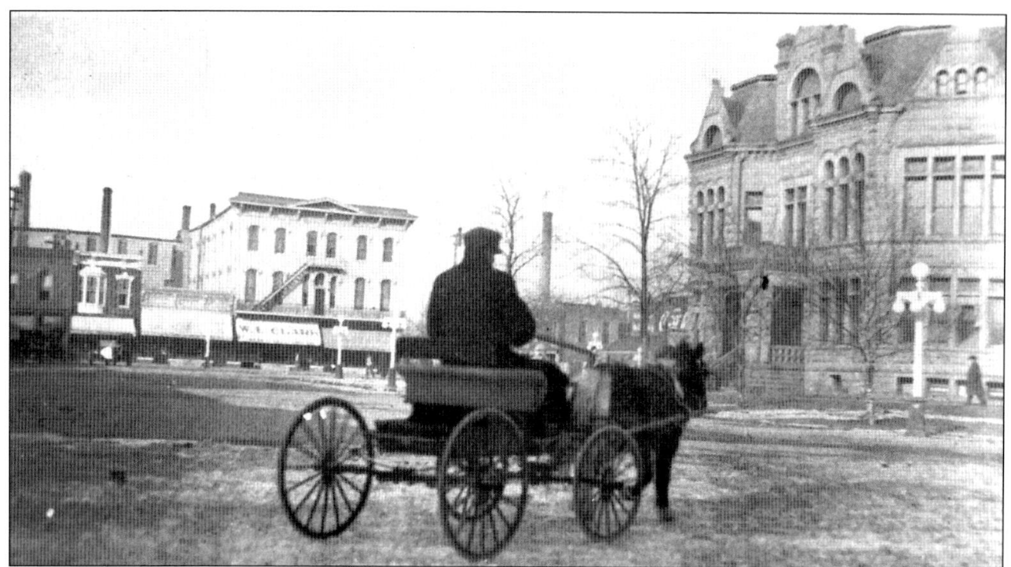

A man with his horse and buggy drives across the west side of Clinton Square in the early 1900s. Directly to the man's left stands the Magill Hotel with a fire escape ladder running diagonally down from the middle two windows. The awning for W.E. Clark's tailor shop can be seen under the left windows. Clark moved from the Magill building in 1919. (VWPL.)

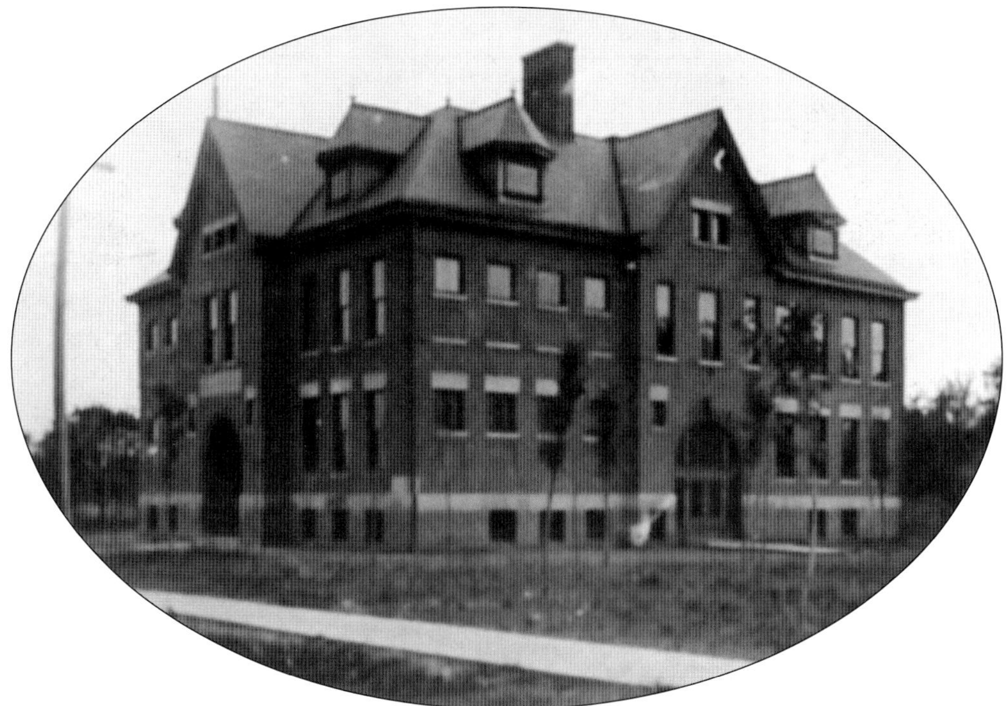

In 1897, the first Lincoln School was built at 400 South Jackson Street with teachers for eight grades. By 1902, with too many students at Lincoln, Washington School took the overflow. Lincoln School was replaced in the early 1900s. In 1953, residents voted in favor of constructing another new school. Construction began the following year, with completion in time for school in autumn 1955. (VWPL.)

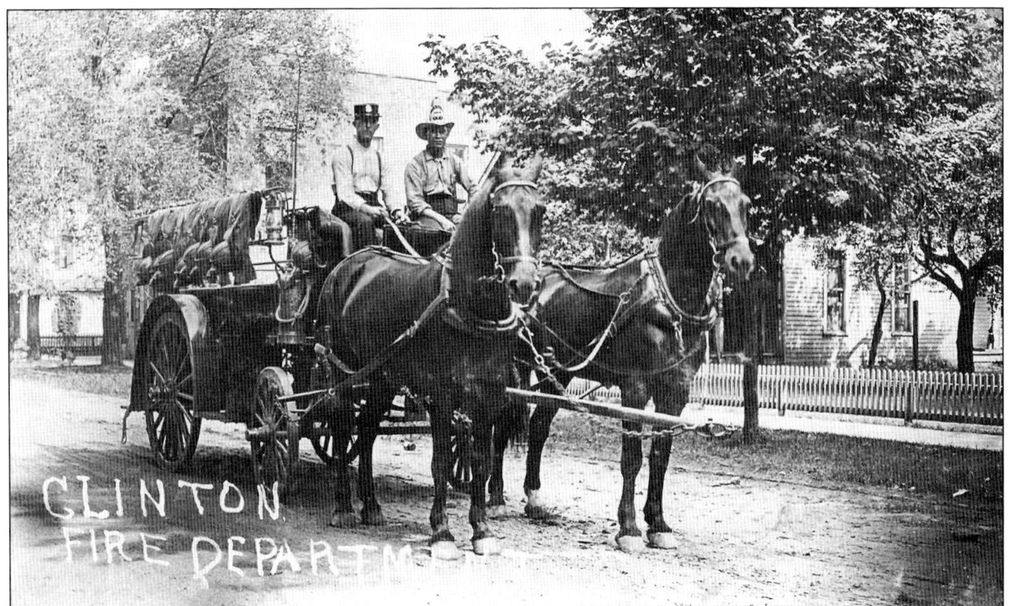

Two members of the Clinton Fire Department pose around 1900–1915. The man on the left may be a Mr. Dallas. The horses, named Ben and Frank, were said to be smart enough to back themselves up to the fire wagon when the siren sounded, waiting for the firemen to arrive. The department's uniforms are draped over the side of the top rail. (KA.)

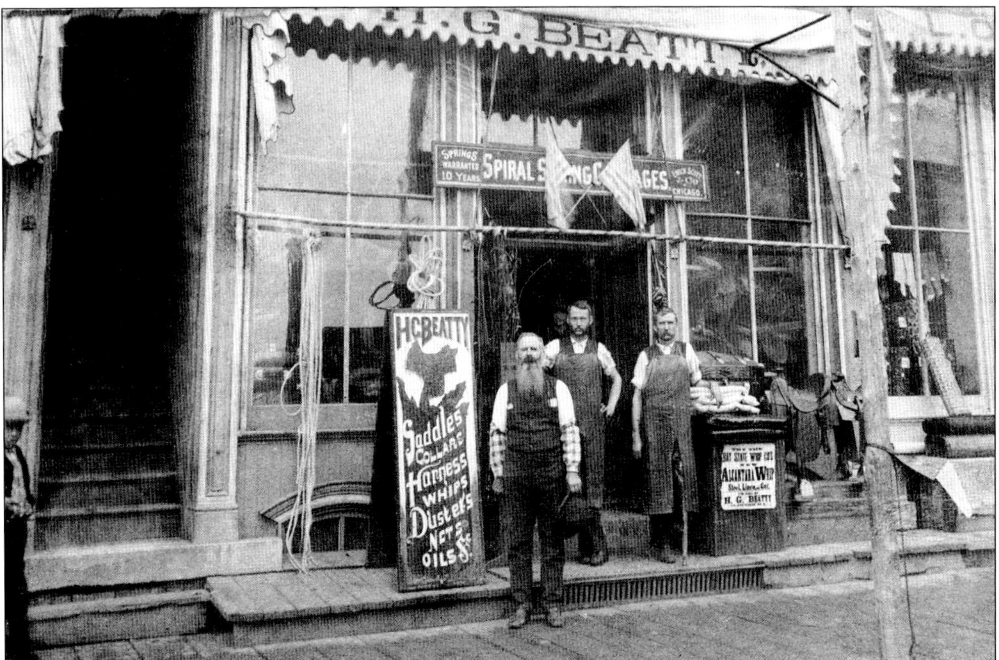

Henry G. Beatty (1845–1926) worked with his father and twin brother operating Beatty harness businesses in Moweaqua and Kenney until moving into a storefront east of his father's original store on the south side of Clinton Square. The man to the far right, missing an arm and a leg, probably fought in the Civil War. Beatty descendants ran the business until its 1967 closure after 119 years of operation. (DCM.)

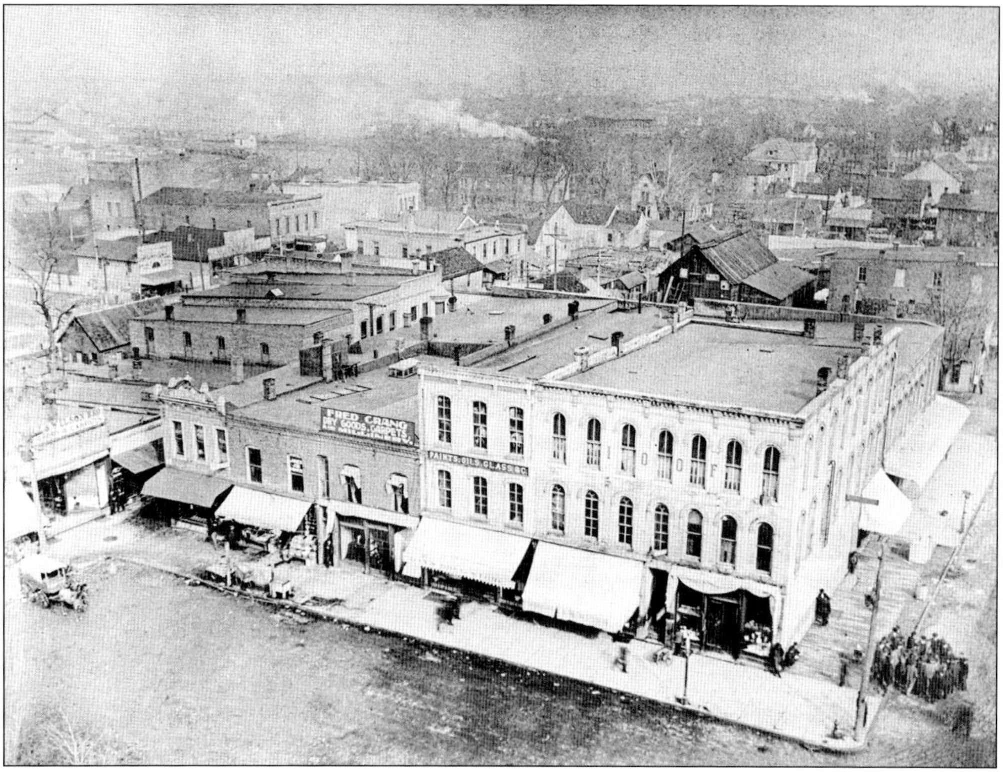

An aerial view of the east side of the square displays "IOOF" (Independent Order of Odd Fellows) between top windows of the corner building. Currently, the building displays "THE OHIO" instead. Fire destroyed the building to the left (showing "Paints, Oils, Glass") in November 1914. The other structures to the left are not drastically changed. (DCM.)

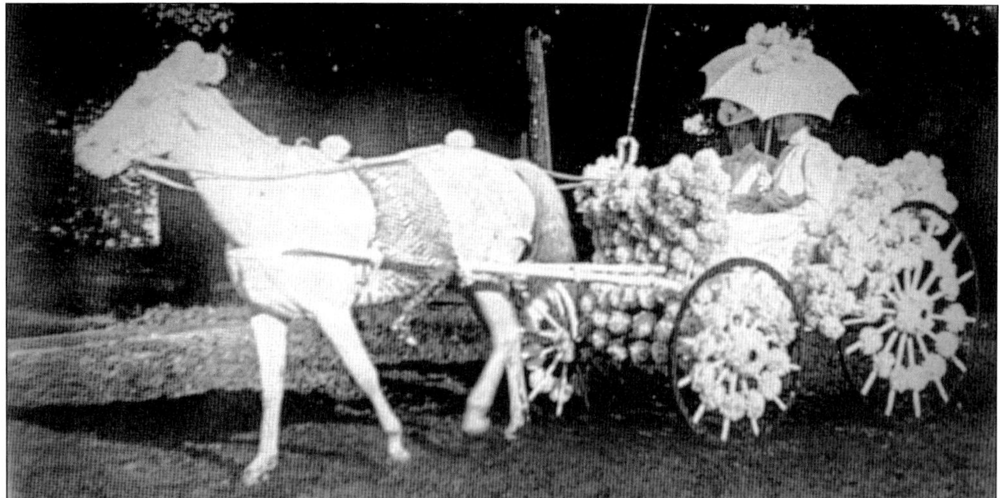

In 1899, Clinton enjoyed a Fourth of July floral parade with flower-decorated carriages. The first carriage, covered in hydrangeas and drawn by a snow-white horse, was driven by Nellie Magill, daughter of Robert and Clara Magill. Accompanied by Emma Lewis and escorted by John Q. Lewis, mounted on a similar horse, Magill won the first prize. She married Oscar Pond in 1903 and died at the age of 100. (DCM.)

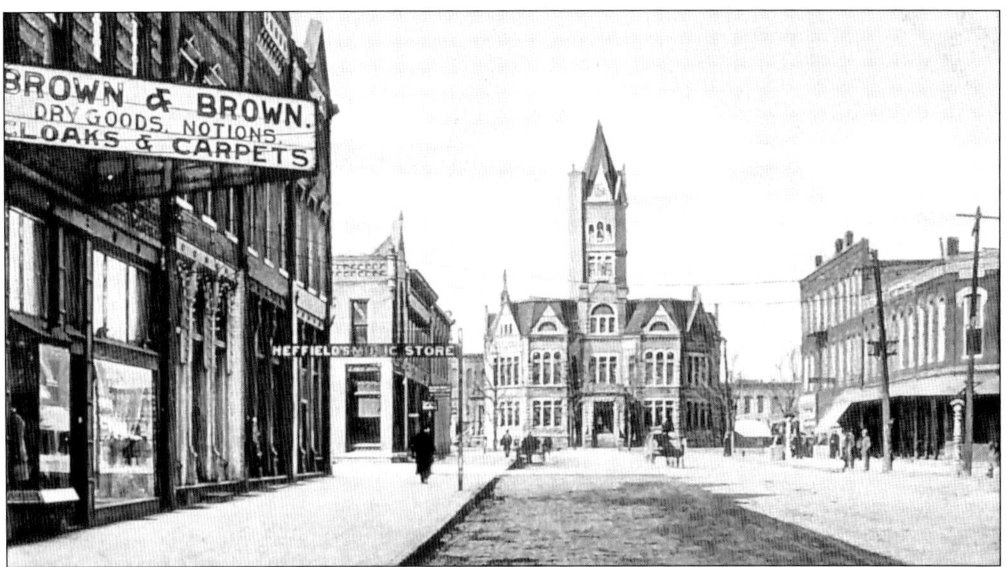

Stores along East Main Street appear around 1901–1909. One sign advertises Sheffield's Music Store, and another advertises Brown & Brown Dry Goods, which opened in 1901 at 206–208 East Main Street. Later, the Clintonia Theater occupied some of the area. Across from the courthouse, on the right corner, stands the current Ohio Building, with the 1884 Cackley building east of it. (VWPL.)

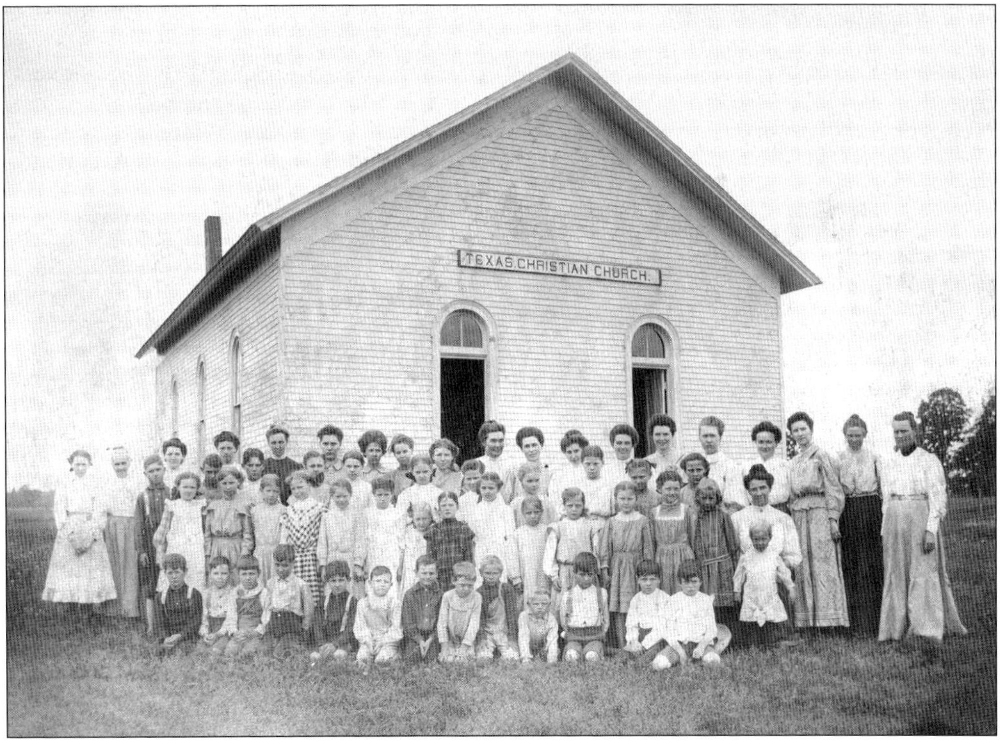

Organized in 1850 by Walter Bowles and William Springer, Texas Christian Church then consisted of approximately 12 members. After using a Baptist church for their services for 25 years, they obtained a land grant in 1875. Soon they had their own church four miles south and one mile west of Clinton. (DCM.)

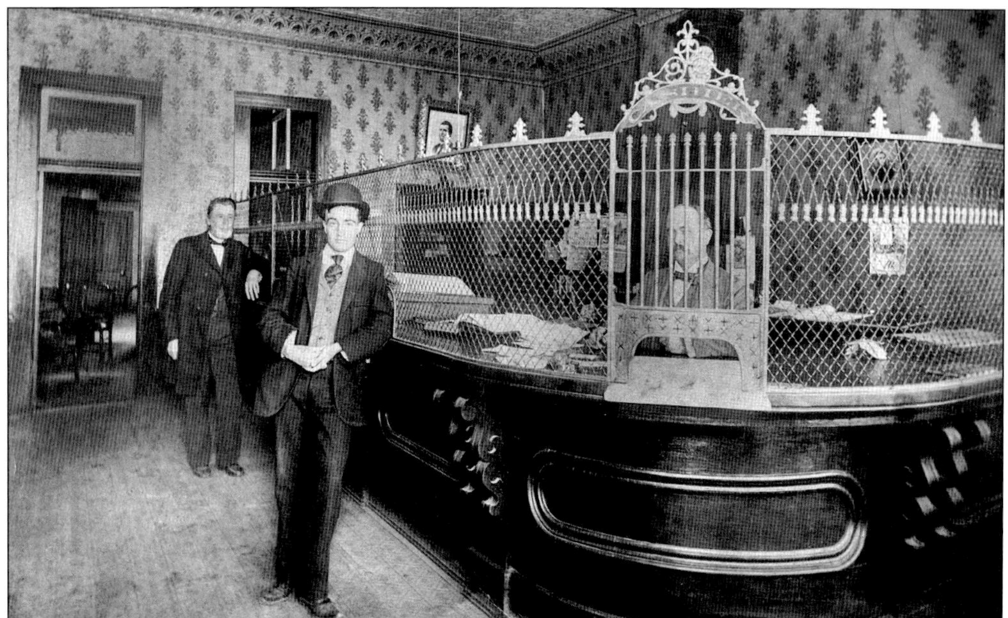

In 1867, Dr. John Warner and his partners, James McKinley, Henry Magill, J.R. Warner, and Lawrence Weldon, established Clinton's first bank under the name John Warner and Company. Inside the bank, Dr. Warner stands in the back left, and he also appears in the framed portrait on the far wall. The man in the hat is unidentified, but John Lewis, a bank employee, stands behind the counter. (DCM.)

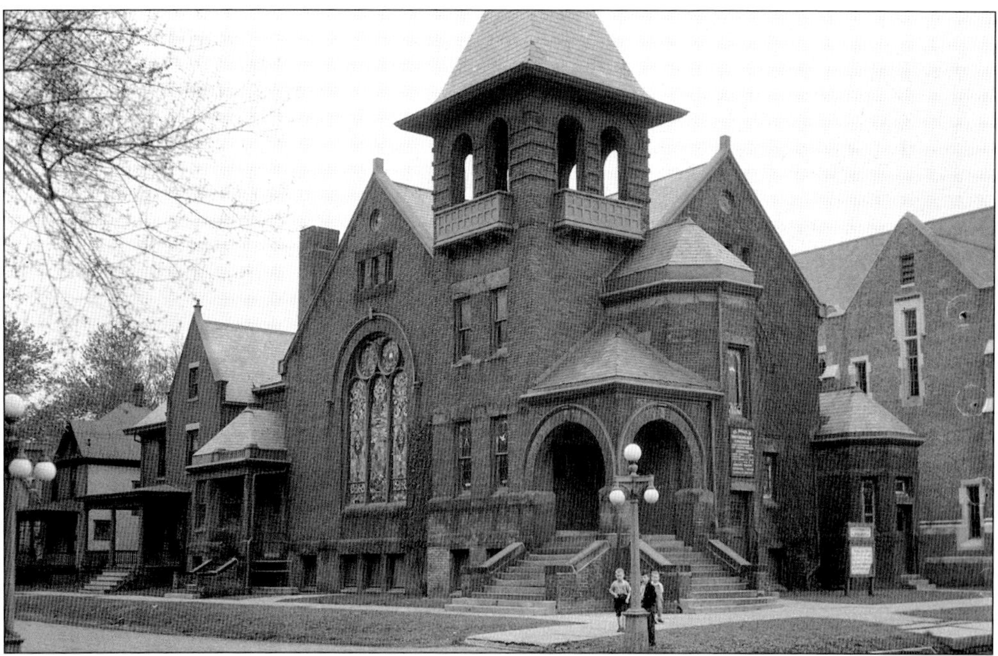

By the 1870s, residents formed a Universalist church named St. Paul's. Services were held every fourth Sabbath, usually at the Christian church. Construction at 107 South East Street began in 1899 with a 1900 dedication. Dr. John Warner donated a pipe organ. Newspapers last mentioned the church in the late 1980s and its address as 320 East Main Street. (DPL.)

At various times starting in the early 1900s, James R. Carroll owned several grocery stores in Clinton, including one on the north side of the square. His store at 602 West Side Square (pictured) was in business from approximately 1904 until 1914. Another store stood at 317 West Johnson Street and another on West Macon Street. He retired in the 1920s and eventually moved to Bloomington. (VWPL.)

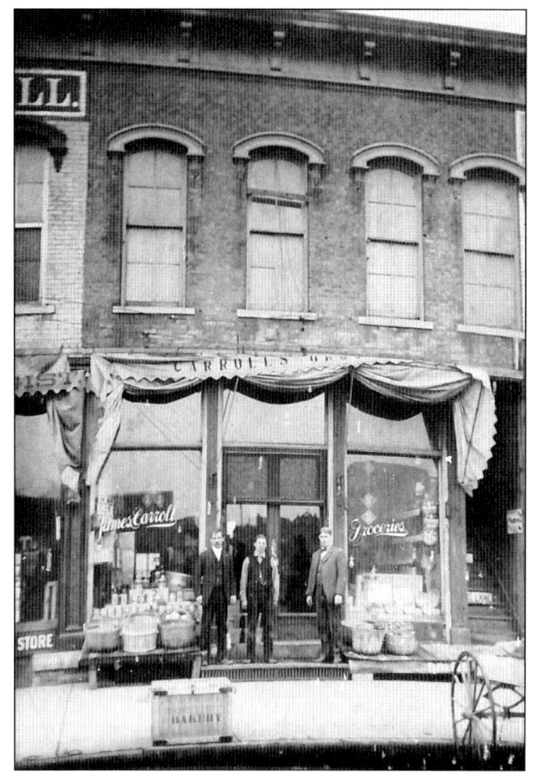

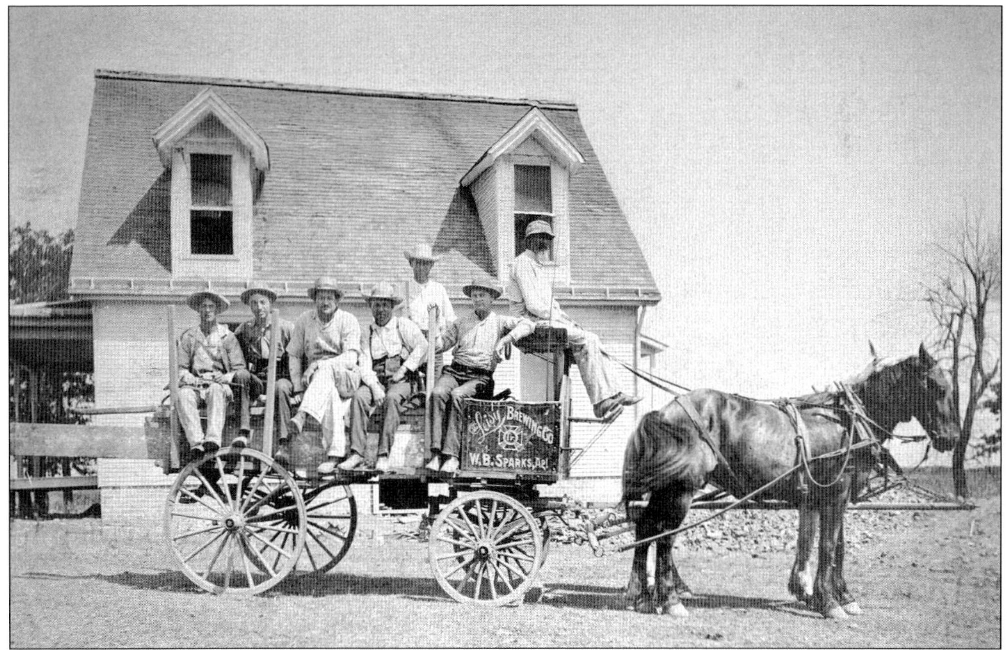

In 1899, planning to open a saloon and restaurant near the Central Hotel, W.B. Sparks joined with J.A. Phares to lease a room being used as a billiard parlor. In 1901, Sparks sold his interest to his partner and bought a half interest in another saloon. He eventually became an agent for Peoria's Leisy Brewing Company. (DCM.)

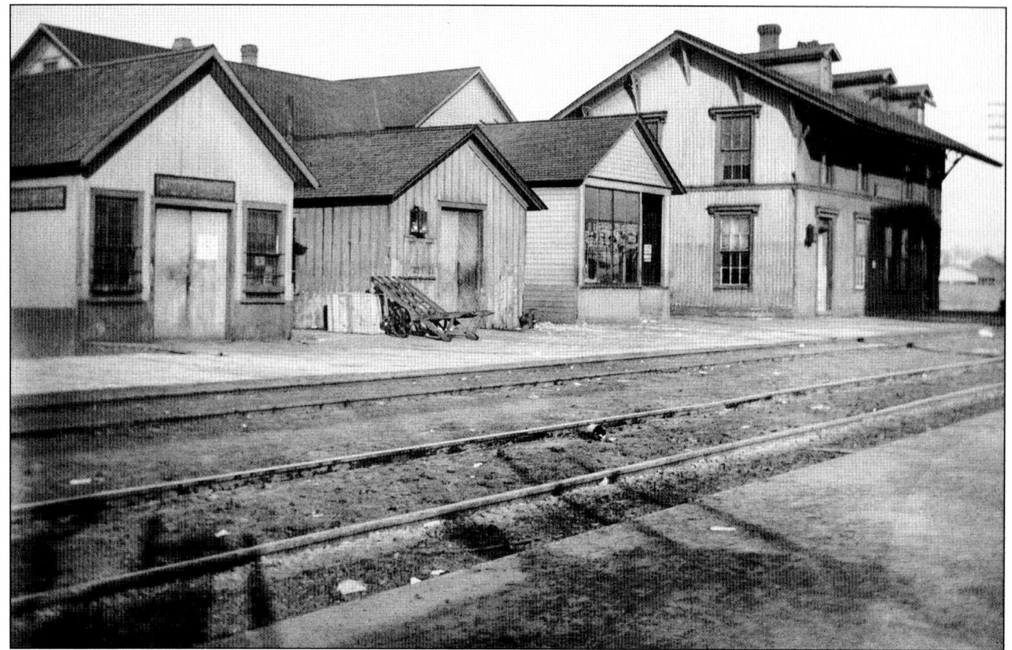

The Clinton rail yard buildings, including the 1894 freight depot, were near Macon Street. Writing on the window of the building to the left of the depot reads "Lunch Room." As of 1968, the building was abandoned, and it was eventually razed. The Clinton yards and offices built in 1915–1916 to house the yardmaster and other staff were located near East and Washington Streets. (DCM.)

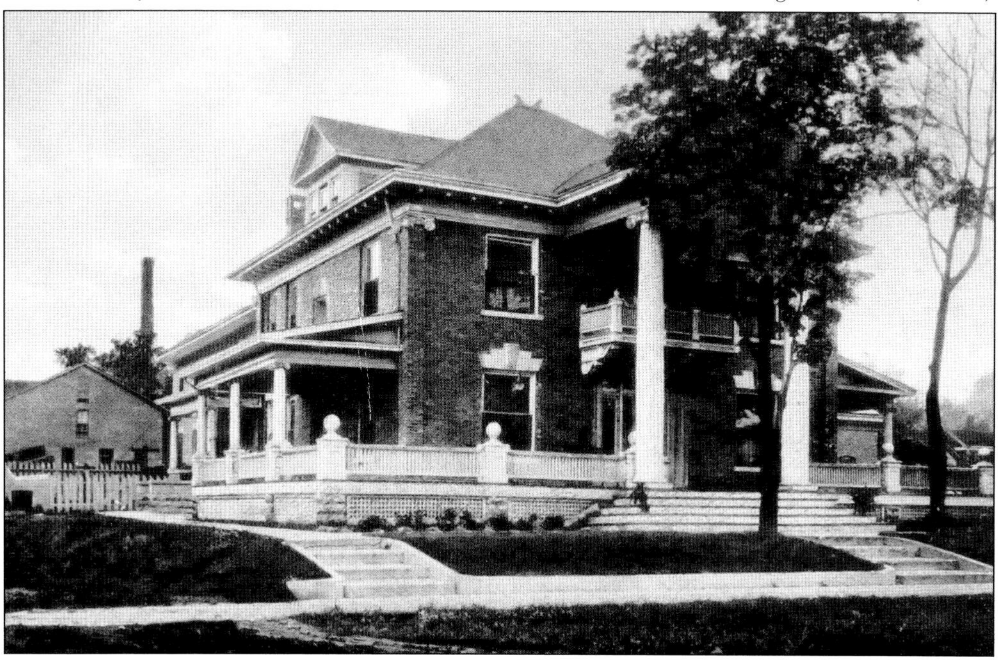

DeWitt County's jail was built in the 200 block of North Monroe Street in 1903. The county's only execution occurred prior to that, in 1882, when Thomas Coyne (also known as Patsy Devine) was hanged at the former jail for murdering a Bloomington citizen. By 1991, a newer jail was built nearby. The 1903 facility was demolished in 1997. (MWC.)

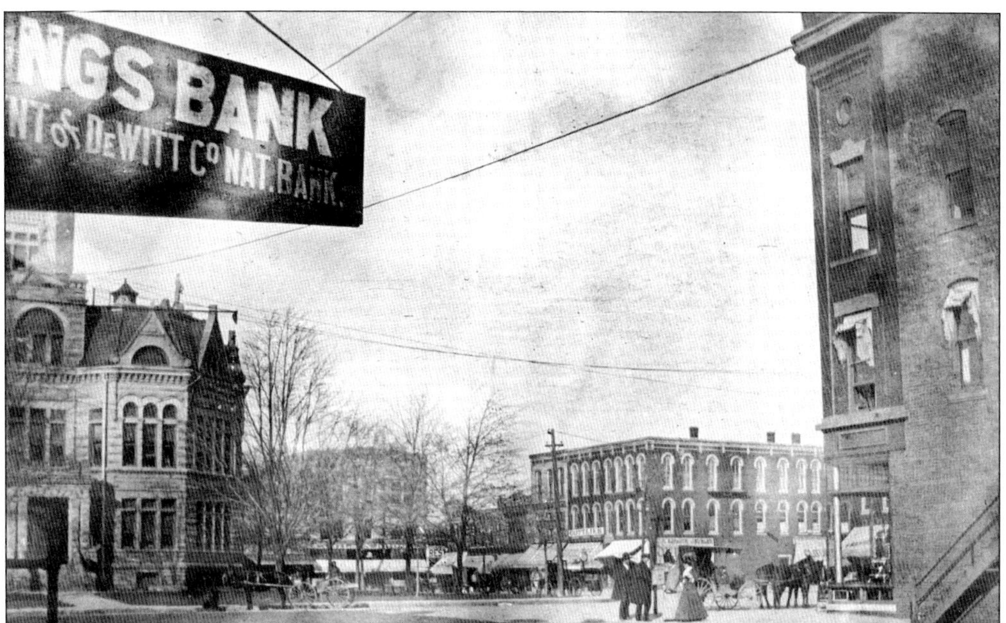

This early-1900s photograph shows the square and the sign for the DeWitt Savings Bank across Center Street from the current chamber of commerce. Several people stand at the opposite corner near what appears to be a postal box. Gottlieb's department store occupied the current Ohio Building at East Main Street and the square. (DCM.)

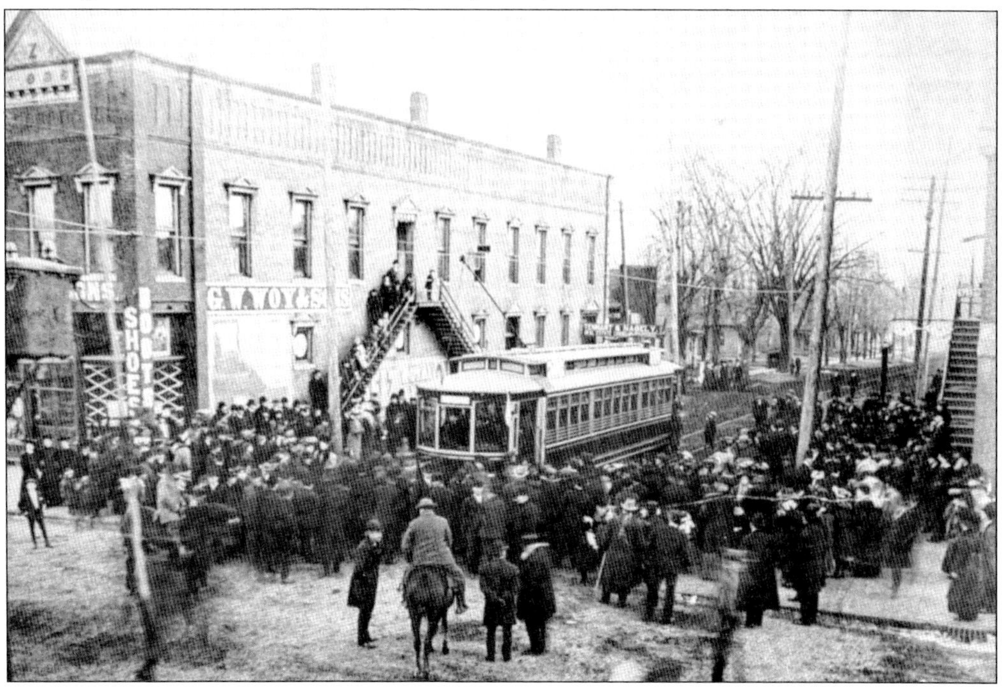

Clintonians crowd around the first interurban train arriving in Clinton in 1905. The tracks ran on Monroe Street, cutting through land owned by C.H. Moore. Although the tracks were removed years ago, portions of the interurban (the poles, elevated track bed, and a bridge foundation) were on the grounds of the Moore Homestead until 2025. (DCM.)

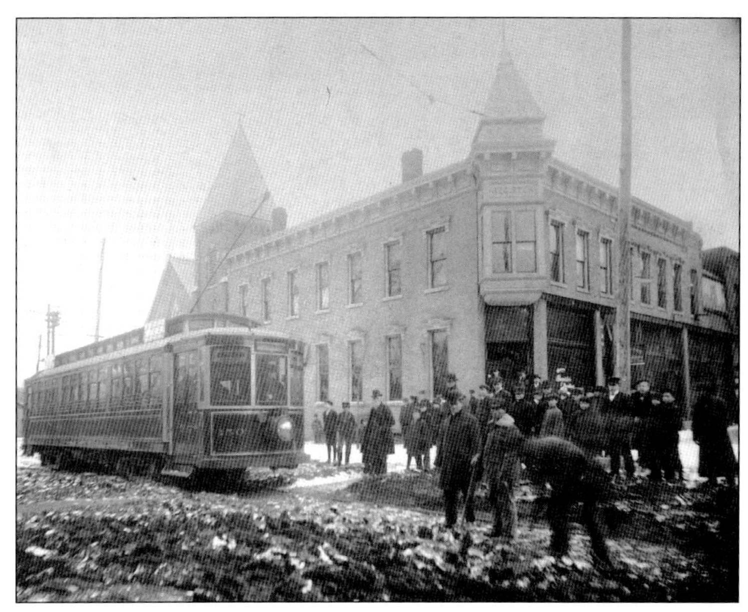
An interurban trolley car stands in front of what is now 122 Warner Court at South Monroe Street. The word "Register" can be seen above the windows on the tower of the foreground building, home then to the *Clinton Register* newspaper offices. The word "Register" is still seen today. The background steeple belonged to the First Christian Church, destroyed by fire in December 1945. (VWPL.)

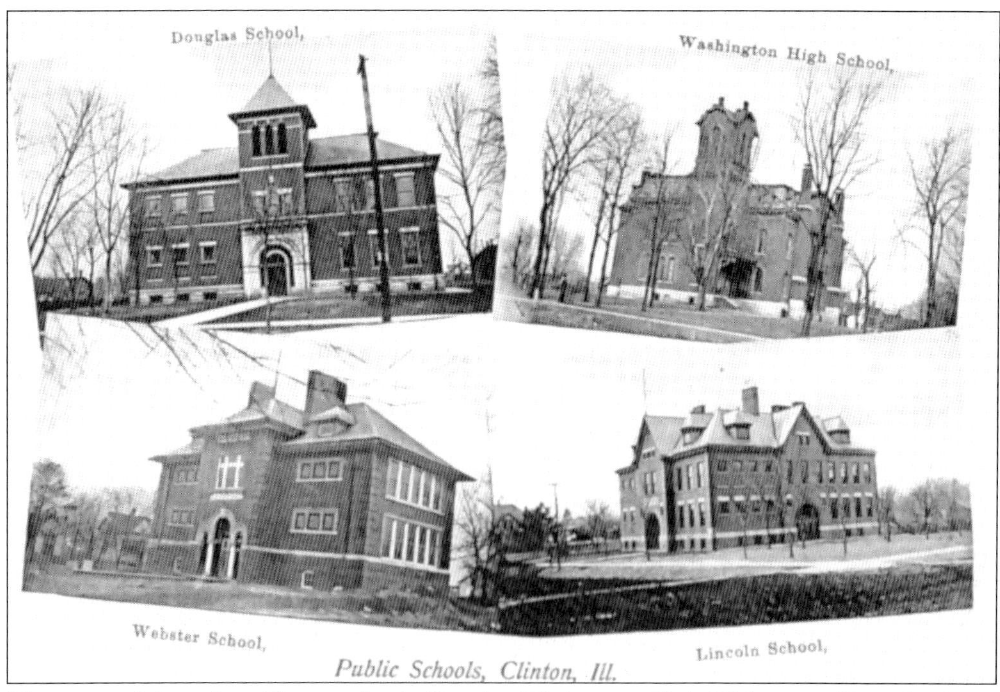

This postcard shows four Clinton schools: Douglas, Washington High, Webster, and Lincoln. Open by at least the 1880s, Douglas School (between Main and Washington Streets) was remodeled in 1902. By 1905, both Douglas and the first Lincoln School were demolished. Built in 1905 at George and Webster Streets, Webster School was demolished around 2015, as was another Washington School on Mulberry Street. (AC.)

Two

Clinton into the 2000s

As Clinton approached the 1900s, more businesses and public buildings were constructed, and the recently built opera house, railroad depot, and courthouse filled vital roles. Grocery establishments, shoe and clothing stores, restaurants, dentists, and doctors crowded the square, with homes spread out nearby.

By 1910, the town included over 83 streets, all brick-covered. Fires constantly threatened, consuming two churches in separate events in the early 1900s. One blaze swept through buildings around the square in 1913.

Eleven daily passenger trains passed through Clinton in the 1920s, but car dealers were eying the future and affordable vehicles. When the Great Depression hit, railroads dropped in popularity. The Illinois Central Railroad offered fewer trains, and by the late 1950s, the Illinois Traction Railroad's interurban system linking small towns finally died.

Fortune magazine's June 1940 issue included a complimentary article naming DeWitt County as "The Ever-Normal County." In addition to referencing people and places in the area, it reported details about elections from 1848 through 1936, noting that except for lacking seven votes in 1884, DeWitt voters always picked the person who became president.

Fortunately, with encouragement of civic leaders throughout the decades, more businesses arrived, some to an industrial park on the east edge of town in the 1950s. Within 20 years, Clinton's population of 8,000 people covered four square miles and 120 streets. The town offered four elementary schools, a middle school, a high school, 17 churches, 2 nursing homes, 2 newspapers, 1 radio station, 9 city parks, and 1 state park. The nuclear power plant east of town brought growth and job opportunities. The 1980s found Clinton with more businesses extending the town's west edge, including Walmart, McDonald's, restaurants, and a hotel. With dedication and hard work from residents and businesses, the growth continues.

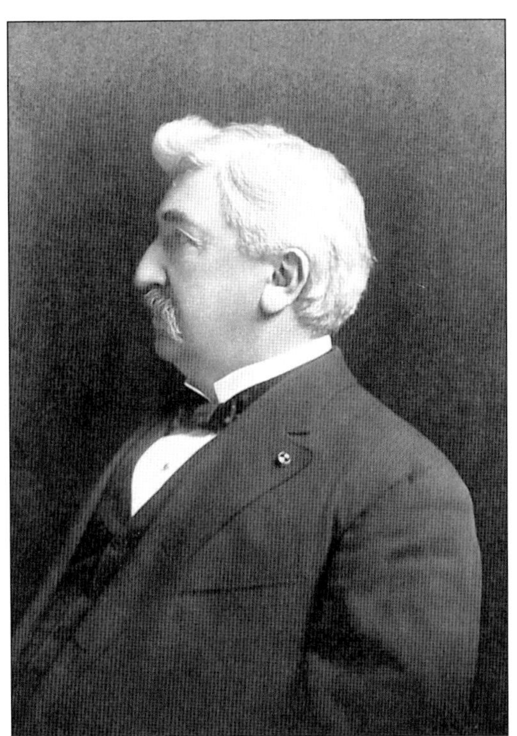

Raised in Clinton, Vespasian Warner (1842–1925) was born to Cynthia and Dr. John Warner. As of 1868, he was in law practice in Clinton with his father-in-law, C.H. Moore. From 1895 until 1905, he served in Congress, then he ran unsuccessfully for Illinois governor. Pres. Theodore Roosevelt appointed Warner commissioner of pensions from 1905 until 1909. (VWPL.)

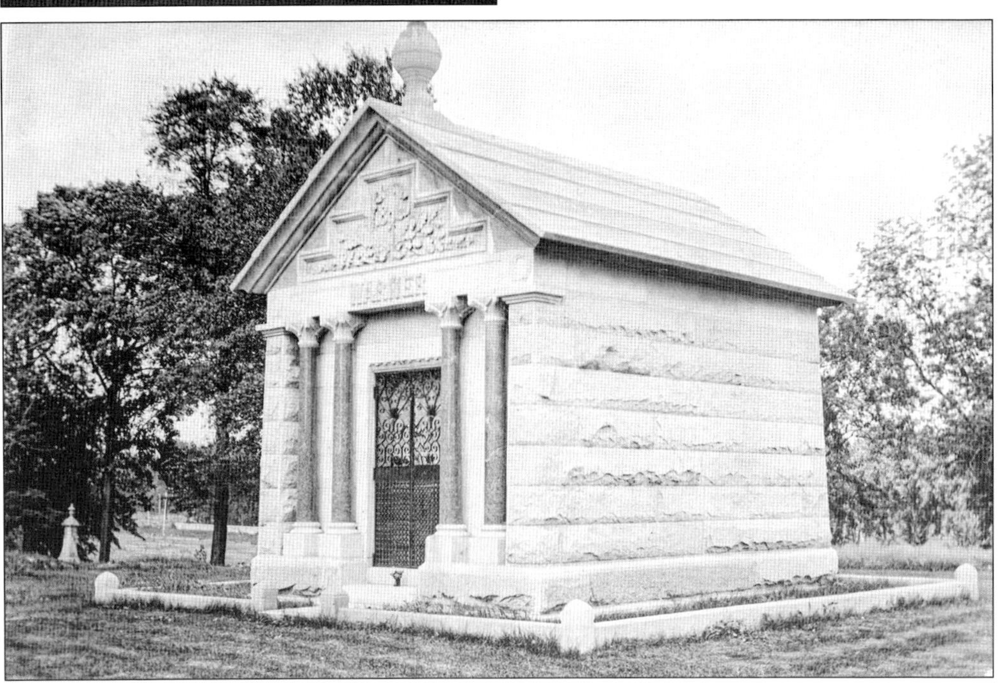

Dr. John Warner (1819–1905) is entombed in this mausoleum to the right of the original gated entrance to Woodlawn Cemetery. After practicing medicine in Farmer City for two years, he moved to Clinton, practicing for another 12 years before going into banking. At his death, he possessed DeWitt County acreage, a farm near Olney, and several farms in Indiana, Nebraska, and Iowa. (DCM.)

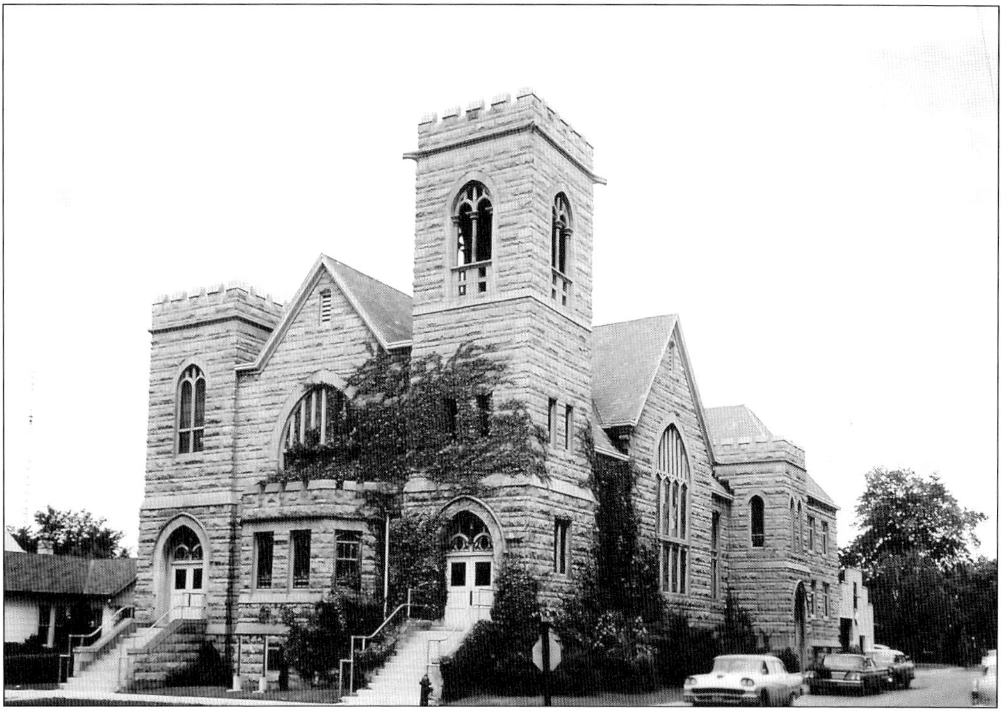

Clinton's Presbyterian residents first held services in 1853 in various churches, the courthouse, and a hall on the square. The next year, Presbyterian women purchased land for a church on the northwest corner of Madison and Washington Streets, with a dedication in 1860. In 1905, it was replaced by the North Center Street church to which C.H. Moore donated a pipe organ. (VWPL.)

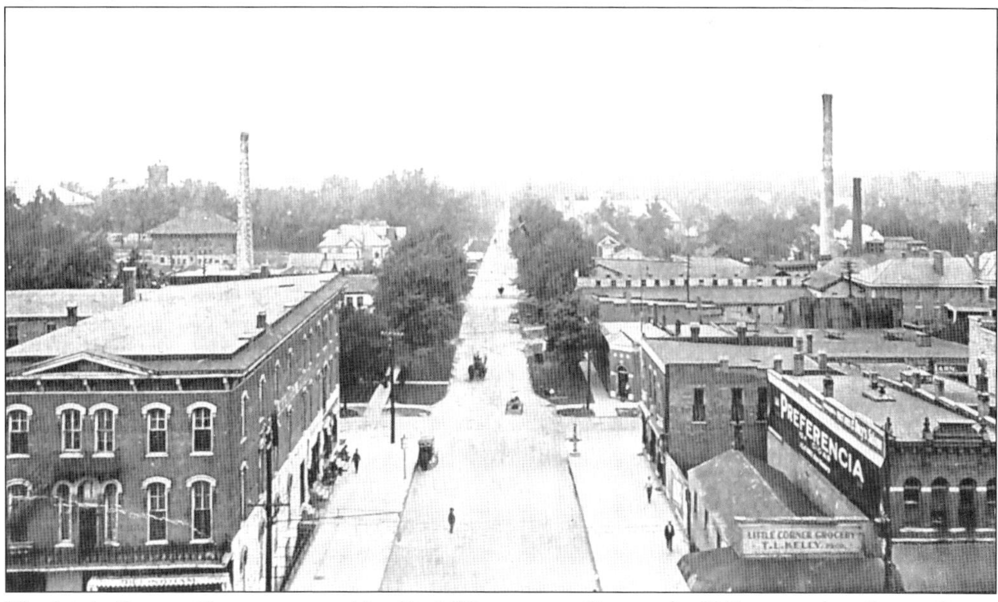

The Little Corner Grocery, owned by Civil War veteran Thomas L. Kelley, stood at Center Street and the north side of the square. The store opened for customers in early 1905. An advertisement for Preferencia Cigars appears on the east building's wall. The building currently occupied by Sorrento's Pizza is a block beyond, and the Magill Hotel is across the street. (VWPL.)

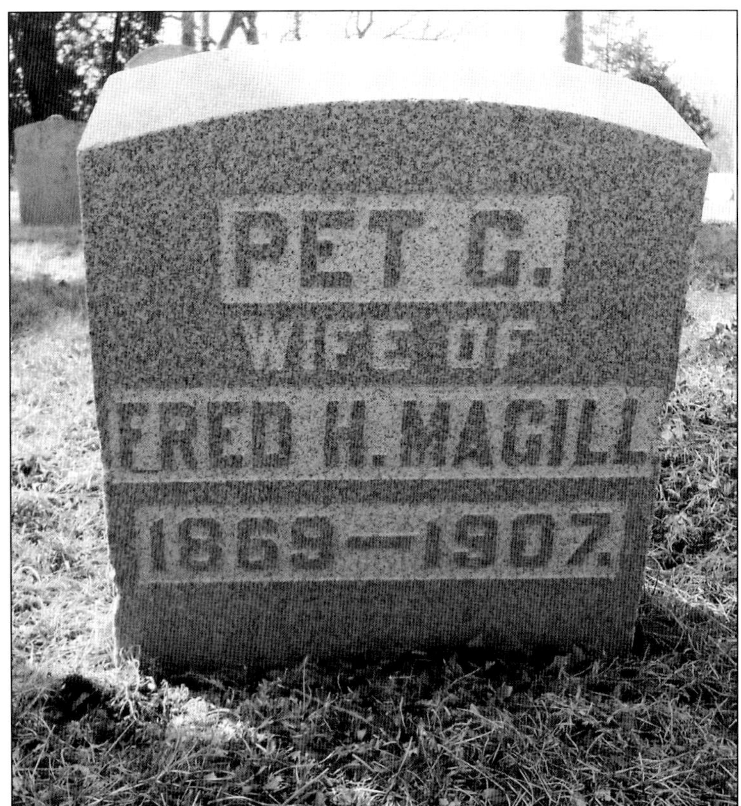

In May 1907, after claiming he found the body of his wife, nicknamed "Pet," next to a bottle of chloroform, Fred Magill obtained a quick inquest. Her death was ruled a suicide. In Denver with his daughter three weeks later, Magill married his daughter's young friend Fay Estelle Graham (later Johnson). They were arrested, tried, and acquitted for Pet Magill's death. Fay Magill Johnson died in 1978 in California. (AC.)

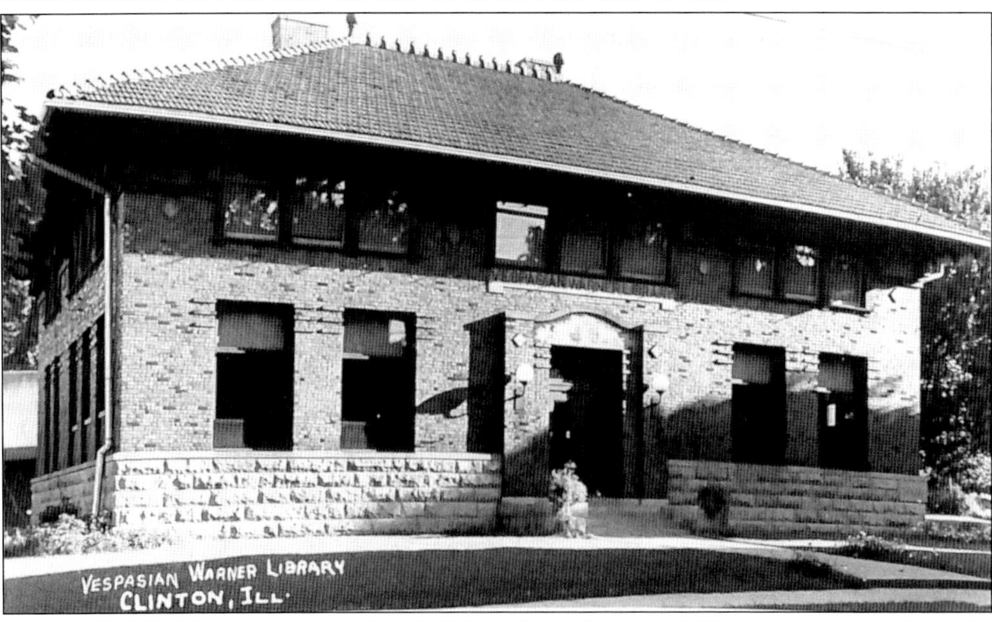

In his will, C.H. Moore bequeathed his 7,000 books to the city of Clinton but required they be placed in a proper library building. After Vespasian Warner, Moore's son-in-law, donated money and land for the project, construction of the Vespasian Warner Public Library ran from 1906 until October 1908. In 1992, a Prairie-style addition enlarged the building. (VWPL.)

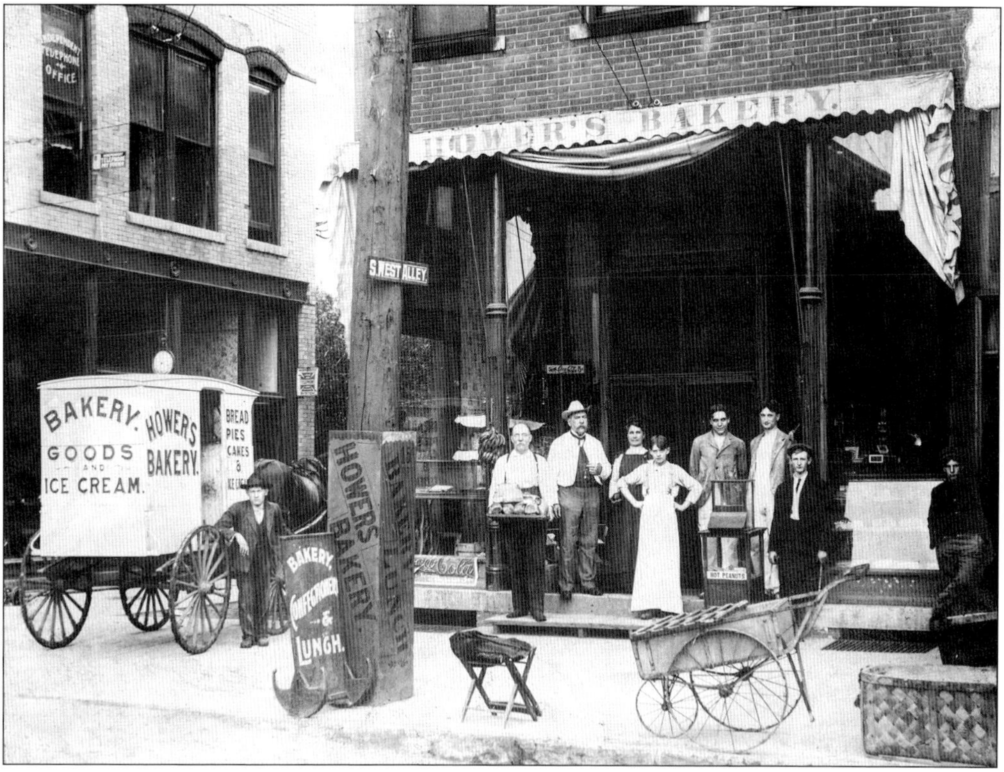

Grant Hower's Bakery occupied the southwest corner of Clinton Square. Photographed from left to right are Roy Lane, M. Nicholi, George Hower (Grant Hower's father), a Mrs. Baker, Earl Austin, George Langenbacker, baker Frank Crump, Fred Laisure, and Russell Bogardus. Jones Watch and Clock repair shop stands to the left, with the telephone company on the second floor. (DCM.)

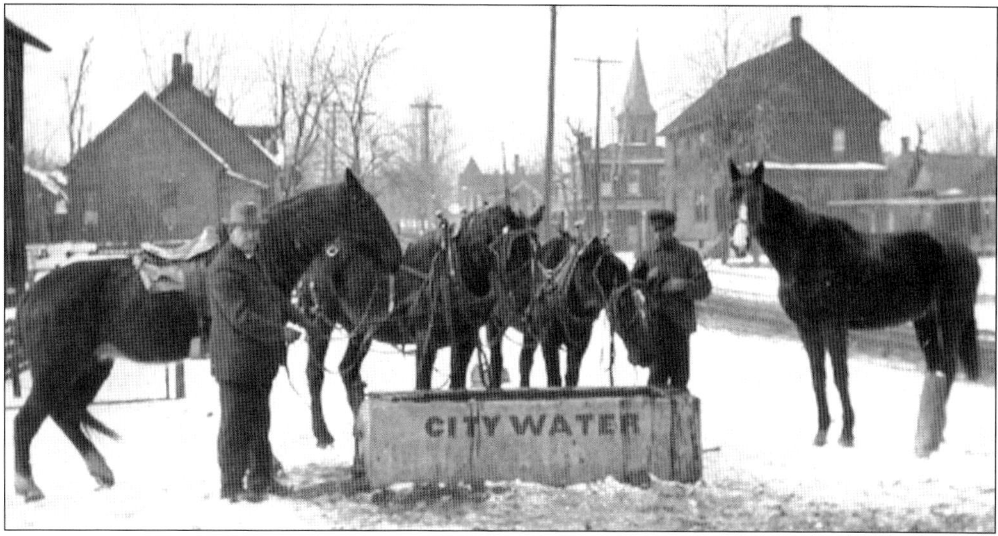

Fred Kent (left), owner of Kent Lumber, and an unidentified man (right) stand with horses beside a city-owned water trough on East Macon Street near Kent's business. St. John's Catholic Church's steeple is visible in the background. Born in 1862, Kent died in 1932. In 1859, his father, Emmett Kent, founded the Kent Lumber Company, DeWitt County's oldest firm. (VWPL.)

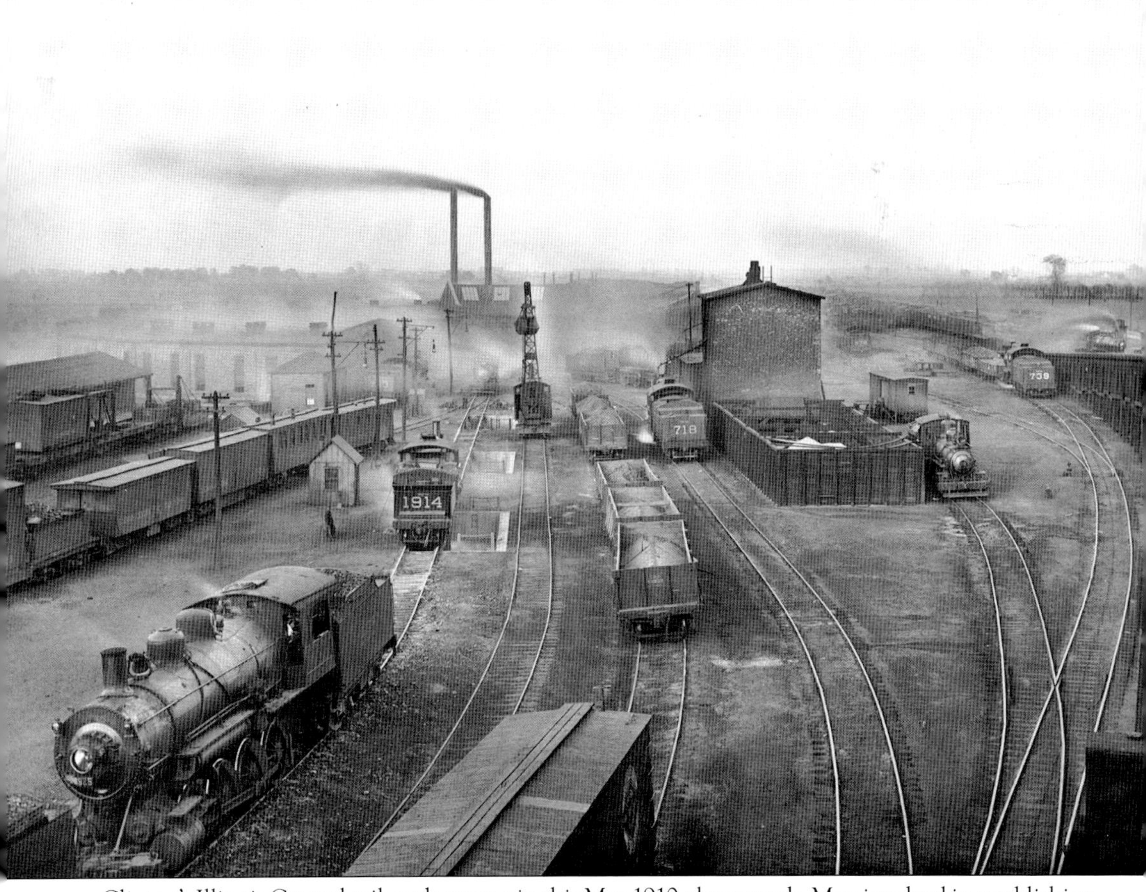

Clinton's Illinois Central rail yards appear in this May 1910 photograph. Men involved in establishing the railroad in Clinton included C.H. Moore, Judge Lawrence Weldon, David Davis, Thomas Snell, and the Magill family. By 1877, Clinton was the crossing point for three lines of the Illinois Central Railroad. Many residents wanted the shops and roundhouse moved to Clinton from Wapella to establish Clinton as a railroad town. At one time, the railroad was the largest employer in DeWitt County. The background smokestacks are seen to the right of the brick roundhouse, partially destroyed then resurrected after an 1875 storm. Diesel engines brought an end to the need for the roundhouse. Demolition began in 1959, but portions existed into the late 1960s. A wedge of the roundhouse survived through the 1970s. The roundhouse crane was eventually moved to Monticello, Illinois's Railroad Museum. (H-R.)

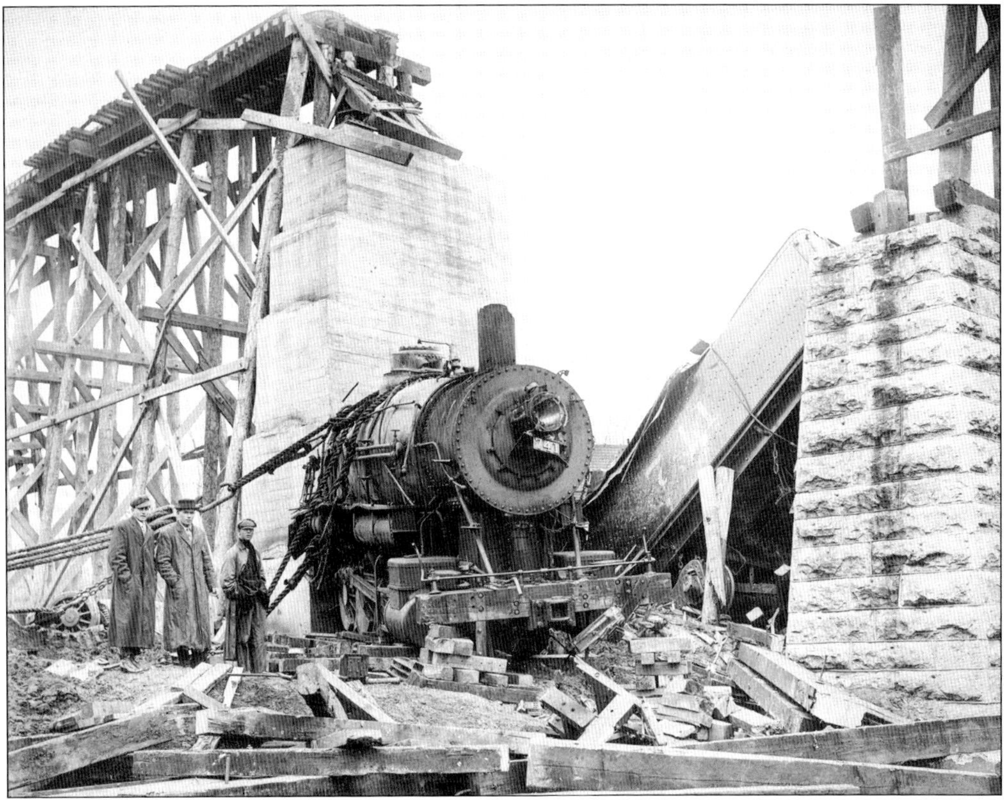

On November 3, 1911, an Illinois Central train engine struck the center span of a temporary bridge over Salt Creek. The engine and two railcars fell 45 feet, carrying four men to their deaths. The men were engineer Harry Emmett and three firemen: Herbert Grissom, Arthur Metzger, and Amnel Crum. (DCM.)

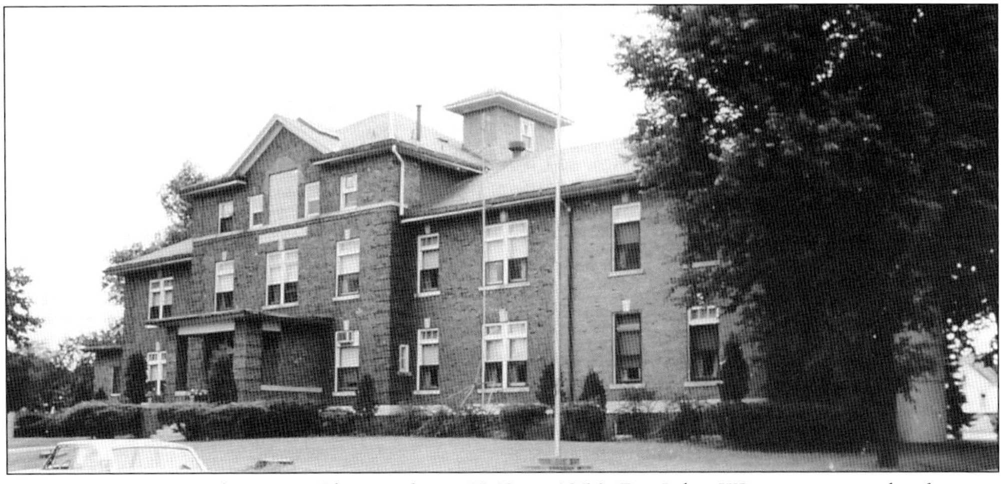

After practicing medicine in Clinton from 1842 to 1856, Dr. John Warner amassed a fortune through banking and investments. Months before his 1905 death, he planned to build a hospital to donate to the city, but his will did not mention furnishings or maintenance. After its construction, the building stood idle until taxes and donors came to the rescue, allowing the Dr. John Warner Hospital to open in 1911. (KA.)

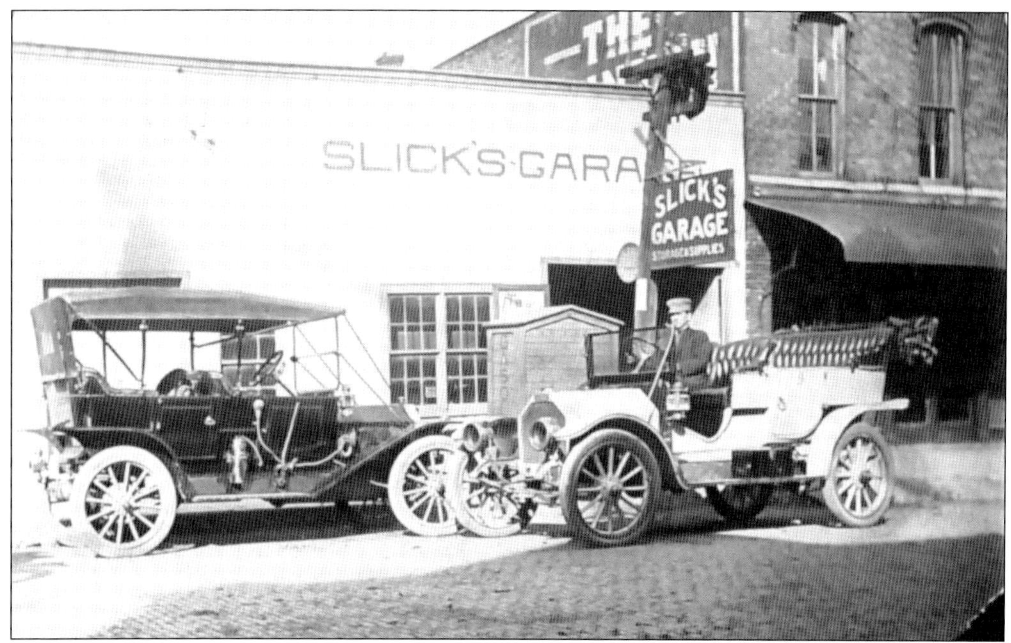

Located on East Main Street, Len Slick's Garage offered storage and livery facilities in addition to car repairs and blacksmithing. It also gave automobile agencies space to display their vehicles. Eventually, Slick relocated to 302 North Center Street. He sold the building and Chevrolet franchise to Frank Moots in 1926. Later, the Clintonia Theater occupied the garage's former site on East Main Street. (VWPL.)

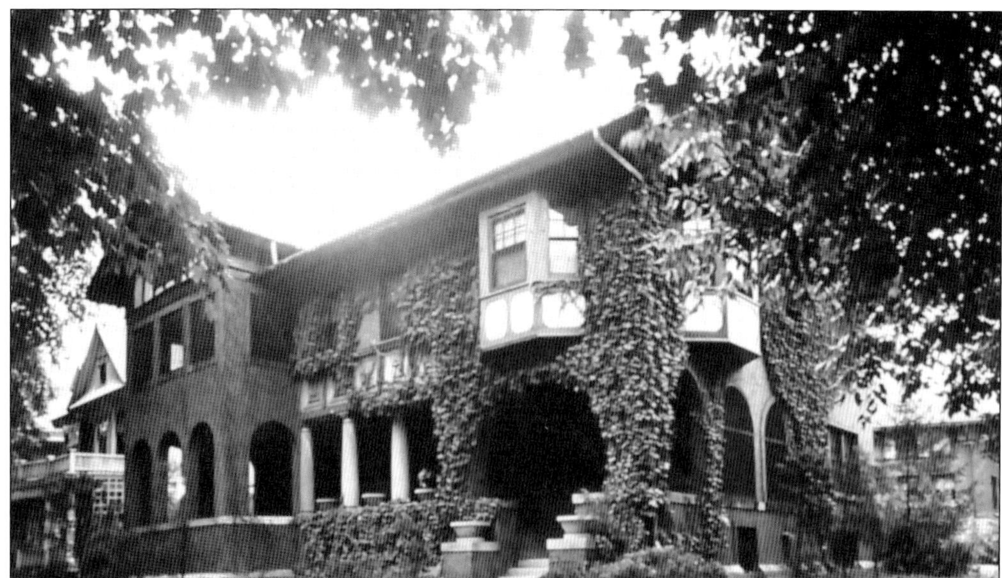

Vespasian Warner's house at 321 North Center Street was built in 1912; he lived here with his second wife, Minnie Bishop, until he died. Upon her 1942 death, it went to the Presbyterian church, but it is now a private residence. The architect also designed the house of Warner's son, Clifton Moore Warner, at 109 West Macon Street. Built in 1905, it became the fine arts center in 1960. (VWPL.)

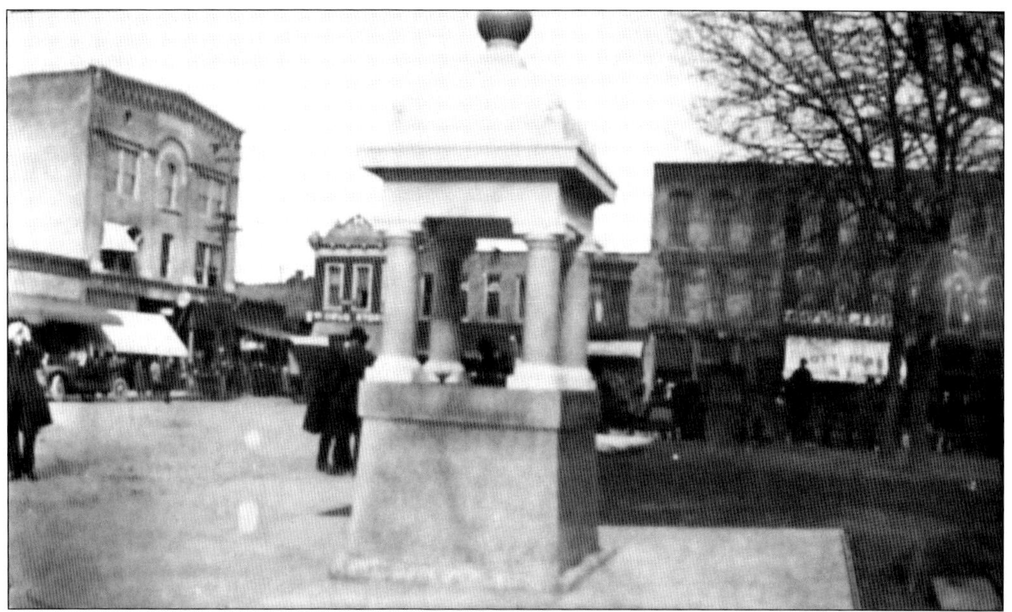

In 1912, Oscar J. Woodward obtained a permit to erect a public drinking fountain on the square to honor his mother, Isabel. It is located on the square's north side. The inscription reads, "In Memory of My Mother, Woodward 1812–1896." Woodward also donated funds to the city for Woodward Park, built in 1939. (VWPL.)

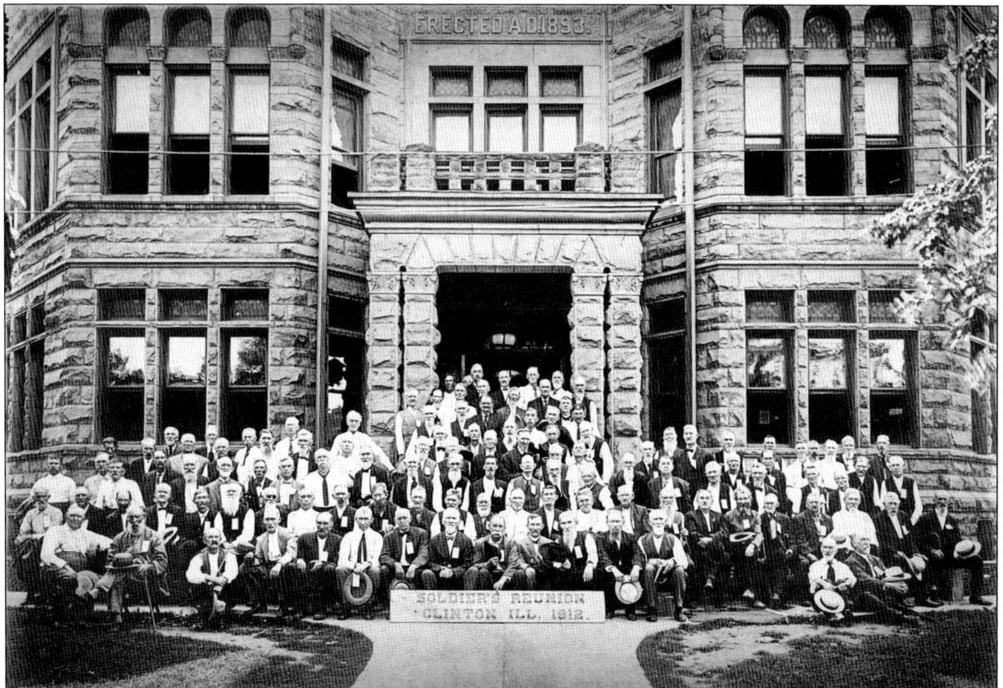

DeWitt County's Civil War soldiers, photographed on the steps of the courthouse, held their 15th reunion in September 1912. Along with an estimated 165 men, their wives and descendants also attended the reunion, with dinner provided by the Woman's Relief Corps (WRC). The soldiers had served in an artillery regiment, two cavalry regiments, and nine infantry regiments. (DCM.)

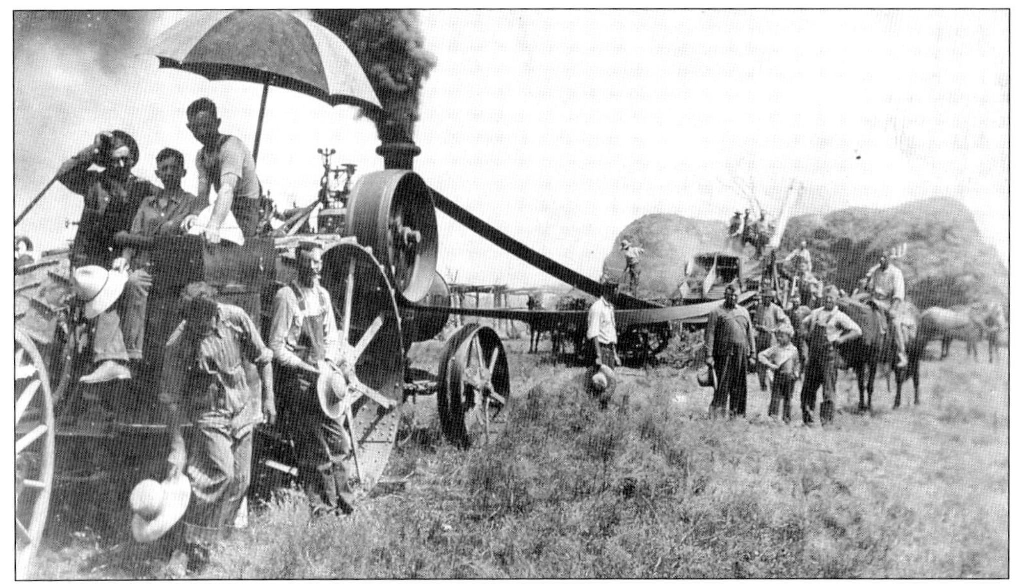

As threshing equipment evolved over the 19th century, neighbors usually shared costs to hire engine crews and machinery to complete the work. In 1850, manual labor needed 23 hours per acre to do the work. In 1900, using such machinery, labor dropped to eight hours per acre. This 1912 photograph shows a threshing team. The annual work was usually completed by early September. (VWPL.)

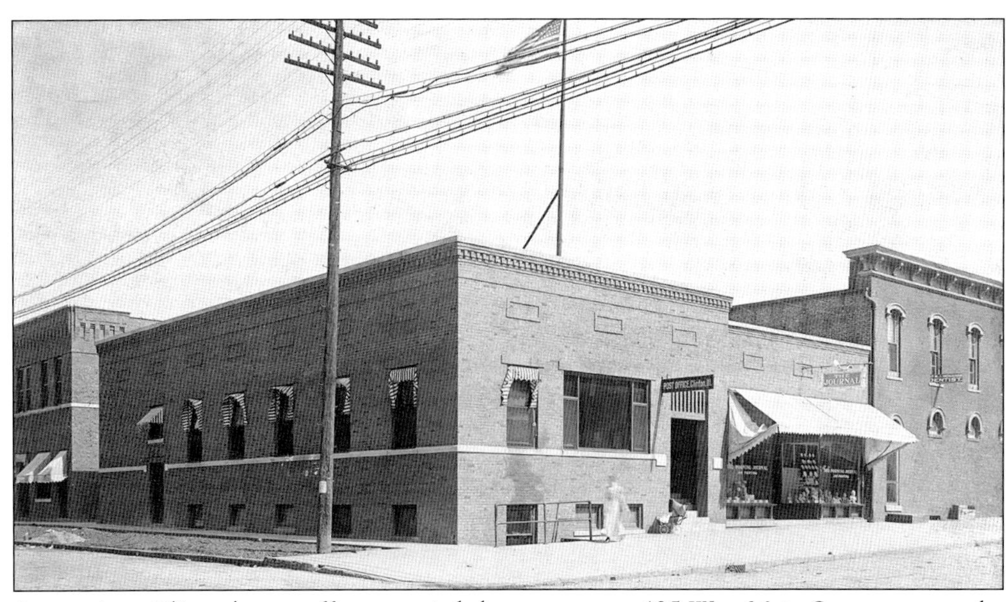

At one time, Clinton's post office occupied the structure at 125 West Main Street, next to the *Morning Journal* newspaper building. To the east of that structure, a sign hangs from a second-floor window announcing M.J. Monahan's dentist office above the building's Leader Cash Store. Monahan ministered to patients from July 1911 until 1913. (MWC.)

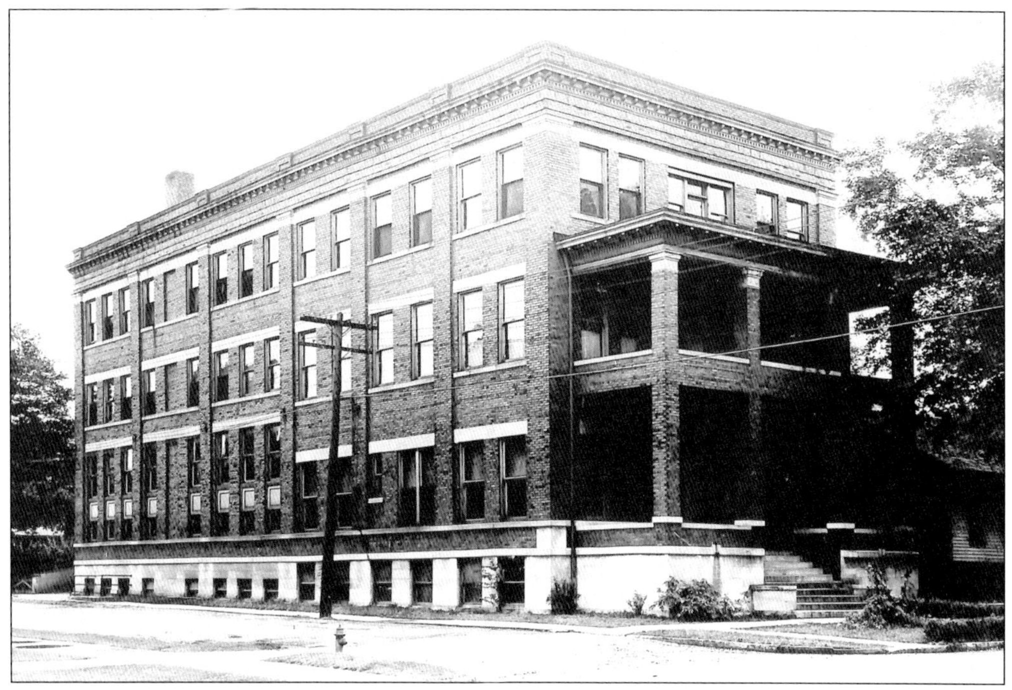

In the 1870s, Fred Kent organized the Young Men's Christian Association (YMCA) in Clinton on the north side of the square in various locations. It operated periodically until 1913, when a three-story building was finally constructed on North Center Street south of the Presbyterian church. A new YMCA on Alexander Street replaced it in 1963. The Center Street location is now a parking lot. (VWPL.)

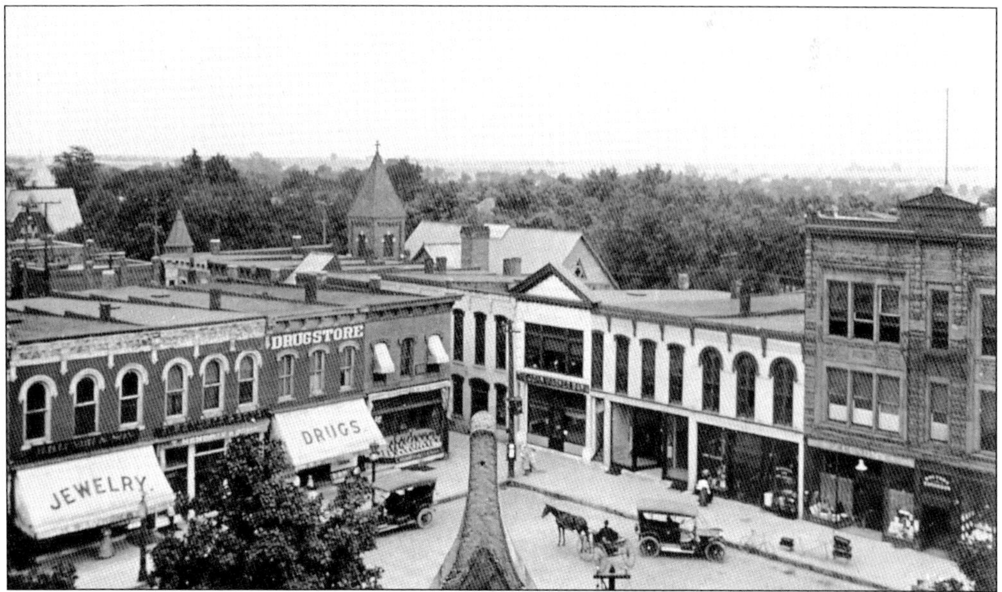

The businesses on the southeast corner of the square around 1915 were H.B. Lundh & Sons Jewelry, T. Hendrix & Sons, a drugstore (probably Chambers Drugs), a shoe store, the John Warner Bank (with a smaller storefront), more businesses, and the Rennick Opera House. The (not-yet-burned) First Christian Church's steeple stands in the background. (KA.)

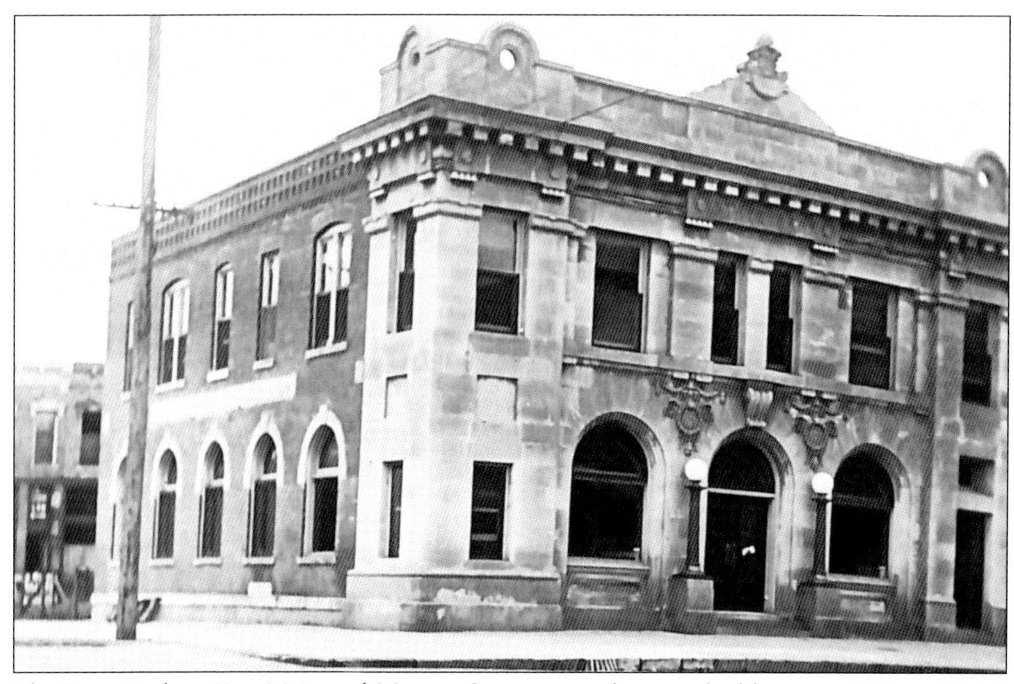

The State Bank, at East Main and Monroe Streets, was photographed between 1915 and 1925. In 1890, it was located in another building on East Main Street. After closing in January 1932, this corner bank was sold in 1935 to the DeWitt County Farm Bureau. It is now an apartment building. (VWPL.)

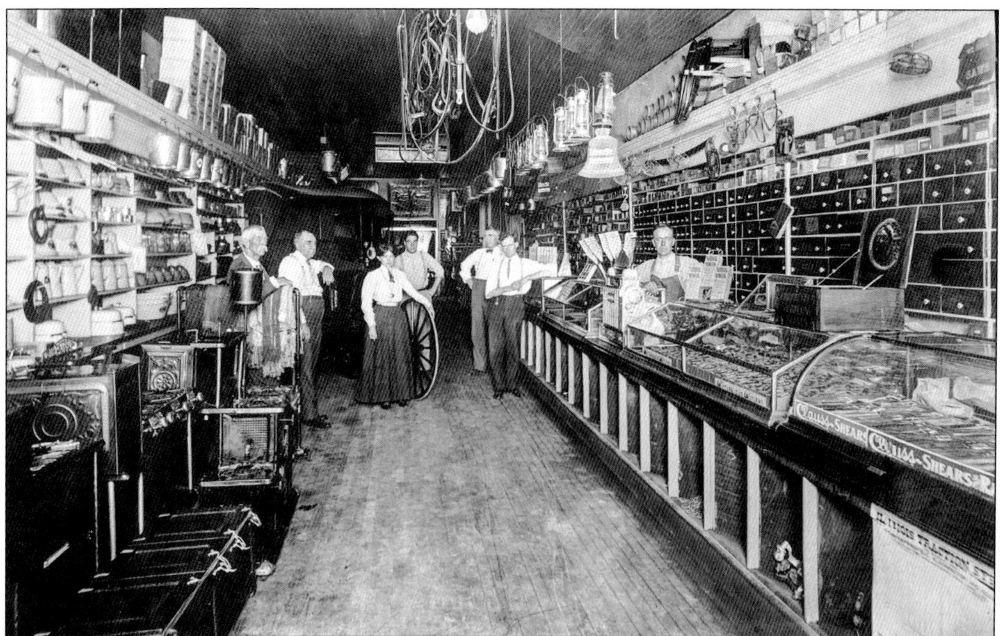

Isaac Bailor's hardware store, at 504 West Side Square, photographed around 1915, was built in 1872 for Philip Wolfe's hardware business. A wooden pump stood outside to help quench thirsts for people and animals. Bailor died in 1922 after 39 years in business. By 1923, it housed a grocery store, C.N. Hammond & Son. (DCM.)

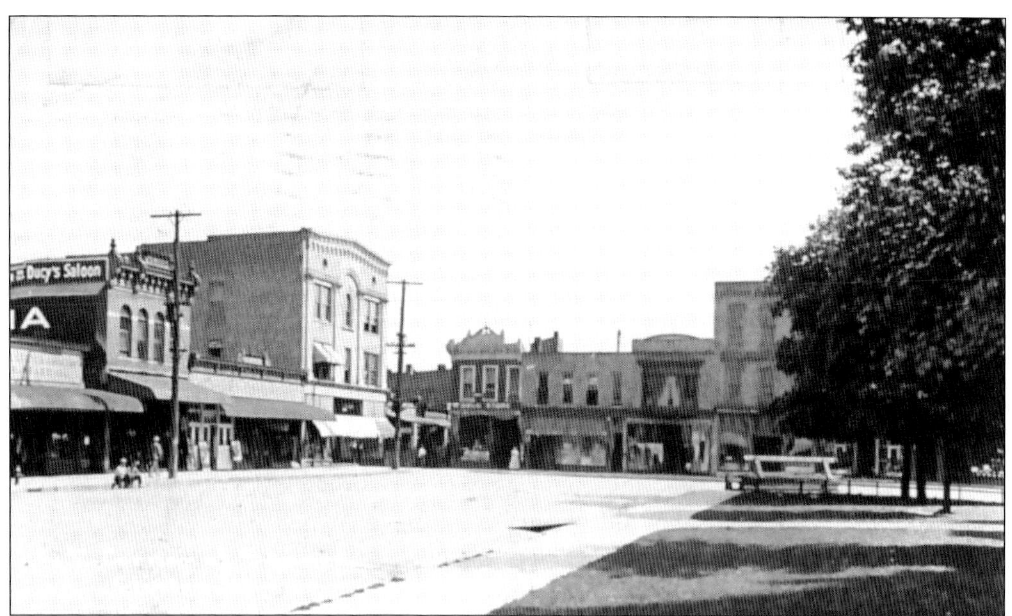

Boys sit on the curb in front of the Little Corner Grocery on the north side of Clinton Square and Center Street next to a building with an advertisement for Ducy's Saloon. The Shapiro building replaced the Little Corner Grocery in 1925. This is before the 1914 fire that destroyed the building north of the rightmost structure, now the Ohio Building. (VWPL.)

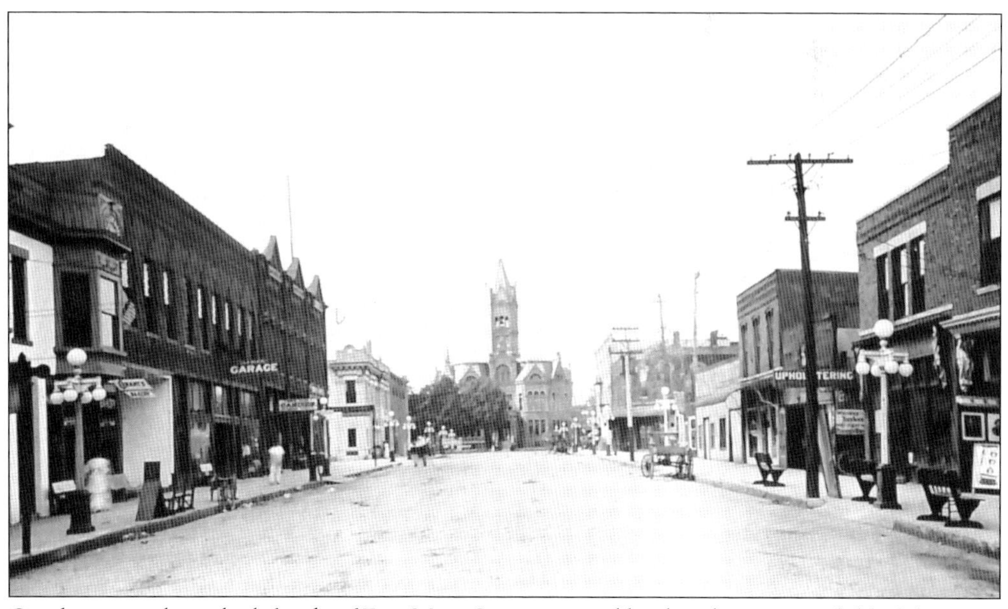

One business along the left side of East Main Street is noted by the white sign with black lettering advertising Grant's Bakery at 212 East Main Street, with another sign for a garage. Farther down, another white sign advertises that they sell candies. The light-colored building at the corner on the left is the State Bank. (VWPL.)

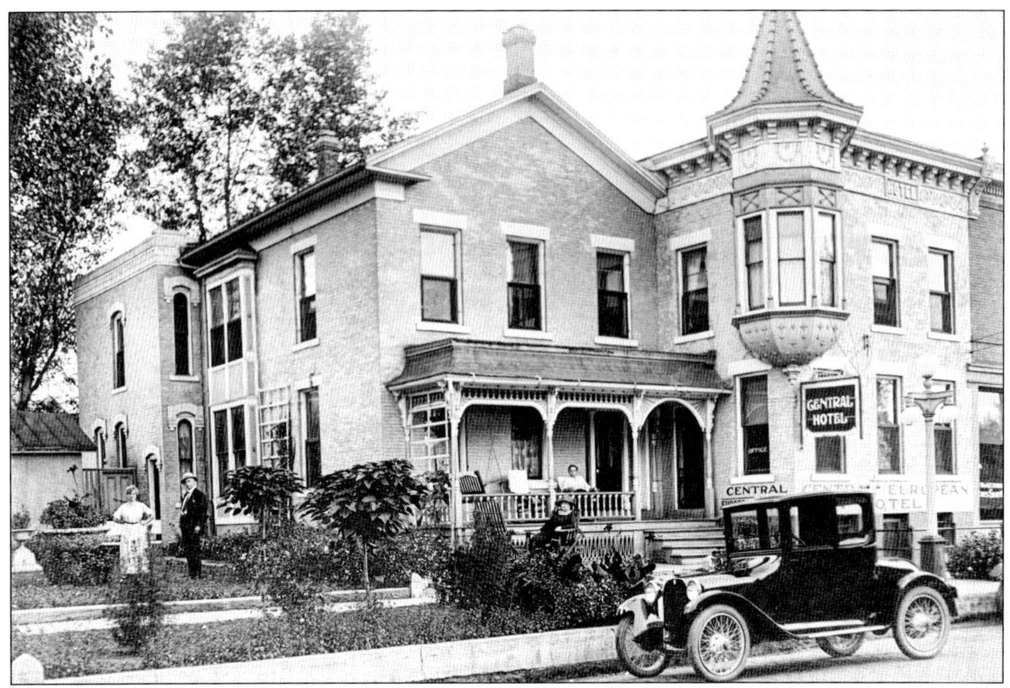

Photographed in the 1920s, the Central Hotel, at 208 East Washington Street, offered meals and accommodations as early as 1857. Located across the street from the county jail and near the crossing of the Great Western and Illinois Central Railroads, the hotel was also an apartment building into the 1900s. Now across the street from a parking lot, "Hotel" is still at the top of the building. (DCM.)

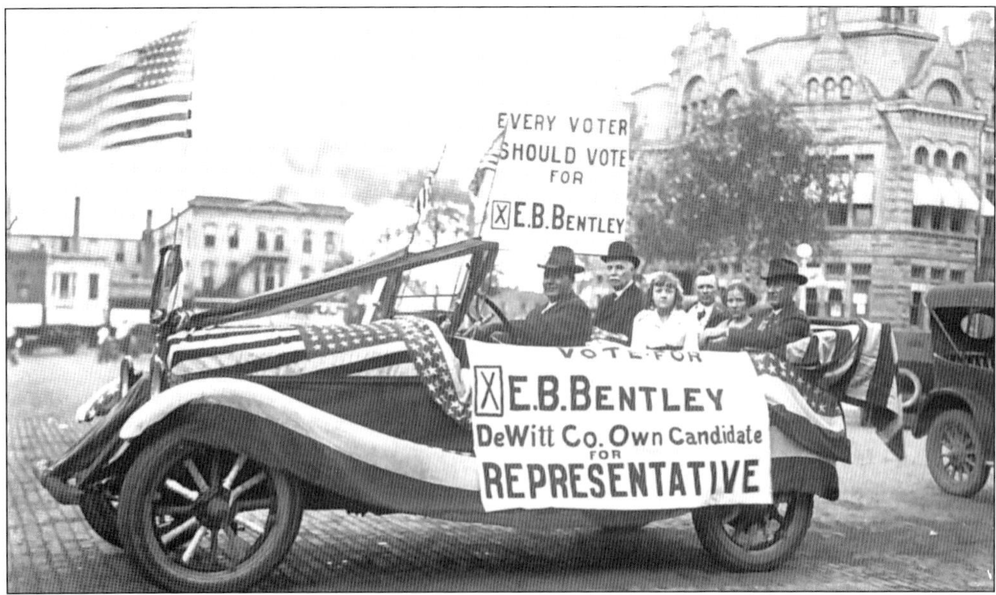

Running as a Republican, Clinton school superintendent Emory Bentley was photographed in his campaign car during either the 1920 or 1922 campaign for the Illinois State House of Representatives. He is the man with the hat to the far right in the back seat. The Magill Hotel appears in the background. (VWPL.)

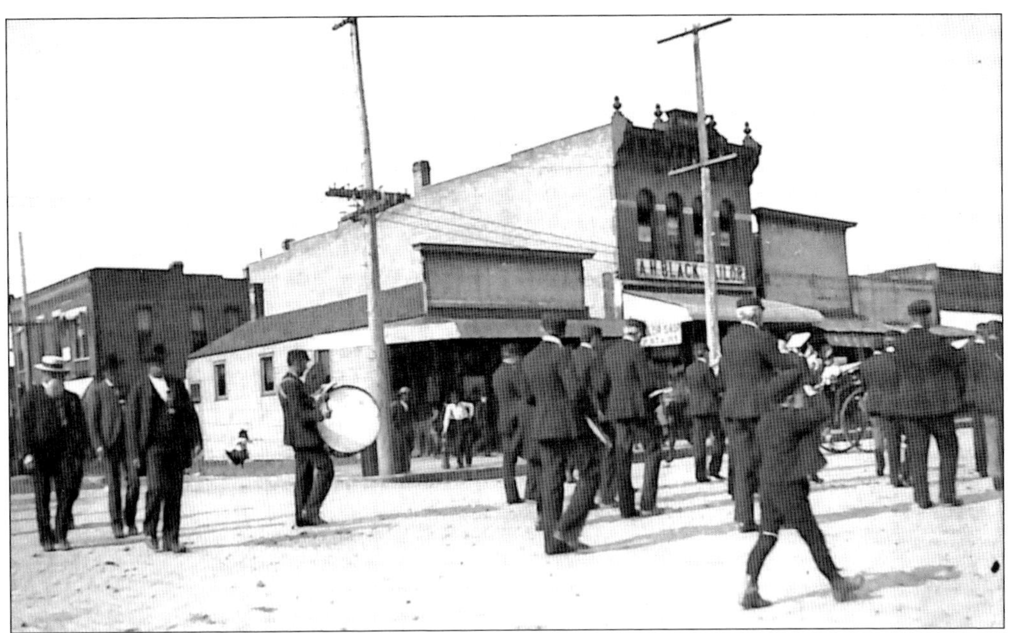

In this pre-1925 photograph, men march in front of the building on the north side of the square where A.H. Black ran his second-floor tailor business. By the look of the windows and architectural pieces, this structure appears to be 801 North Side Square, next to today's Shapiro building (constructed in 1925). (VWPL.)

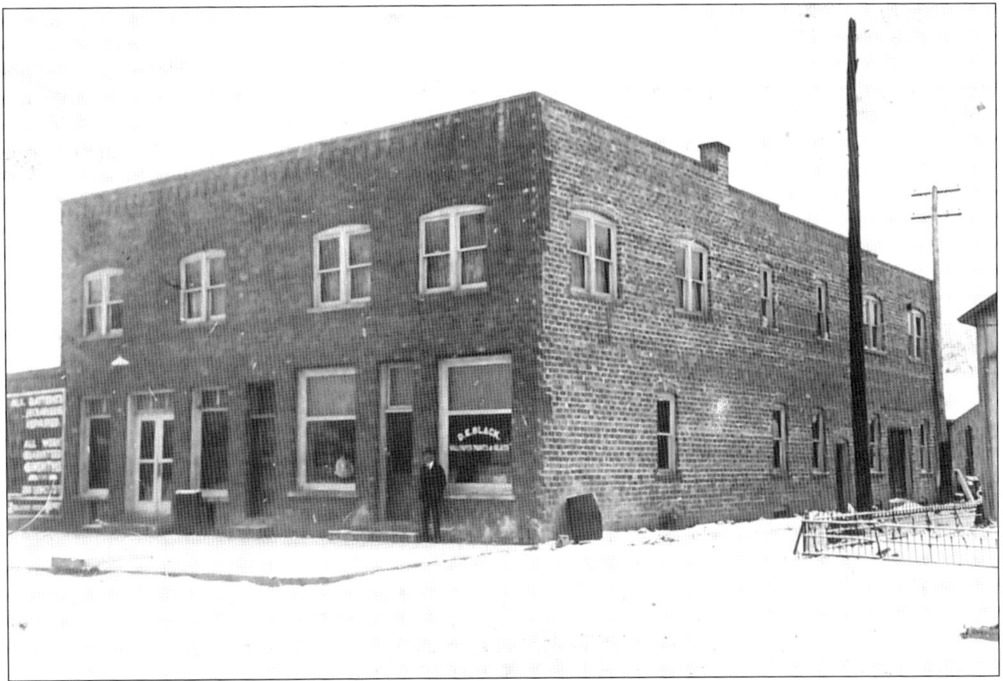

The Clinton wallpaper and paint store of Dudley Black, at 115 South Quincy Street, was photographed around 1920. His partner, Charles Huffman, had sold his interest to Black the previous year. In 1920, Black announced plans to build a brick storeroom on the lot, with the lower floor to be occupied by his business. (VWPL.)

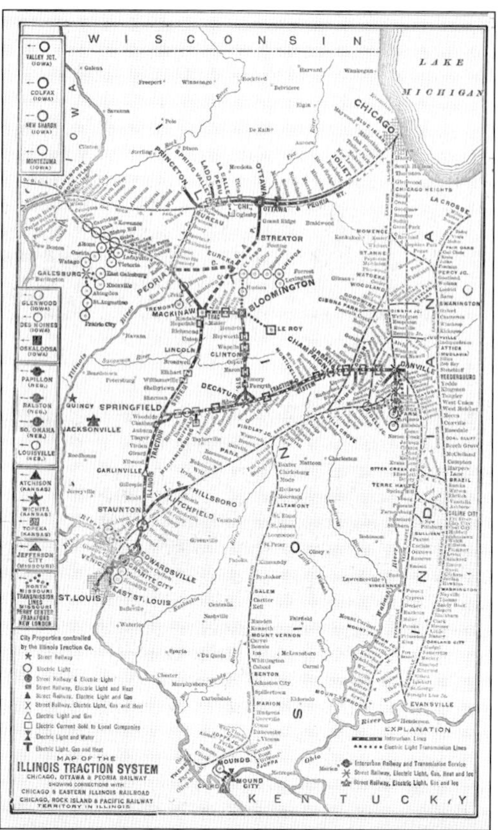

The Illinois Traction Co. System (ITS) shows several rail lines in 1921, including a predecessor to the Illinois Terminal Railroad. After peaking in 1928 and then being affected by the Great Depression, the ITS was reorganized into the Illinois Terminal Railroad Company, focusing on carrying more freight than passengers. (ILDC.)

A child appears with Gowdy Store staff around 1922. H.S. Gowdy had several stores over his 15 years in business, but the last, Hull & Gowdy, was located where the Sav-A-Lot parking lot is now. One of Clinton's largest groceries, it included a bakery. Gowdy retired and closed the store in 1928. (VWPL.)

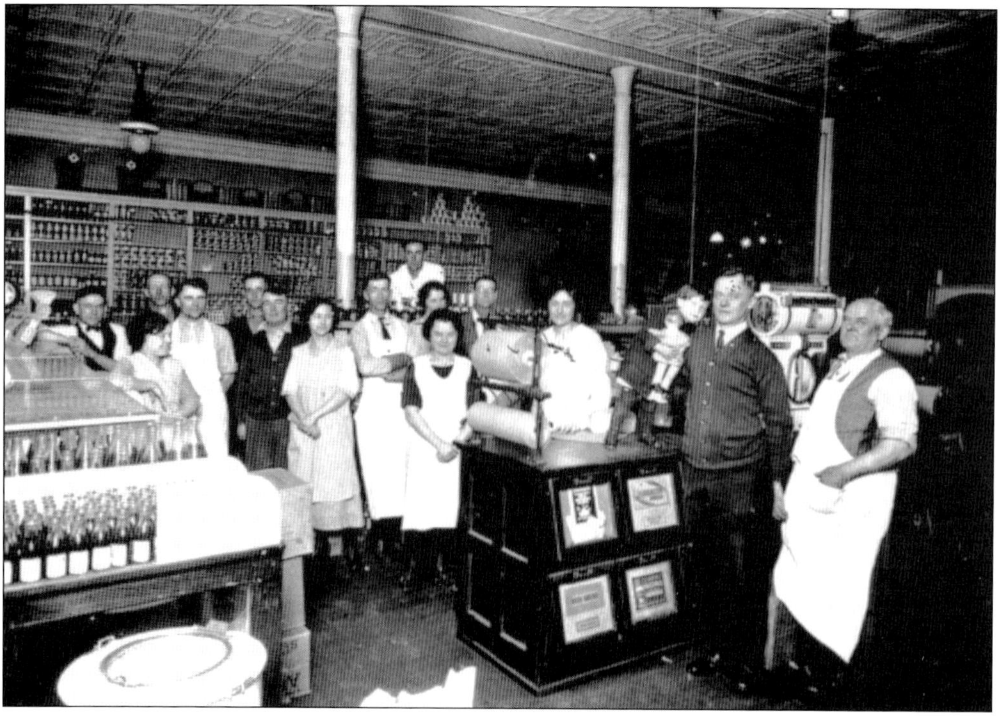

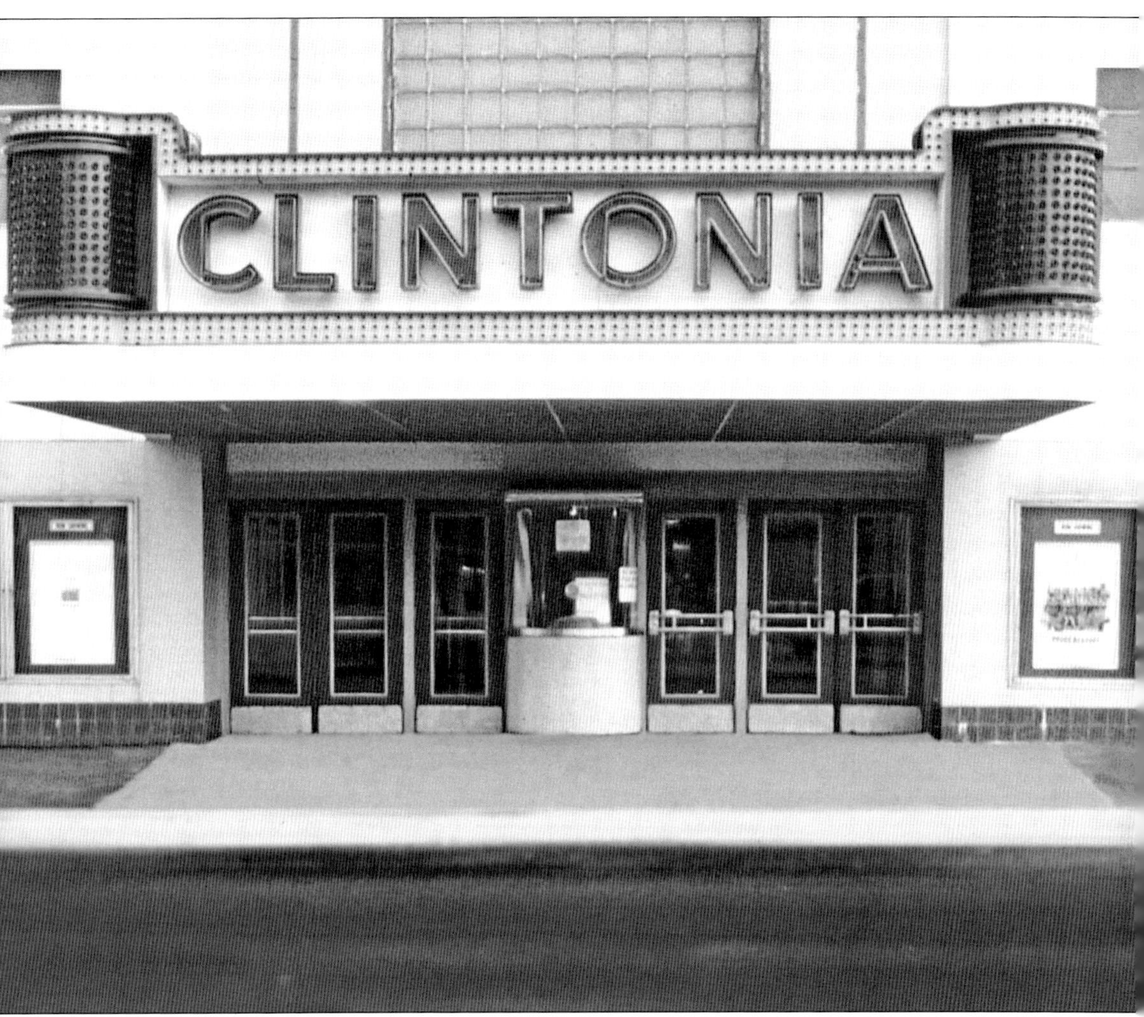

Built by W.F. Corrington and Son at 206–208 East Main Street, the Clintonia Theater opened in December 1921. In 1937, after a renovation, it reopened as the New Clintonia Theater, with air-conditioning and upholstered seating of black, chrome, and burnt orange for 750 people. The foyer included three-piece davenport sets in gold and aquamarine in addition to an easy chair and a kidney-shaped davenport in chartreuse and maroon. There were also two coffee tables in black lacquer with silver trim and another in walnut and stainless steel. In 1973, J.C. Nelson, the owner since 1965, retired and sold the Clintonia and the Clinton Drive-In Theatres to Merle Wagner. It closed as the Clintonia Theatre in 1982 and stood unused. A wall collapsing in March 1989 caused the roof to cave in. The building was demolished in March 1990. (GW.)

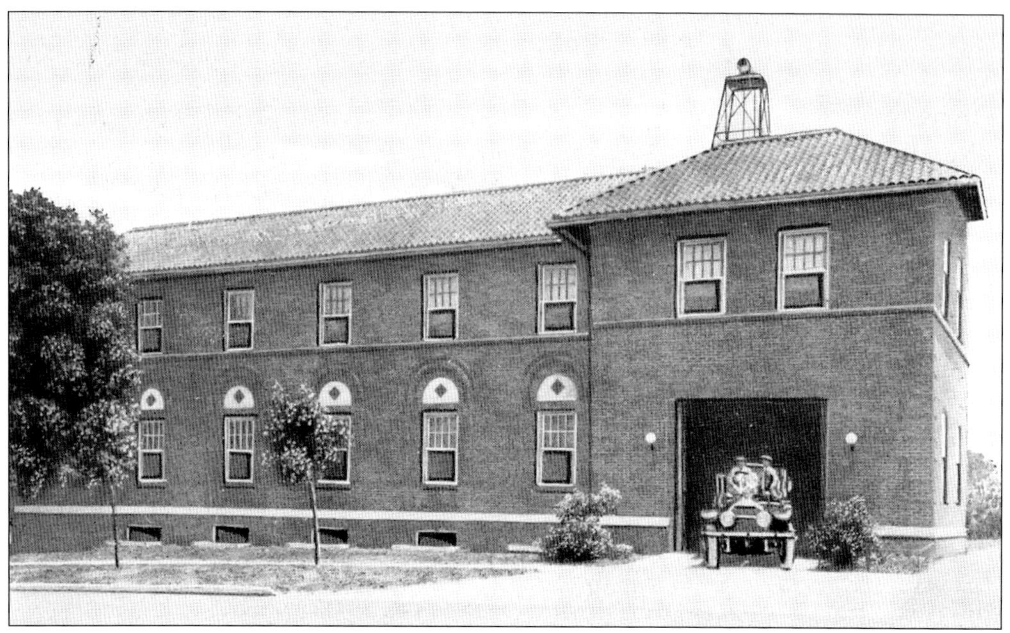

In 1923, Hagerman & Harshman began building the Clinton City Hall and Fire Department at 118 West Washington Street, replacing the 1877 structure on land that had been donated by Eleanor Magill. It included a second-floor assembly hall, a ground-floor restroom, and space for the fire department. The construction was completed in June 1924. (AC.)

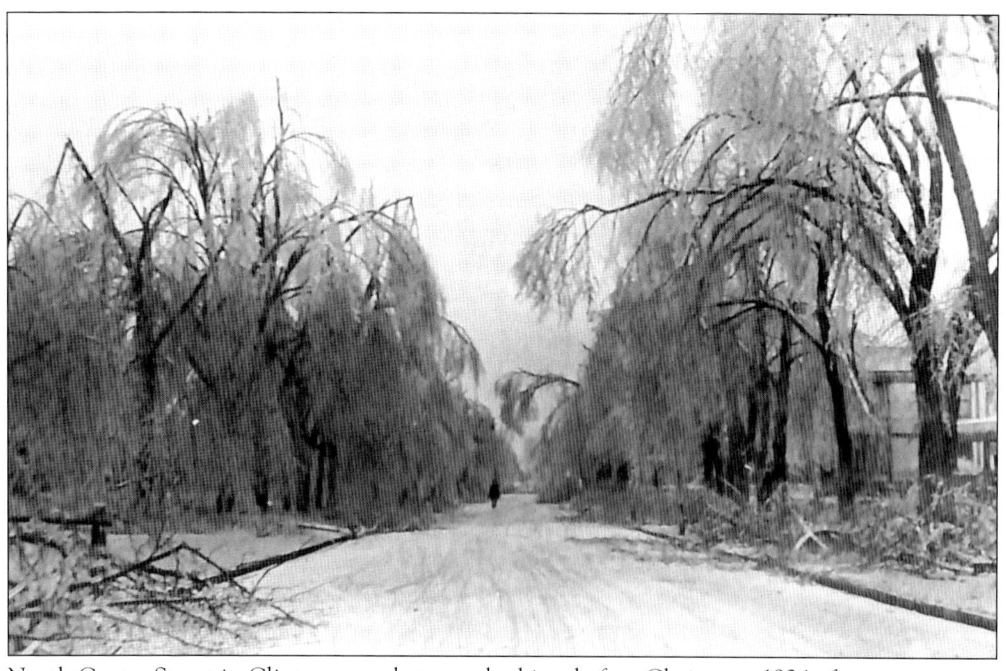

North Center Street in Clinton was photographed just before Christmas 1924 after an ice storm hit the area. Trees and limbs snapped off, and several telephone poles were weighed down by ice. Continuing rain turned to sleet. The roads were drifted full for days, during which time most towns lacked electricity. (VWPL.)

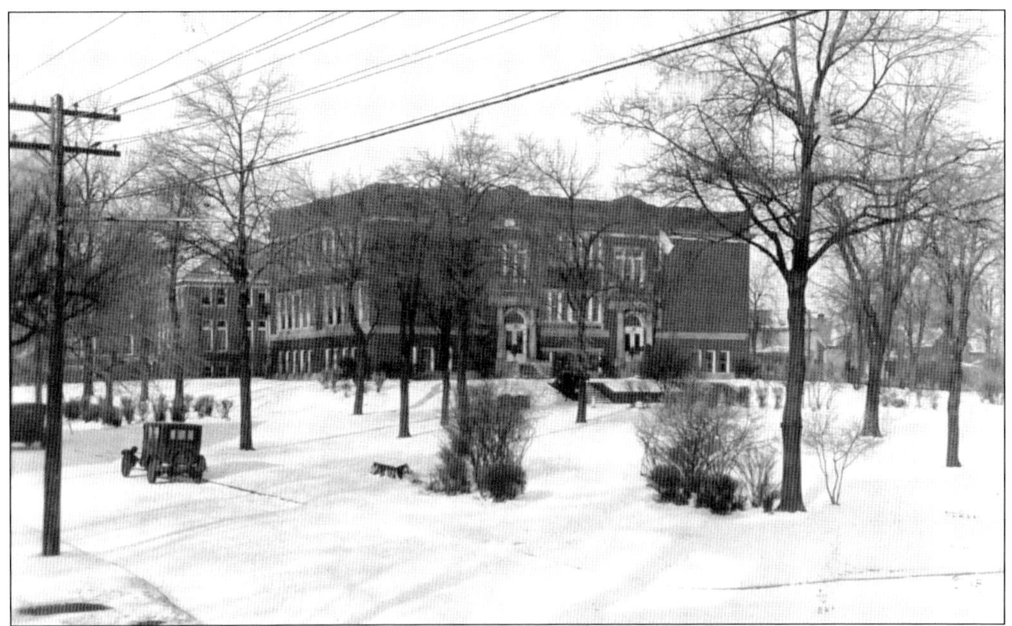

Clinton's high school on North Center Street replaced Old Washington School after its 1908 demolition. As seen around 1925, the high school later served as the junior high school until its 2005 closure. It sat empty until 2008 except for use during special events. That year, items benefitting nonprofit organizations were removed and it was demolished. (VWPL.)

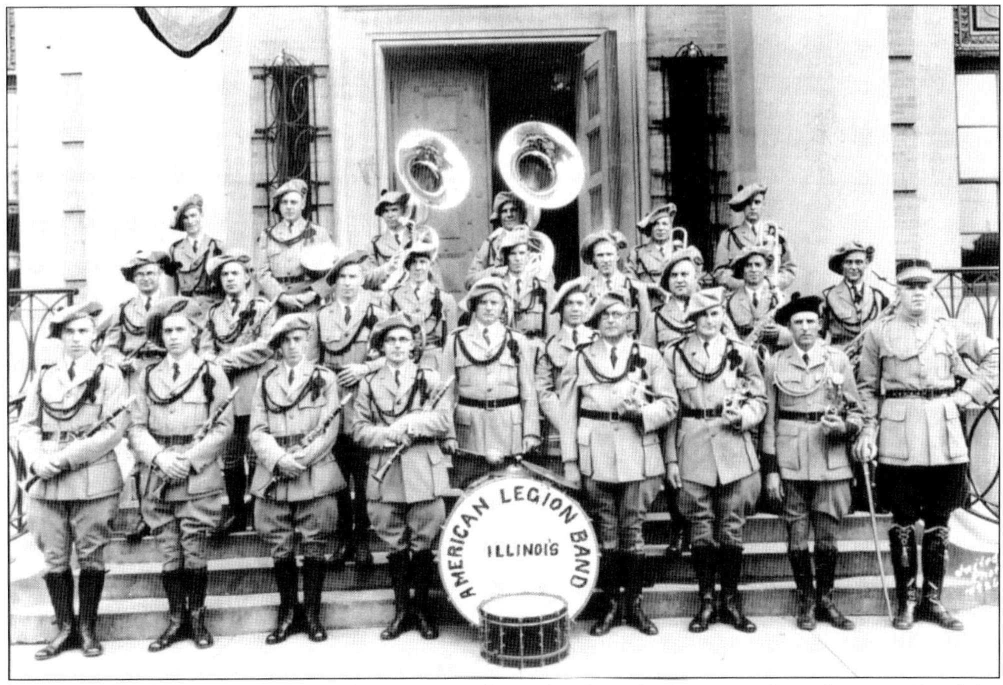

Elmer Hammond of Clinton and Kenney is the only identified man in this photograph of the American Legion Marching Band in Paris, France, in 1927. A former horn player in the Great Lakes Marine Band during the war, he also played with John Philip Sousa's band. The 1927 convention commemorated the 10th anniversary of America's entry in World War I. (VWPL.)

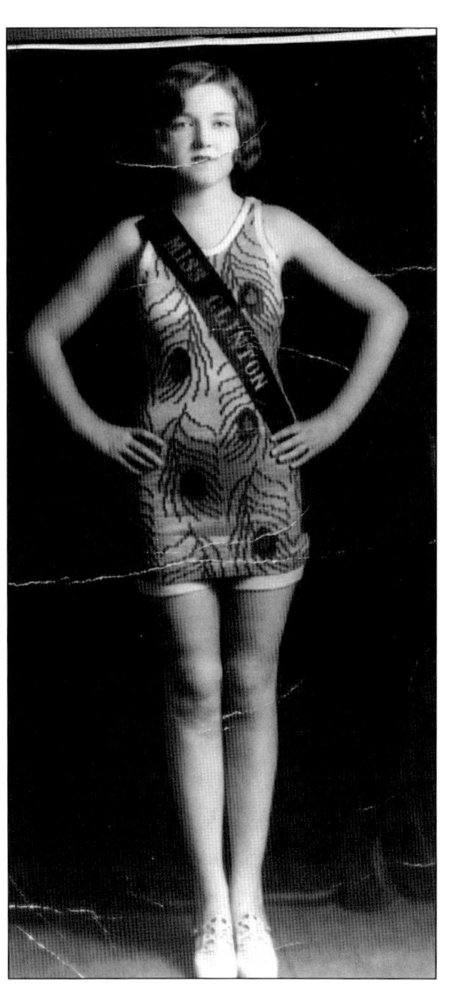

In August 1928, Charline McKinney won first place in the Elks Lodge bathing beauty contest for Miss Clinton held at the Clintonia Theater. That same week, she won $25 in Decatur's Miss Elks contest. The first-place prize was a bathing outfit. Although scheduled to participate in the Miss Illinois contest that year in Havana, Illinois, McKinney withdrew upon her mother's request. (VWPL.)

Built in 1889 and photographed around 1930, the First Christian Church stood at the corner of Monroe and Adams Streets, near the offices of the *Clinton Register* newspaper. A fire destroyed the church in December 1945. The church's next structure, constructed at the corner of Main and Jackson Streets, was dedicated in September 1949. (VWPL.)

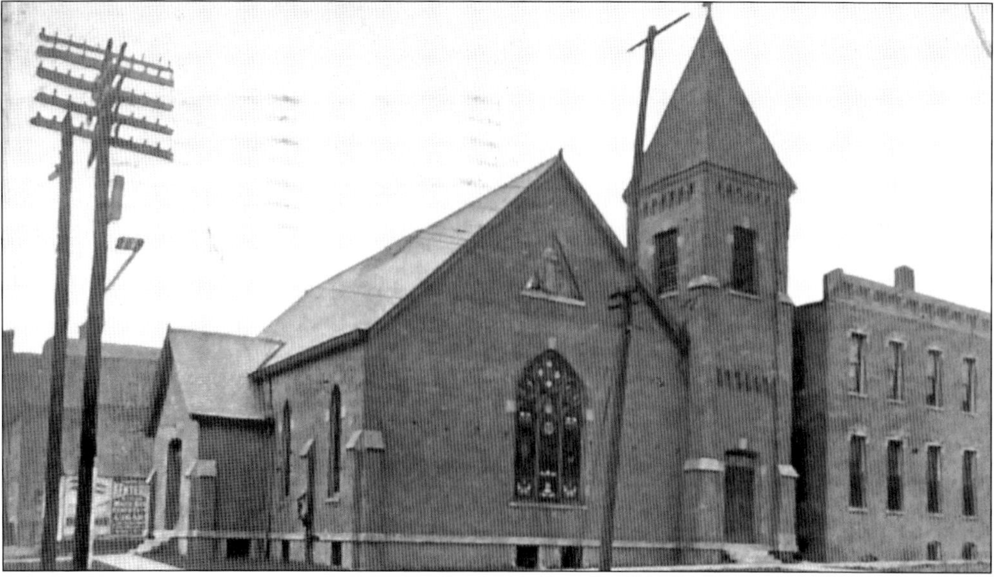

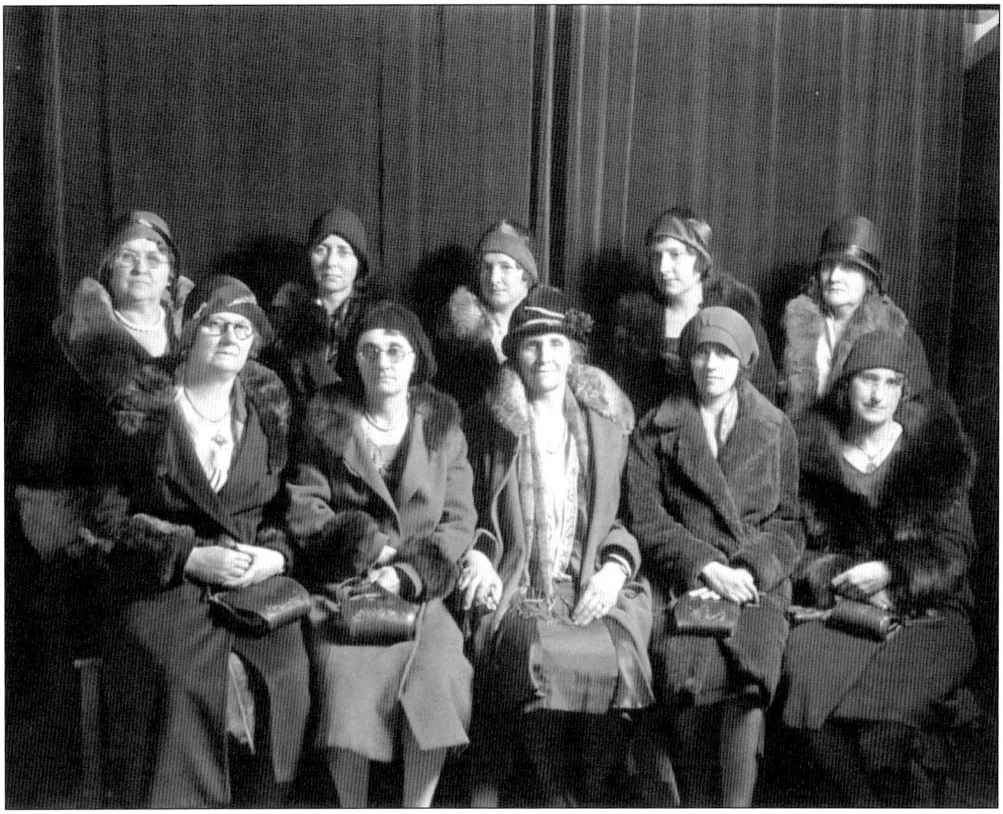

In January 1931, for the first time in county history, women were empaneled for a grand jury. From left to right are (first row) bailiff Mrs. Costley, forewoman Mamie Querfeld, Laura Parks, Consuelo Owens, and Nola Chenoweth; (second row) Edna Greene, Mabel Harper, Enid Trowbridge, Jeanne Miller, and Rena Hillis. Twelve men also sat on the jury. (VWPL.)

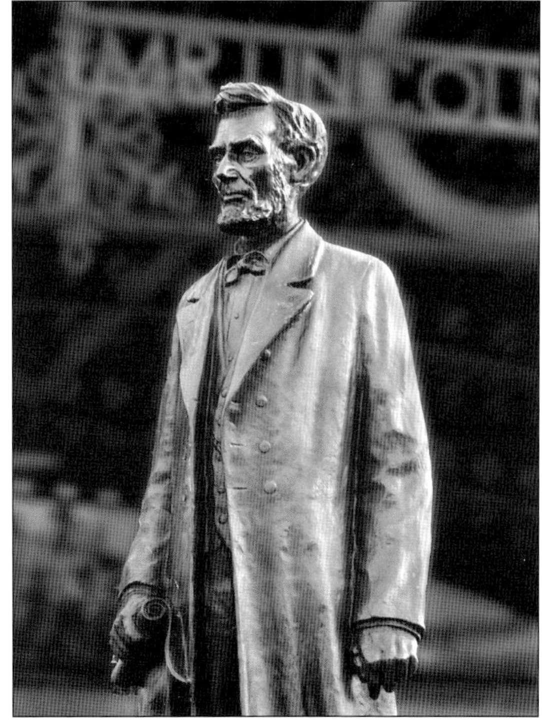

On November 11, 1931, a statue placed in Clinton Square was dedicated to Abraham Lincoln, honoring his work as a lawyer riding the Eighth Circuit from the 1840s through the 1850s. The statue stands where he opened his 1858 senate campaign and is said to have made his "You can fool the people" speech. (AC.)

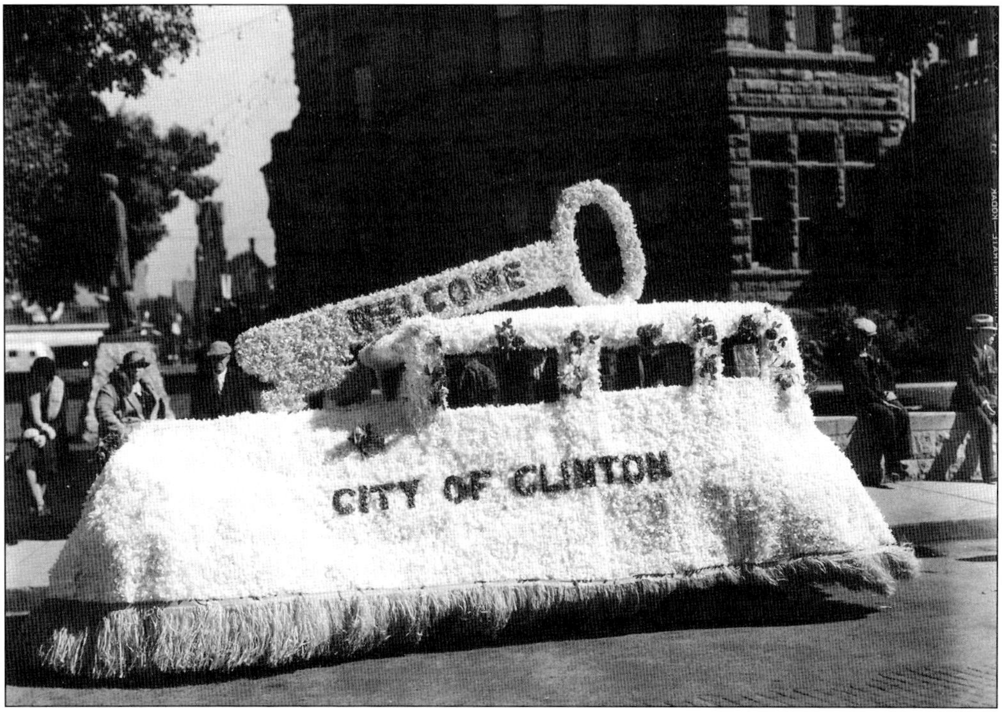

In 1935, Clinton began its four-day centennial celebration with a Friday morning parade. Over 5,500 spectators watched Mayor Bernard M. Pugh ride the City of Clinton float and, on another, the Queen of the Pageant, Alice Wilson, with 12 attendants. The pageant, repeated over three nights, included a ballet and commemorated events in local history. (DCM.)

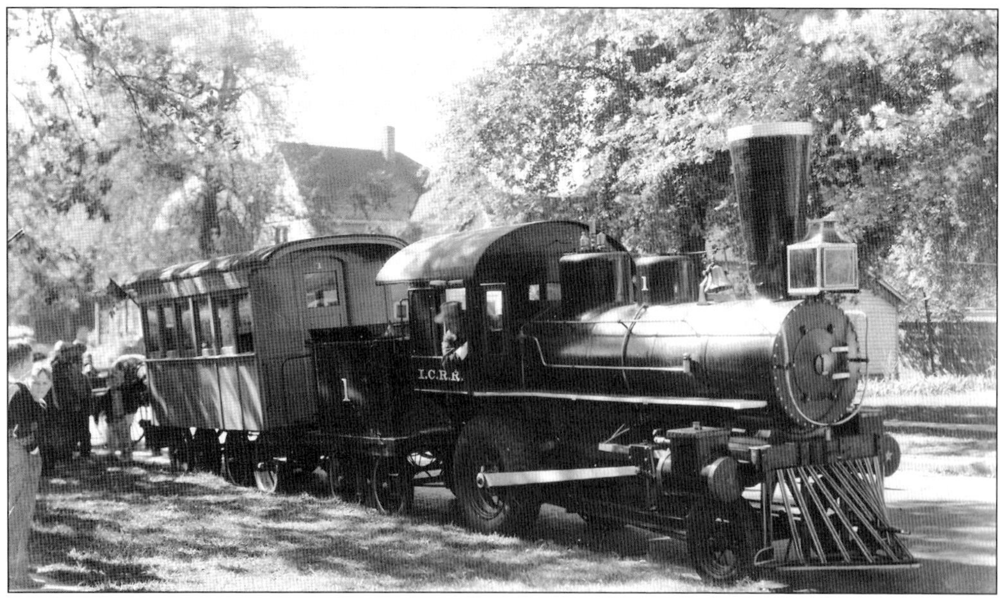

The centennial parade included many floats, including some representing the history of transportation: an ox-drawn covered wagon, a goat and cart, and a small replica of the first Illinois Central Railroad train. Other floats included those by the Rotary International Club, the DeWitt County Farm Bureau, churches, and school bands. (DCM.)

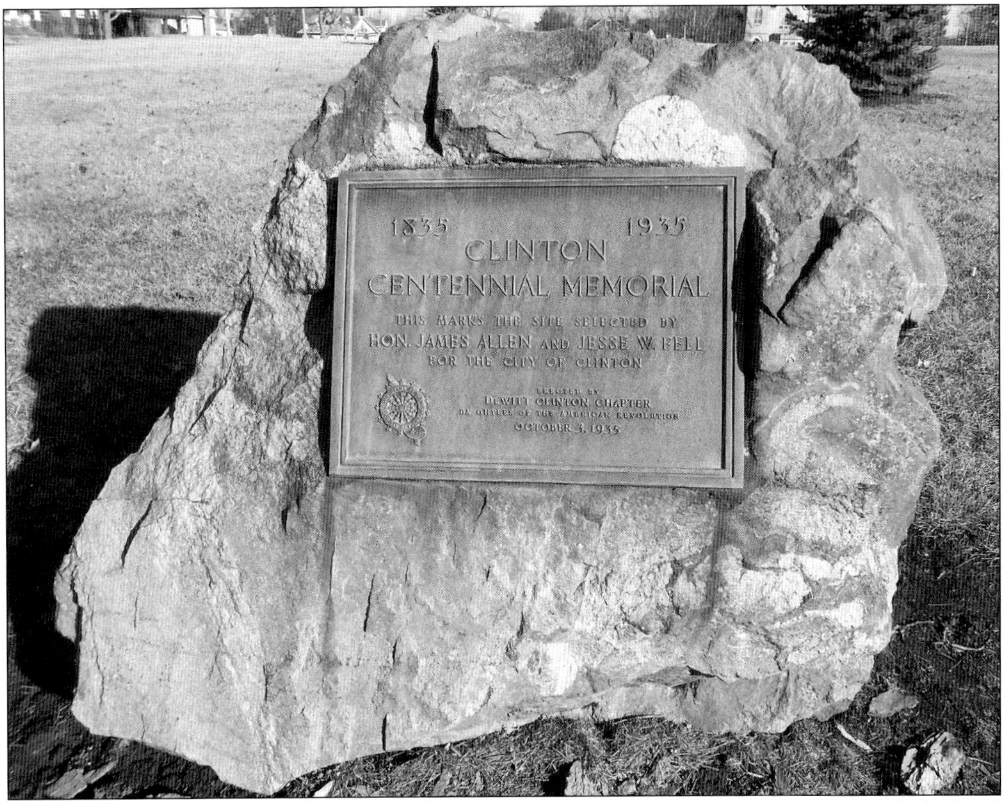

This boulder sits on the green space north of Warner Library. For Clinton's centennial, the local Daughters of the American Revolution chapter presented a plaque commemorating the site and founders. At one time, the property belonged to Rose Douglas, the widow of Stephen A. Douglas. She was also great-niece to Dolley Madison. Rose Douglas donated the land to the city. (AC.)

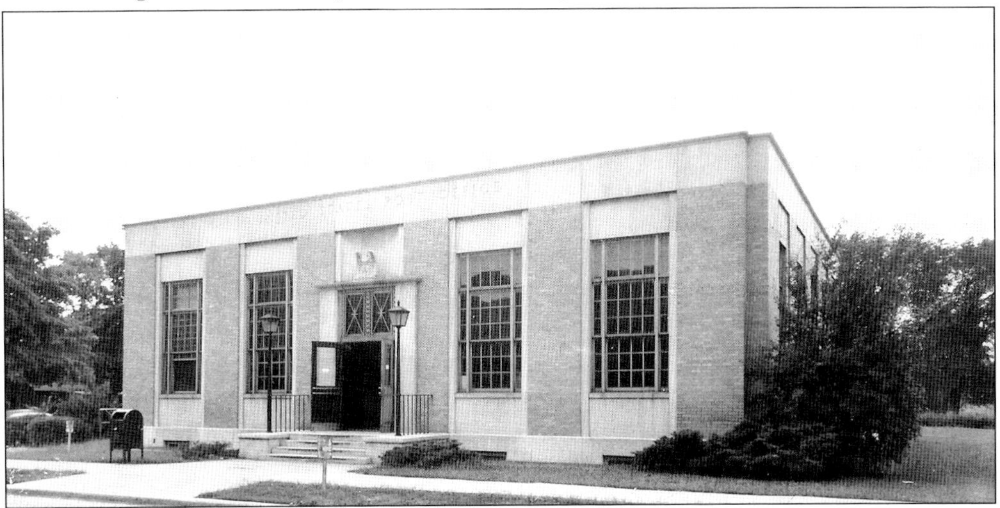

Approximately 5,000 people toured Clinton's new post office at Main and Quincy Streets during its 1938 dedication. It was constructed on property purchased from the estate of Eleanor Magill. A 2006 act of congress named the building in honor of Gene Vance, former All-American basketball player (one of the 1940s "Whiz Kids") with the University of Illinois team. (KA.)

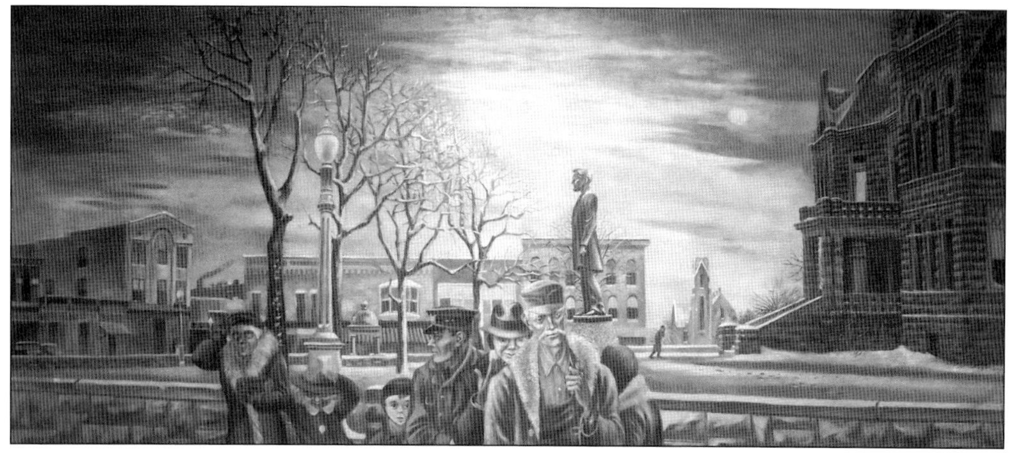

A New Deal color mural painted in 1939, *Clinton in Winter*, hangs on a wall above the clerks in the Clinton Post Office. The artist, Aaron Bohrod, created two additional post office murals, one for Galesburg and another for Vandalia. His 1940 painting that hung in the square's courthouse, *The Courthouse Lobby*, was exhibited in 2007 at New York City's Forum Gallery and was purchased by a private collector. (AC.)

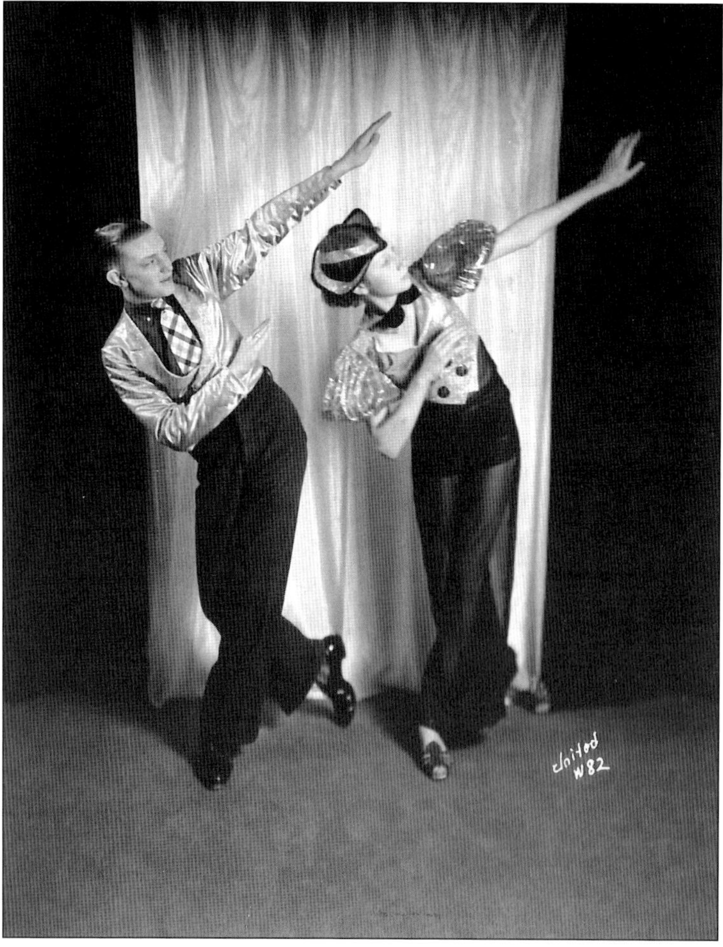

Errald Bob Wilson (1919–1994) was the tap-dancing proprietor of Bobby Wilson's School of Dance in Clinton. After winning many prizes in his teenage years, he studied dance with Hollywood's Bill "Bojangles" Robinson, then joined the armed forces during World War II. He poses in 1939 with an unidentified young woman in matching costumes. He eventually worked with the ITS and retired as president. (VWPL.)

While DeWitt County sheriff Kenneth Westray was in the Army during World War II (from 1943 to 1946), his wife, Myra, became interim county sheriff. Her team solved a string of farm robberies covering five counties. She is flanked in 2011 by DeWitt County sheriff Jered Shofner (left) and Madison County sheriff Bob Hertz, president of the Illinois Sheriffs' Association (right). (JS.)

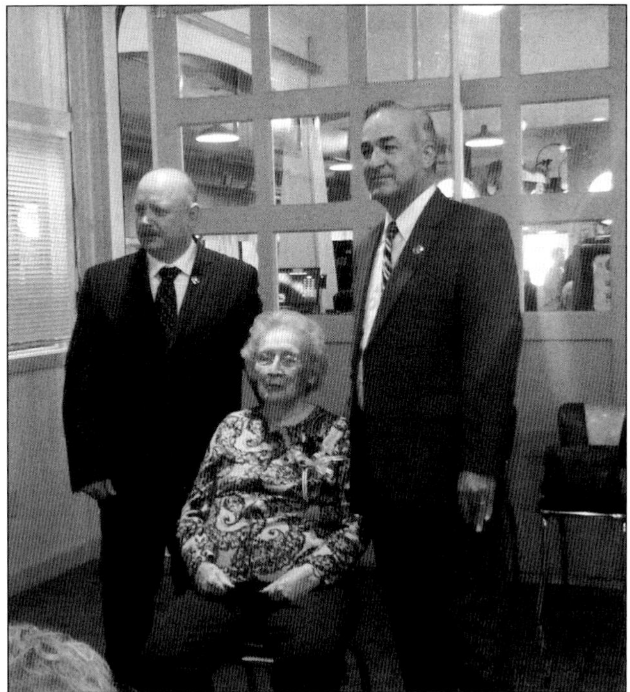

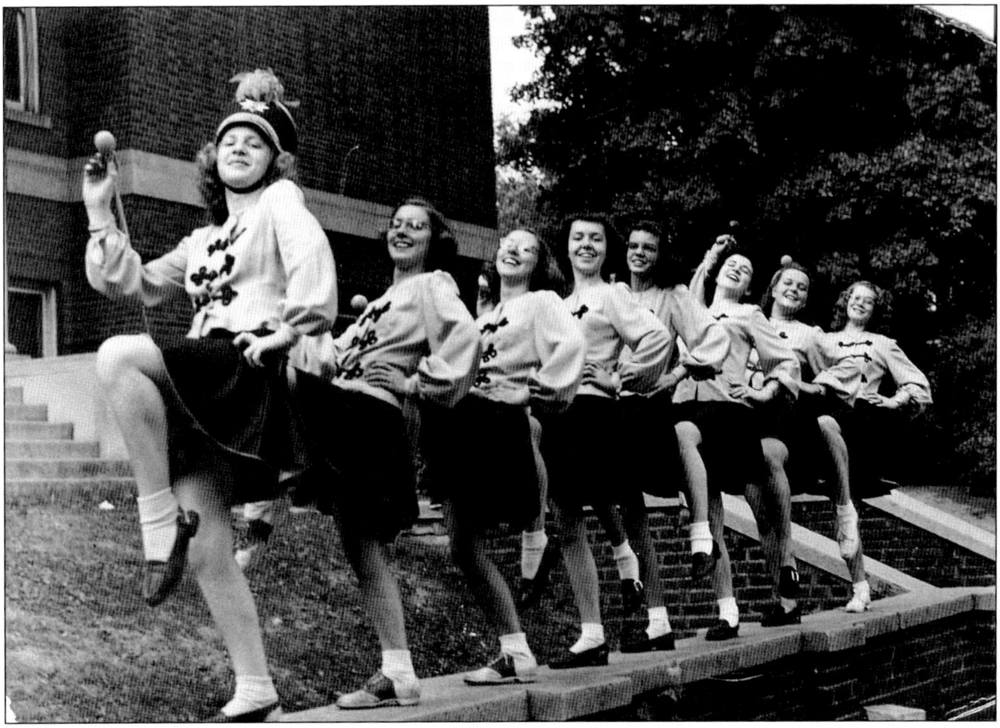

In 1945, Clinton High School enrolled 129 freshmen. By 1949, the high school had several majorettes for its marching band. Of those, eight unidentified young women strike an energetic pose outside the school. Because it was not until 1953 that the word "majorette" appeared under any of the student photographs, these ladies remain unidentified. (VWPL.)

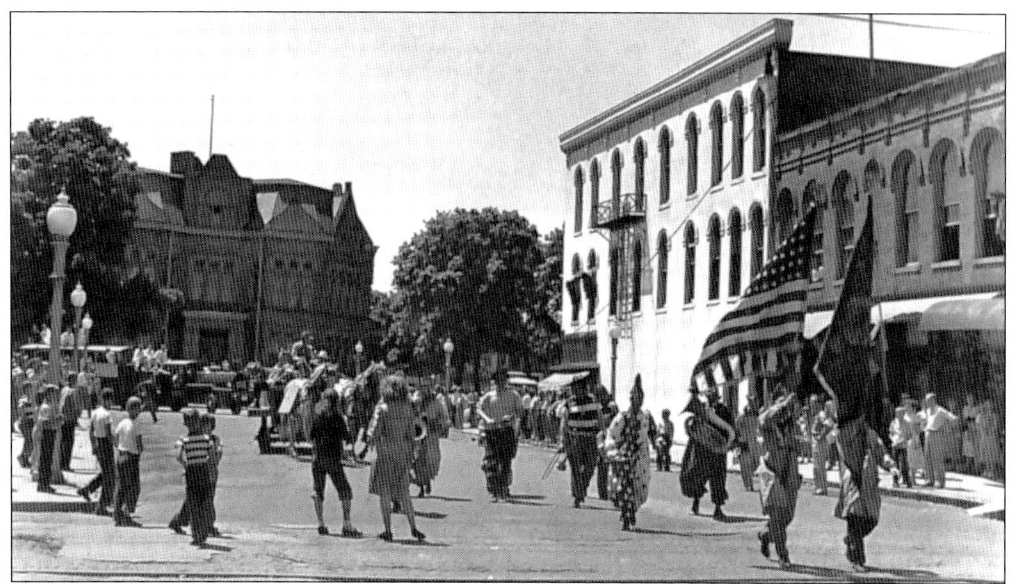

Members of the clown band of the Crang-Bennett American Legion Post No. 103 march in a Legion parade around 1950 (after the 1946 removal of the courthouse's clock tower) along East Main Street. Organized in 1919, the post was named after two Clinton soldiers who died in France during World War I. Welby Crang died in Paris after falling ill, and Archie Bennett was killed in action. (VWPL.)

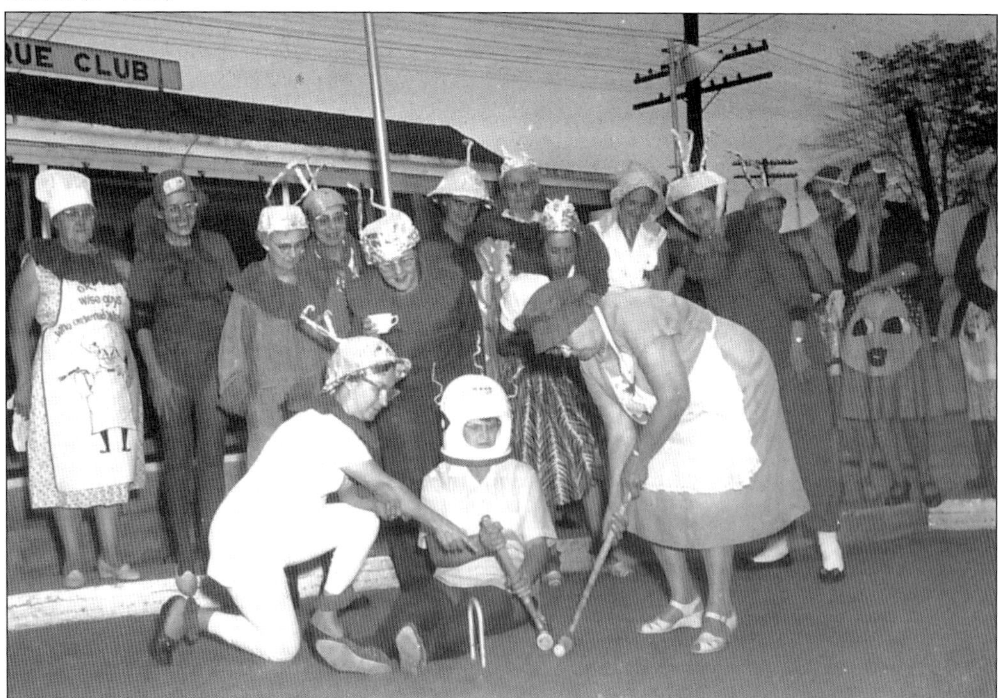

Nineteen women pretending to be space aliens pose in 1950 near the Clinton Roque Club clubhouse, at the end of West Main Street. While the others watch, three show off their stances for roque, a variant of croquet invented in the late 1880s using short mallets on a hard court. It became very popular in the mid-1900s, dying down in the 1980s. (VWPL.)

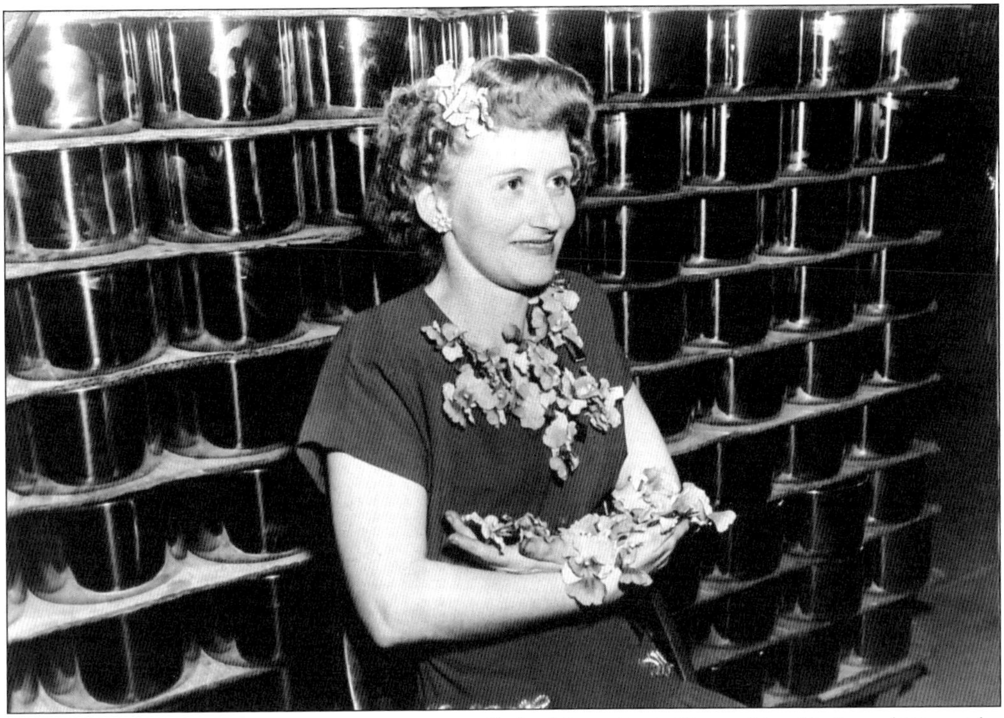

The Revere Copper and Brass Company originally had factories in Rome, New York, and Riverside, California. It opened its third factory in January 1950 at the southeast edge of Clinton. Customers received shipments later that year. Edna Garren was one of the women receiving orchids at Revere's 151st anniversary in 1951. After the Riverside facility closed in 1962, all copper-clad production moved to Clinton. In 1968, the company stopped making cookware in Rome, thinned down the copper and stainless steel, and also changed the logo. Sadly, market changes forced the Clinton factory's closure in 1999. Revere is now a subsidiary of Corning's Consumer Products Division. (Both, CJ.)

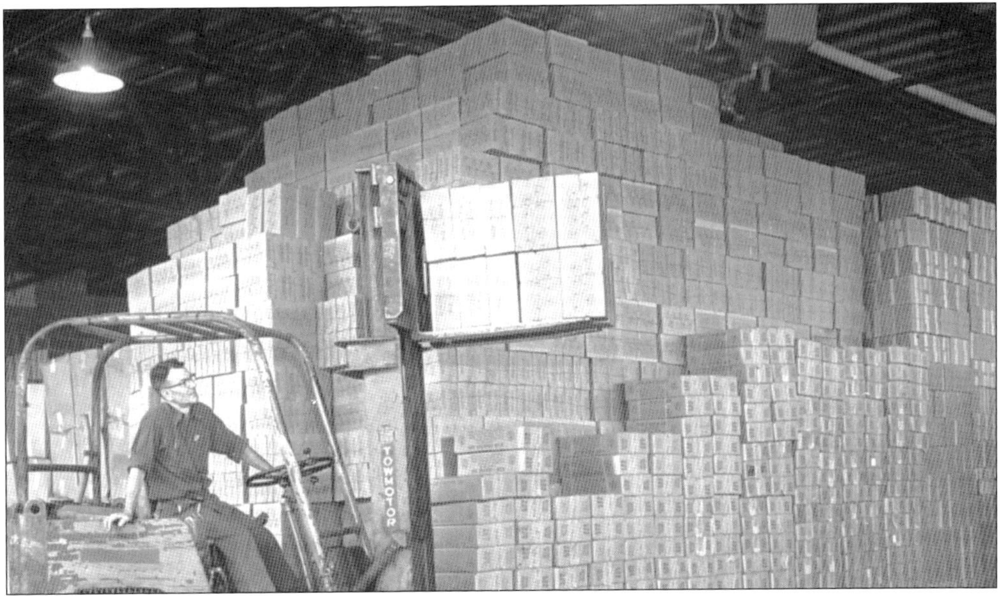

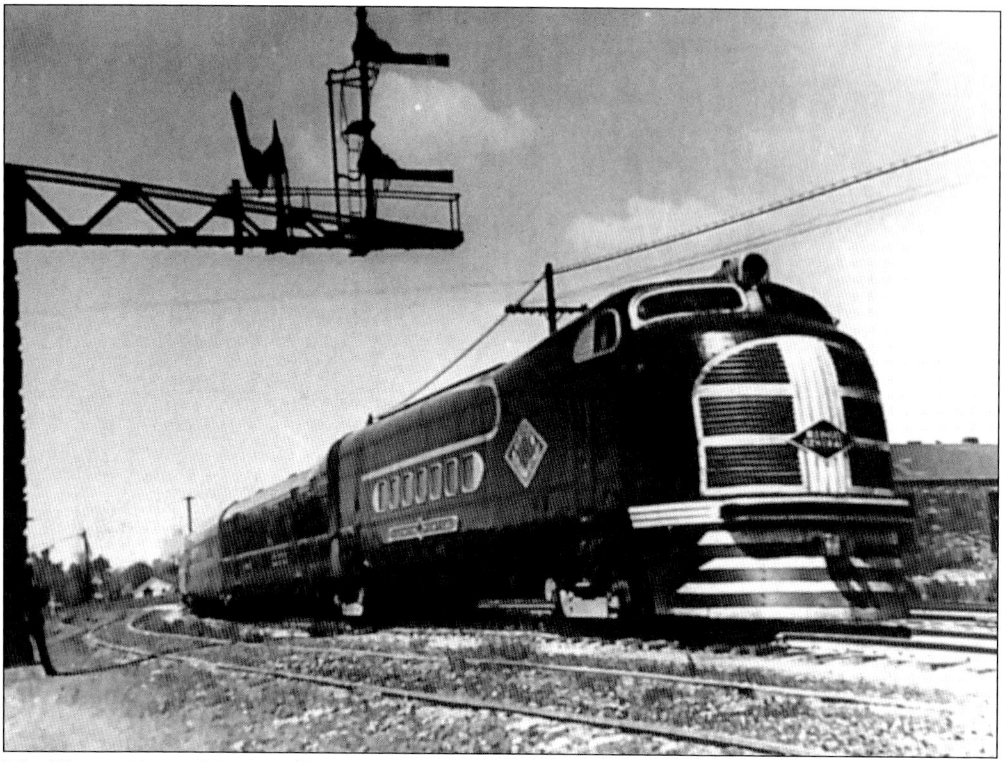

The Illinois Central Railroad's streamlined passenger train the Green Diamond ran from 1936 to 1968 between Chicago and St. Louis, passing through Clinton. The name referred to the diamond shape inside the train's logo as well as the Diamond Special, the railroad's oldest train on the Chicago-to-St. Louis line. From 1968 until 1971, it ran between Chicago and Springfield as the Governor's Special. (VWPL.)

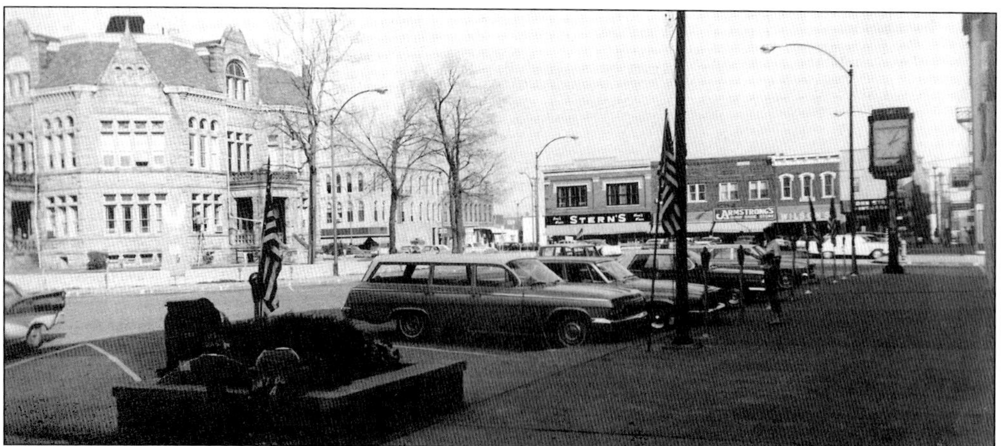

Clinton businesses on the south side of the square in the 1960s included Stern's Clothing Store, Armstrong's Family Shoe Store, Wilson's Hat and Dress Shoppe (site of the former Chambers Drugstore), Starkey Insurance (there for 40 years), the John Warner Bank, and more. Harold and Nellie Wilson served customers at the Hat and Dress Shoppe from 1957 until their 1977 retirement. (KA.)

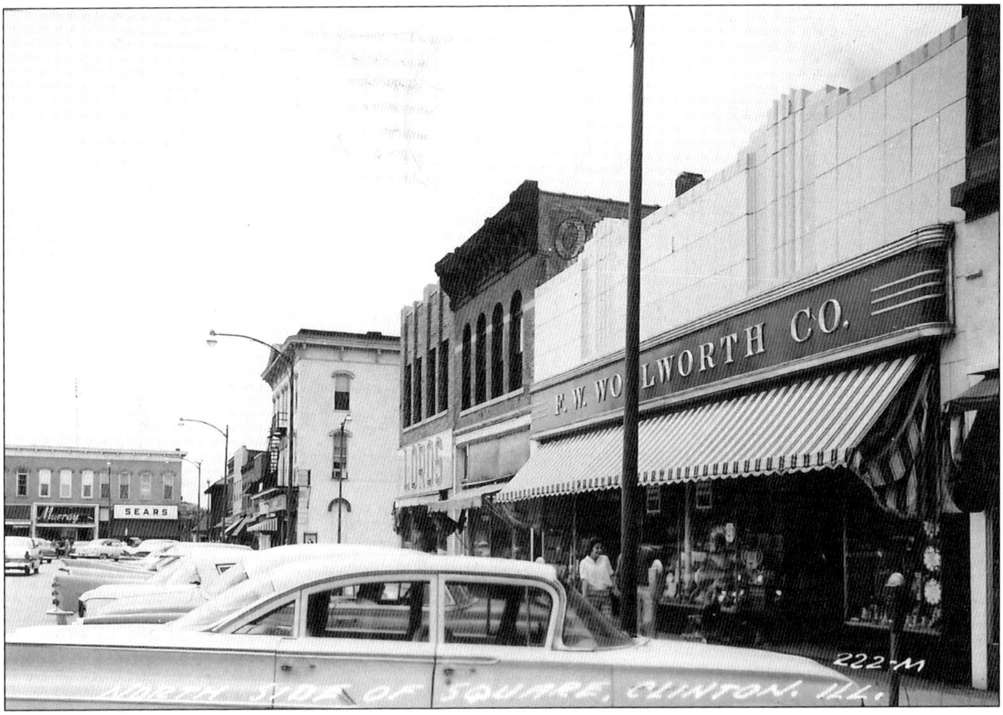

Stores along the north side of the square in the 1960s included Sears Roebuck and the Murray Boot Shop on the west side. Lords' Dress Shop occupied the current H&R Block site on the north side, and F.W. Woolworth Company, with its Art Deco facade, was located two doors east. In 1963, Clinton merchants had a Miss Merry Christmas contest, with Cyndie Armstrong representing Woolworth's. (VWPL.)

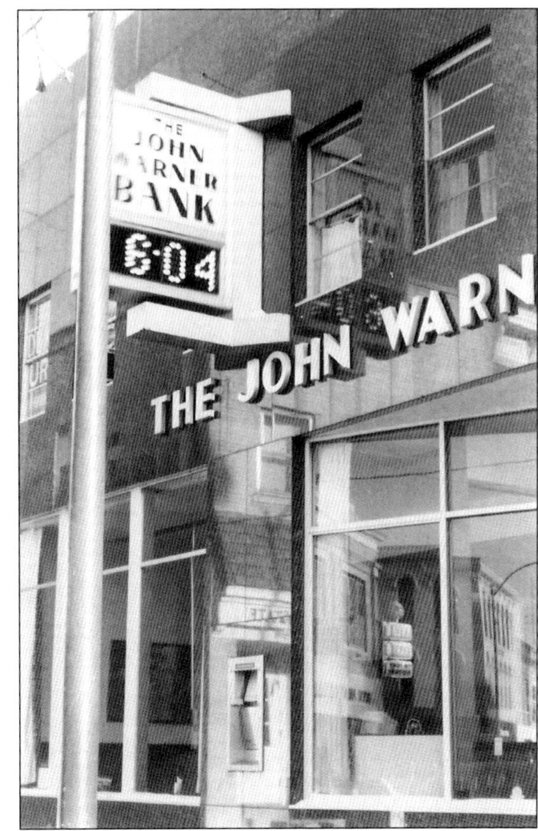

The John Warner Bank, photographed in 1974, was Clinton's longest-serving financial institution until Warner descendants sold it in 2003 to another banking group. By 2009, the new group's six Illinois banks had failed due to investment losses. The State Bank of Lincoln worked with the Federal Deposit Insurance Corporation to assume the bank's deposits. It is now Heartland Bank and Trust. (AC.)

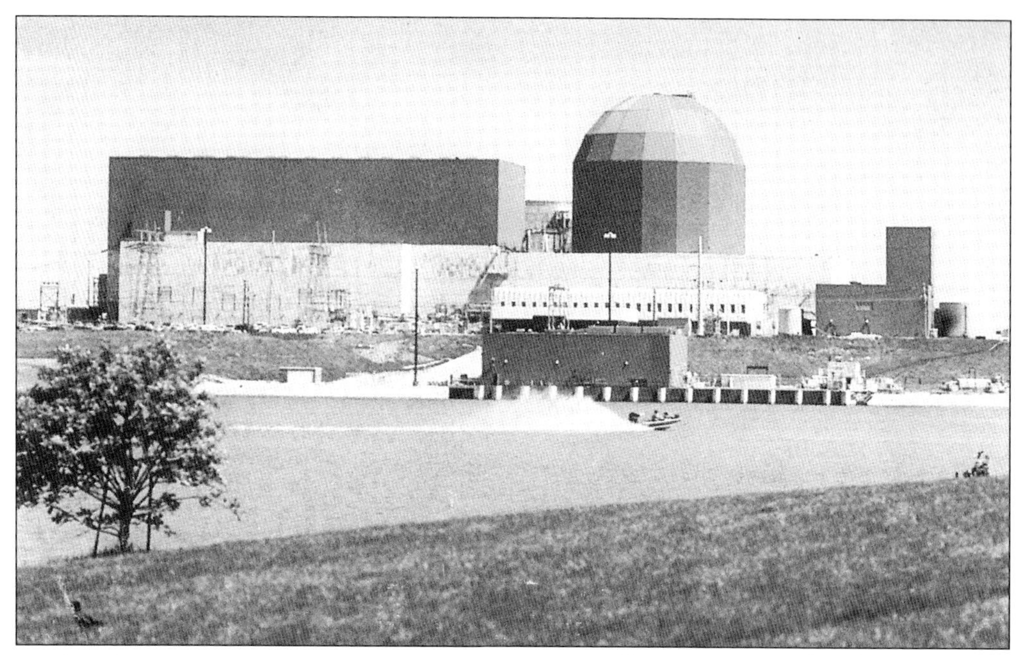

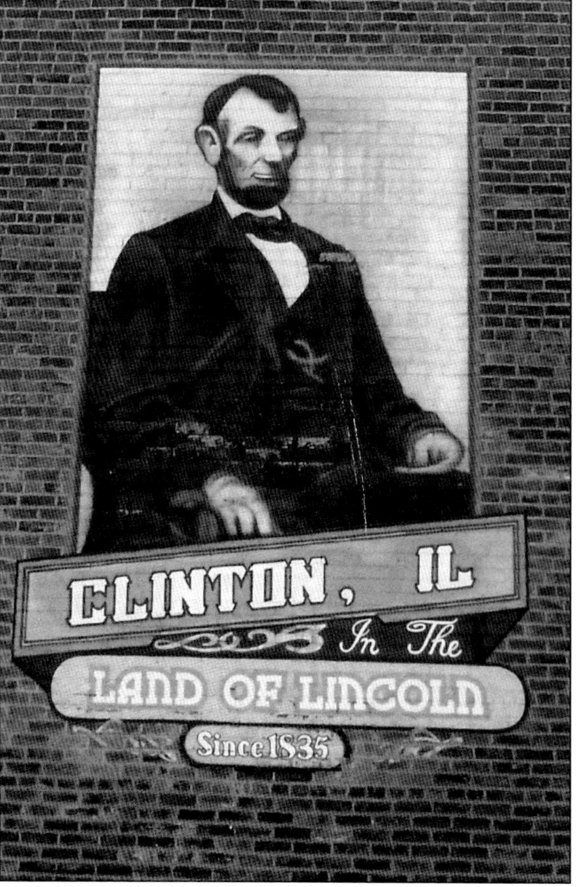

Construction on the Clinton Power Station's nuclear reactor began in 1976. Operations commenced on November 24, 1987, seven years behind schedule. Final construction costs ran 1,000 percent over the original $430 million budget. With frequent maintenance and closure in 1996, Illinois Power sold it to Exelon Corporation. The Clinton reactor's license expires in 2026, but the current owner, Constellation Energy, is seeking to extend it to 2047. (AC.)

Artist Steve Woods's 2010 Clinton mural honors Abraham Lincoln, who rode the Eighth Judicial Circuit twice yearly from 1847 until 1859. During that time, he formed relationships that grew in importance in his life as a lawyer and politician. Sadly, only two Illinois courthouses where he practiced law still exist today: Metamora and Mount Pulaski. (AC.)

Three

Farmer City

When Dennis Hurley became the first permanent settler in 1830 near the future Farmer City, the area was named Hurley's Grove after him. By 1837, when 19 more families had settled in the area, the land was surveyed for a new town, Mount Pleasant, just north of Hurley's Grove, divided into 14 blocks of 12 lots each and a public square. John Smith, one of the founding fathers, opened the first hotel there.

By 1839, a mail route established from Danville to Bloomington included Mount Pleasant. However, another Mount Pleasant already existed in Illinois. To receive mail, citizens decided to use the township, Santa Anna, as the post office name. In 1869, residents finally changed the town's name to Farmer City.

Arriving in 1869, the railroad brought a building boom. Sadly, much of the business district was destroyed by fire in 1879, with another fire in 1894. Until 1907, many of the sidewalks were wooden, but a new city resolution required new ones to be of concrete.

One well-known business, the Arbogast Brick, Tile, and Cement Manufacturing Company, provided bricks used in many local brick buildings. They were also used for Clinton's Warner Hospital and Douglas School, University of Illinois campus buildings, and elsewhere.

Residents used well water until the early 1920s, when a water tower was erected for the 1,600 residents. Meanwhile, kerosene lamps lit the streets until the 1950s. By 1956, Northern Illinois Gas Company provided residents with natural gas. That same year, a flash flood of nearly three feet covered the intersection of Routes 150 and 54.

In the early 1970s, Interstate Highway 74 made it easier to travel through the county, bringing visitors and more residents. In the past, opera houses, theaters, and the fairground provided entertainment. These days, Farmer City celebrates its almost 200-year history with rodeos, fairs, and races.

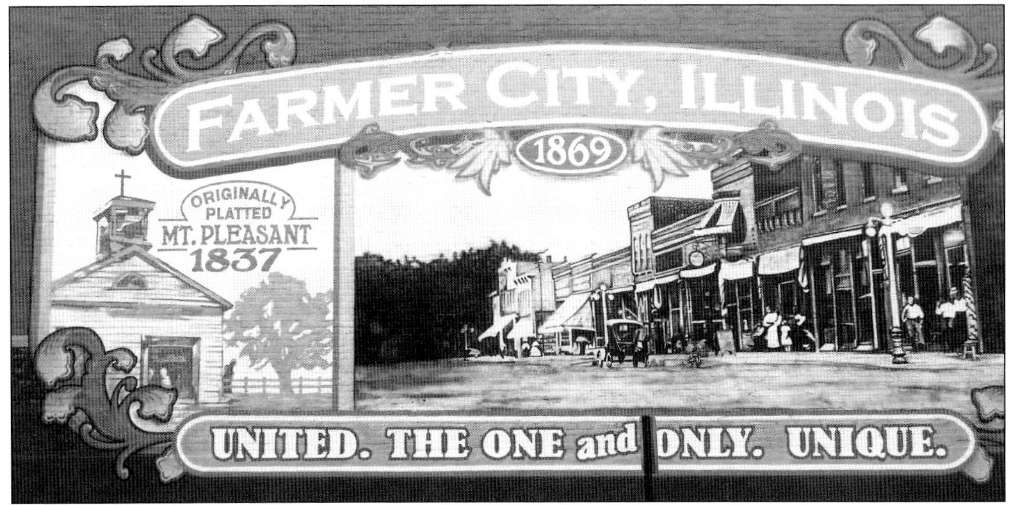

Artist Steve Woods's 2014 mural at Main and Green Streets commemorates the 1837 establishment of Mount Pleasant. Two years later, residents adopted the township name of Santa Anna for their post office to more easily receive mail. In 1869, the town name and post office were changed to Farmer City. (AC.)

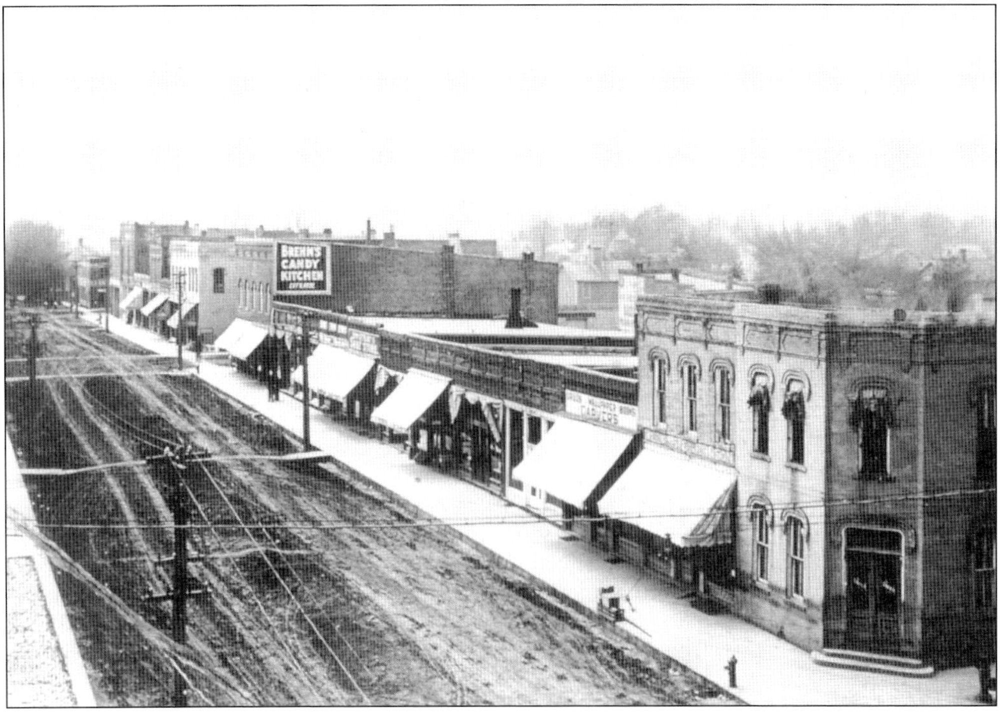

Founded in 1892, Brehm's Candy Kitchen was located at 224 South Main Street, the current home of the Farmer City Genealogical & Historical Society. Brehm's closed in the 1930s. The building at 216 South Main Street housed (Moses) Eppstein and Sons Shoe Store from 1886 to 1973, while the First National Bank stood at the far right from 1874 to 1894. (FCGHS.)

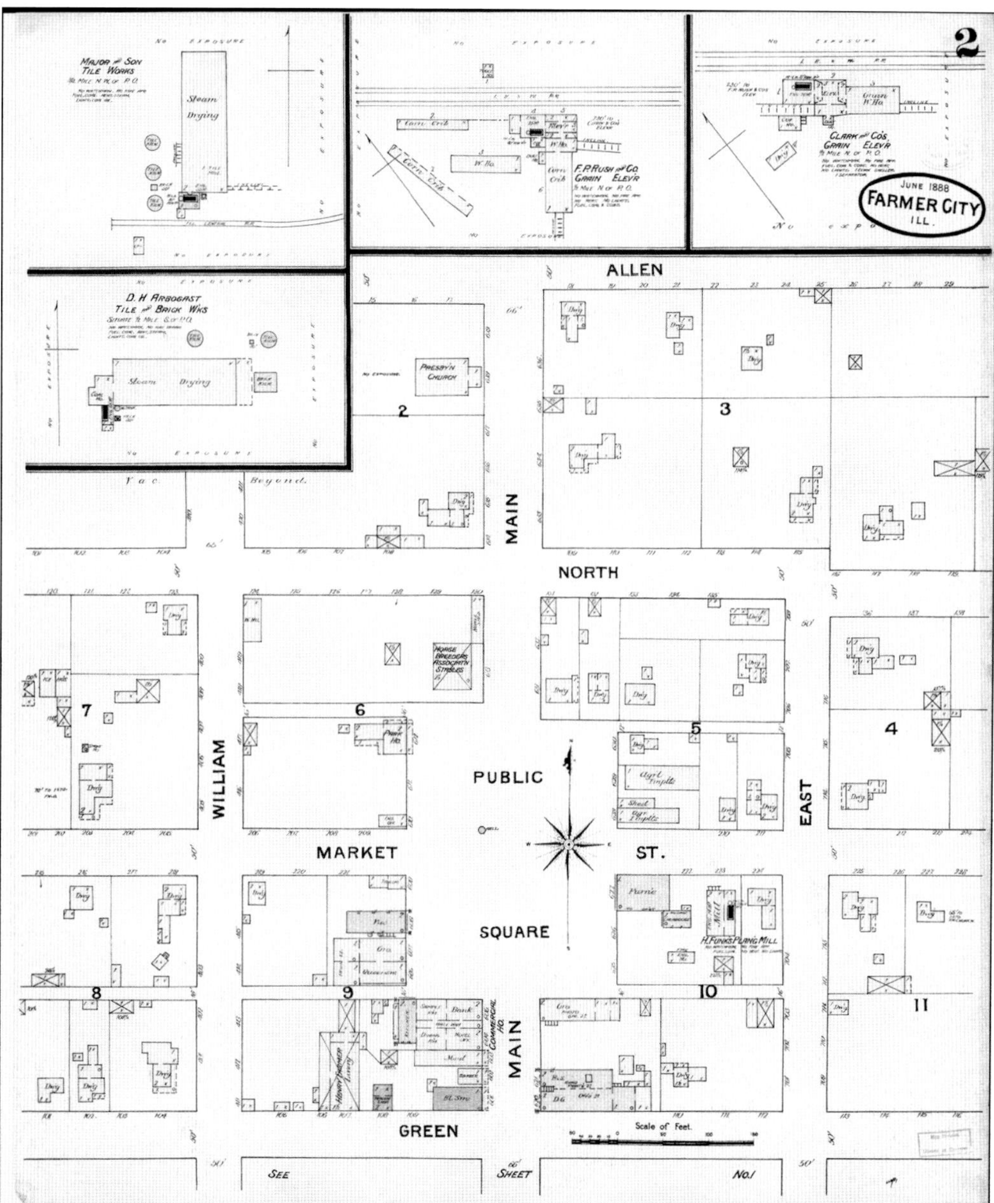

The Sanborn Map Company's 1888 fire insurance map shows the main streets of Farmer City, with businesses clustered around the public square. A tailor shop occupied the southwest corner of Market and Main Streets. The Commercial Hotel and the first Weedman bank stood a block south. Located between three-quarters and one-half mile northwest of the post office, the Major and Son Tile Works and the D.H. Arbogast Tile Works appear in the upper left inset boxes. In the inset boxes to the right of the tile works, notes detail that the F.P. Rush and Company Grain Elevator and the Clark and Companies Grain Elevator were located one-half mile north of the post office. It was clearly important to also note that neither grain elevator had a night watchman, heat, or lights, and both housed fuel, coal, and cobs. (LOCGM.)

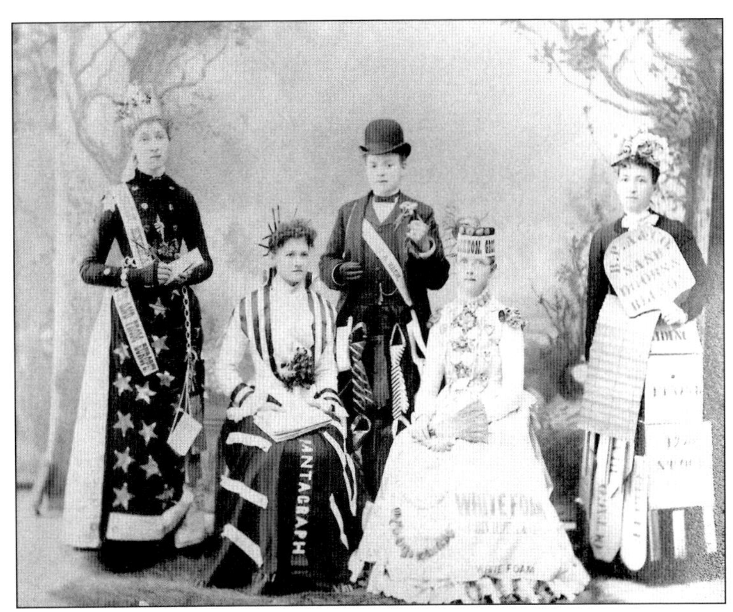

To collect for charities, merchants periodically organized a Merchants' Carnival featuring Methodist church ladies. In 1887, merchants posted are, from left to right, Lella Crum as Miss John Weedman Bank; Amanda ? as Miss *Bloomington Pantagraph*; Paulina Eppstein as Miss Eppstein's and Bach's Clothing Store; Mary Wood Crum as Miss Jim Jackson Grocery Store; and Mrs. Sam Robinson as Miss Lumber Yard. (FCL.)

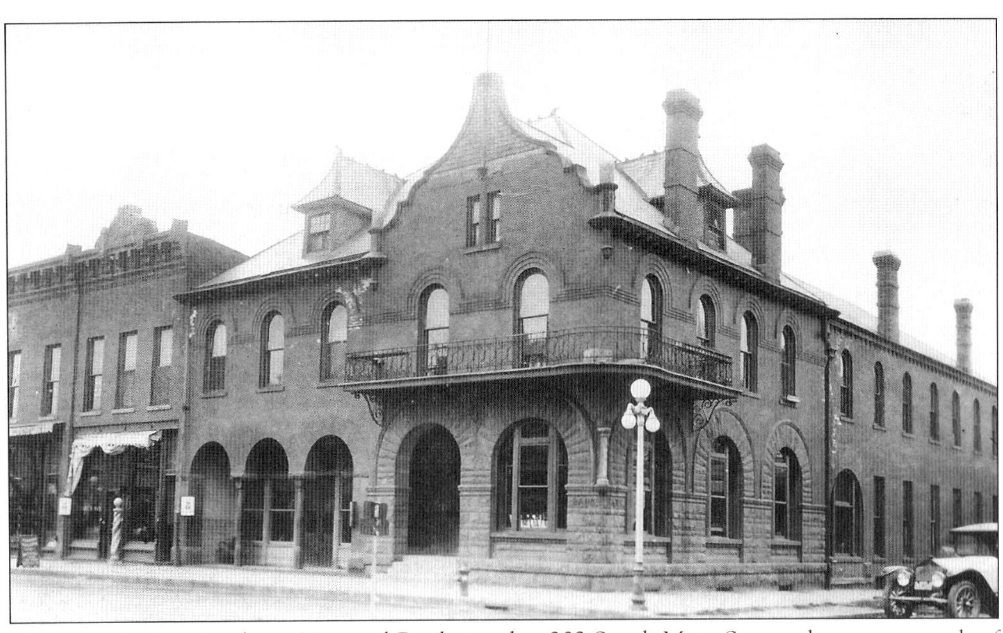

The second John Weedman National Bank stood at 202 South Main Street, the corner north of the Commercial Hotel. Thomas Brothers Bankers owned a private bank there previously, before Weedman's ownership from 1876 until his 1885 death. From October 1885 until its January 1932 closure, it was the John Weedman National Bank. The word "Bank" is seen etched into the building's stone corners. (FCGHS.)

In 1832, seven people gathered at Richard Kirby's log cabin in Hurley's Grove to form a Methodist organization. Churches were built and replaced in 1838, 1843, and again in 1862, when one was constructed at the foot of Plum Street. The current United Methodist church (originally Methodist Episcopal) was constructed in 1898. (AC.)

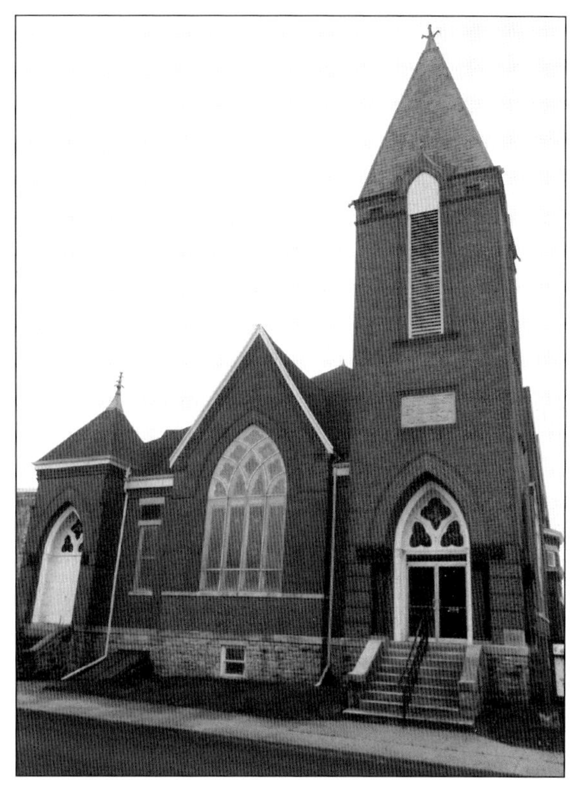

Fire department volunteers stand in front of the city hall in the early 1900s. The opera house appears at the left. Founded in 1905, the fire department was supported for years through donations and benefits. Its first equipment included a hose cart and bucket brigade. Volunteers often lost time when residents tried to outrace them to a fire. (LA.)

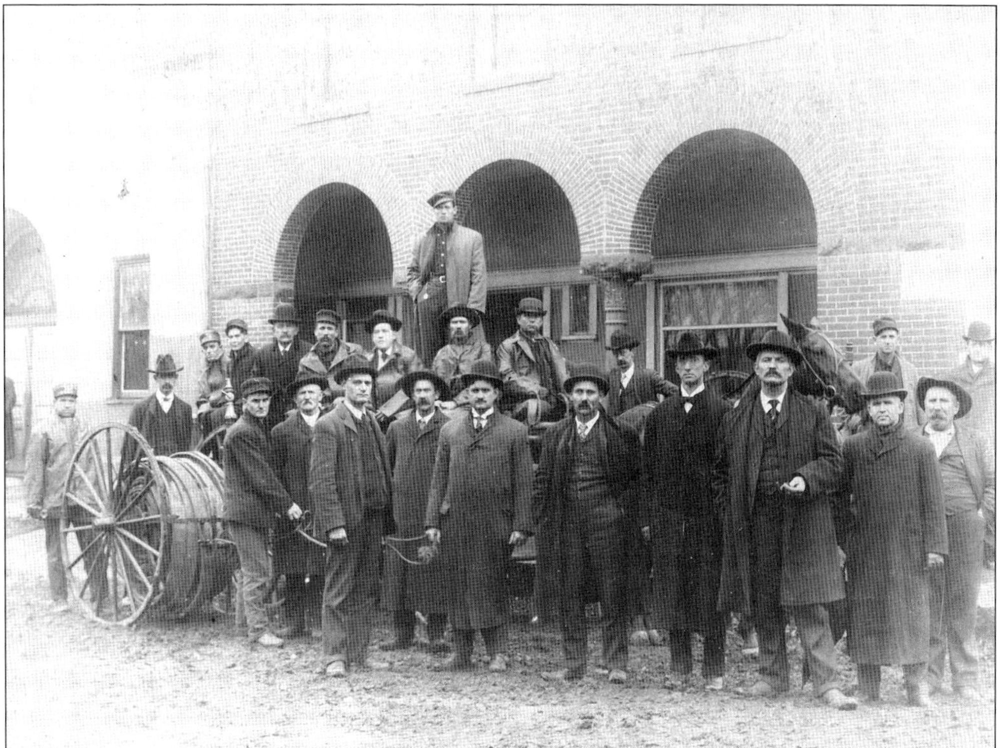

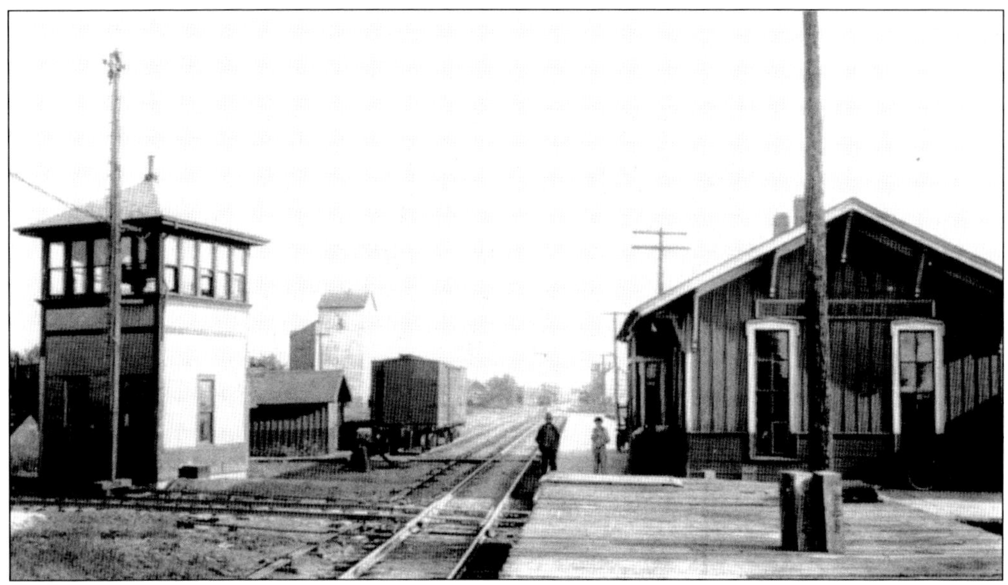

Two men stand in front of Farmer City's Illinois Central and Big Four depot near North and John Streets. "The Big Four" was a nickname for the Cleveland, Cincinnati, Chicago & St. Louis Railway, which formed in 1889 after mergers and acquisitions of several rail lines. The lunchroom stood behind the station. (FCGHS.)

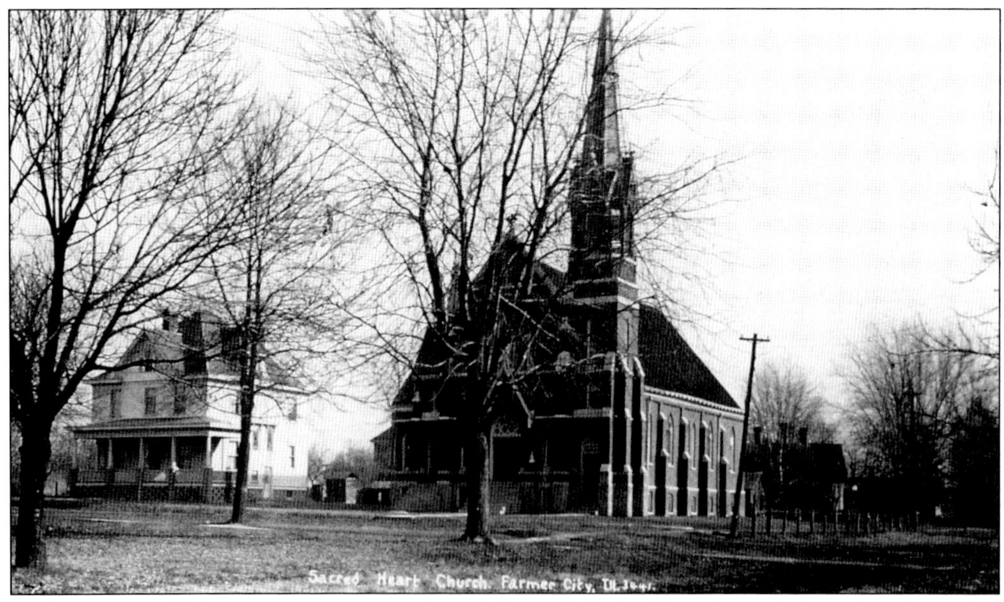

Replacing an 1882 frame structure, a new Sacred Heart Catholic Church was dedicated in November 1900. Prior to 1882, Catholics celebrated mass in parishioners' homes, with services provided by Bloomington priests. The other two area Catholic churches were Clinton's St. John the Baptist, founded in 1879, and Wapella's St. Patrick's, founded in 1853. (FCGHS.)

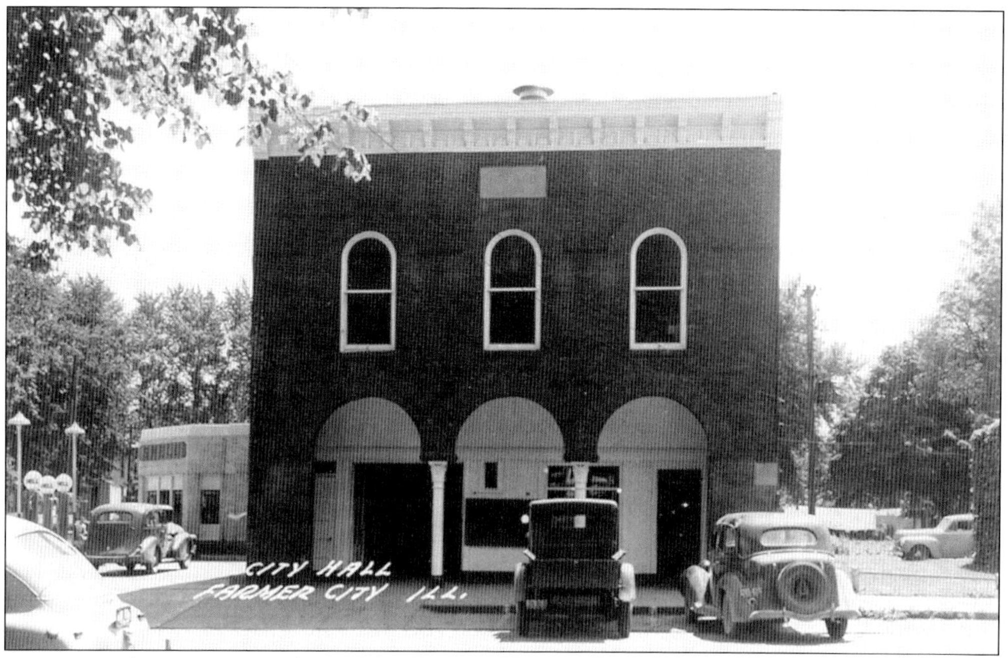

Farmer City's two-story city hall, at 105 South Main Street, was constructed in 1904. The upper story was divided into the hall and police court but hosted the town library during the early years. In the 1930s, the building housed the Works Progress Administration (WPA). In 1974, a one-story addition replaced the neighboring Shell service station. (FCL.)

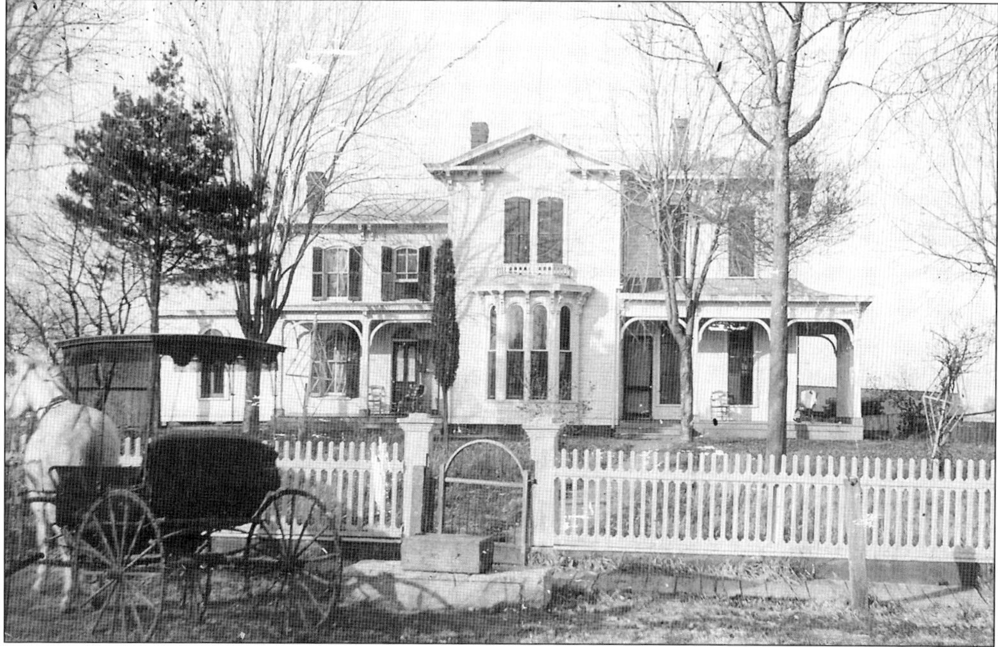

The house of Joseph (1838–1905) and Sabina Moore (1836–1919) stood at the northwest edge of Farmer City. Upon Moore's death, his will gave $2,000 to the library. He also gave 10 acres of the northeast corner of his land to establish the Joseph G. and Sabina Moore Township High School, benefitting DeWitt and Piatt Counties. High school construction began in 1911. (VWPL.)

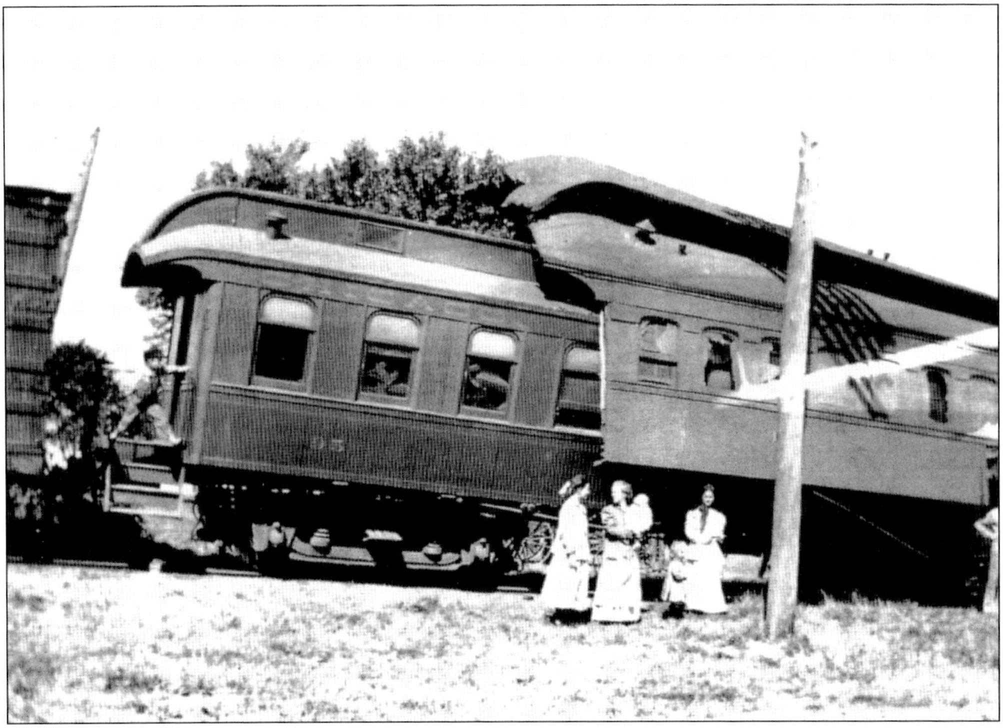

In October 1909, a passenger train car telescoped over the baggage car in a wreck west of Farmer City, photographed by William Leischner. One person died, with more than 40 injured. The people photographed are, from left to right, an unidentified child on steps, an unidentified woman, Winnie Ellis Leischner (Leischner's wife) holding their eight-month-old son John, daughter Darlene Leischner (toddler), and Winnie Leischner's mother, Mary Ellis. (FCGHS.)

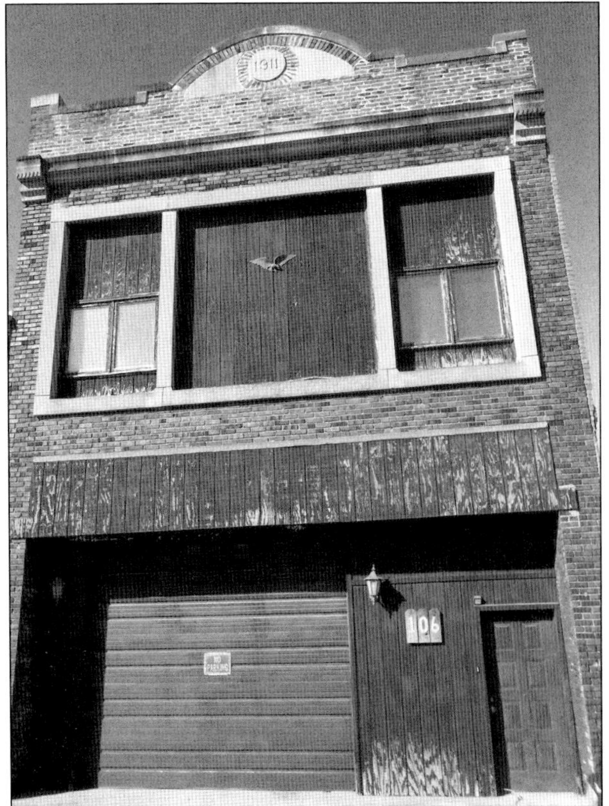

The capstone of the building at 106 South Main Street shows its construction year of 1911. At one time the site of J.N. Moreland's furniture store, the building at various times housed automobile sellers, then the Wartena Sales Company (roofing supplies) before being remodeled in 1930 for Farmer City's volunteer fire department. The fire department occupied it until the 1970s. (AC.)

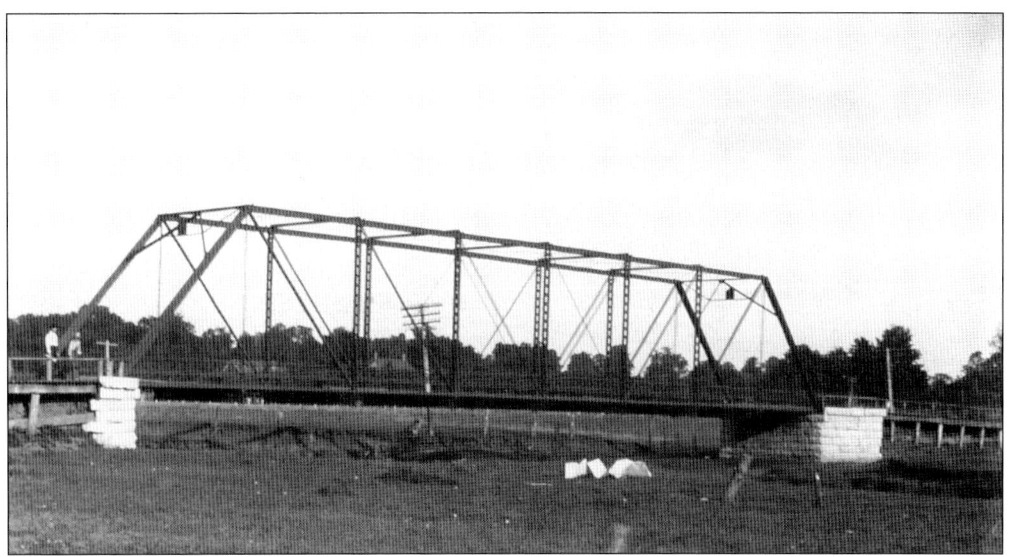

In 1912, the DeWitt County Board of Supervisors authorized replacing the bridge across Salt Creek on the state road running southeast out of Farmer City. The 1880s wooden bridge had been condemned for many years. Two unidentified men stand on the new, reinforced concrete bridge, in commission by January 1913. (FCGHS.)

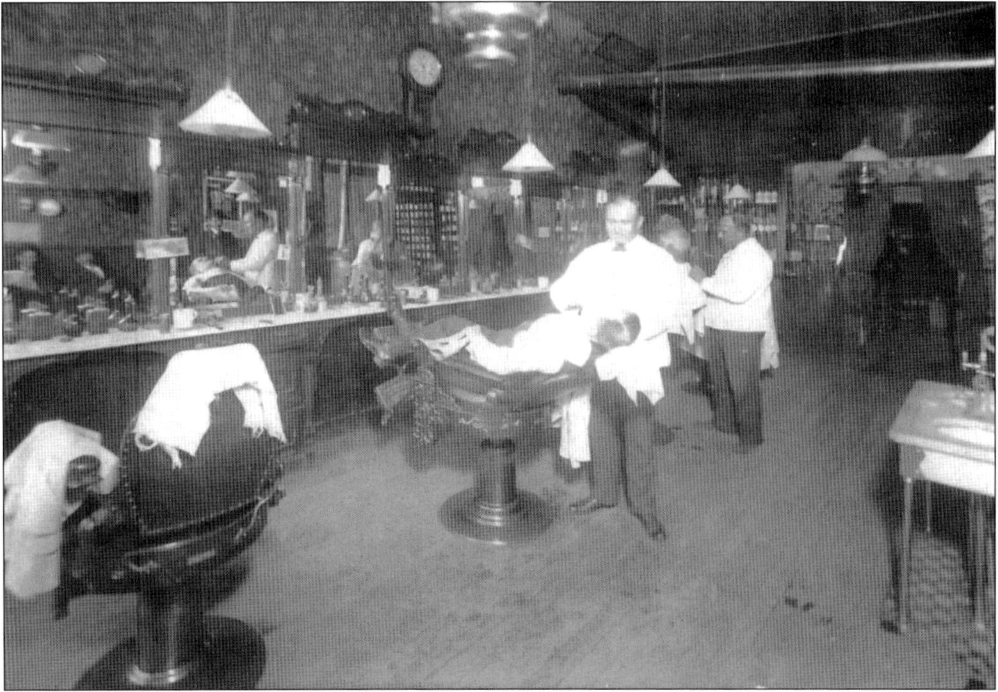

This pre-1912 photograph shows James Reed in his barbershop at 223 South Main Street, where he served customers from the 1900s until the 1910s. From 1921 to 1924, it hosted Jim "Red" Bell's barbershop. Other businesses in past years included a dressmaker, bargain store, cleaners, Collier & Son Hardware, A&B Hatchery, and Vogue Cleaners. (FCGHS.)

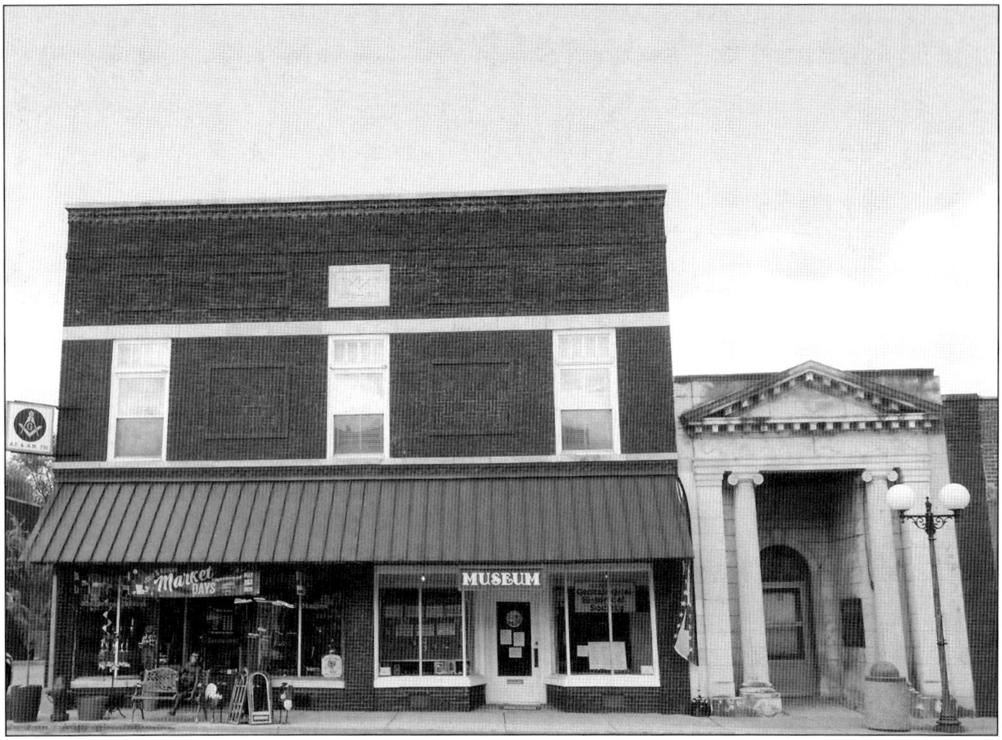

The capstone of 224–226 South Main Street displays "1879" for the Masonic lodge's construction date, plus "1918" for the installation of a new facade. Home since 1993 to the Farmer City Genealogical & Historical Society, the Abe Eppstein and Jacob Bach Clothing store occupied the site in the 1870s. Other former businesses included Brehm's Candy Kitchen (1891–1930s) and the Blossom Shop and Western Auto stores in the 1950s. (AC.)

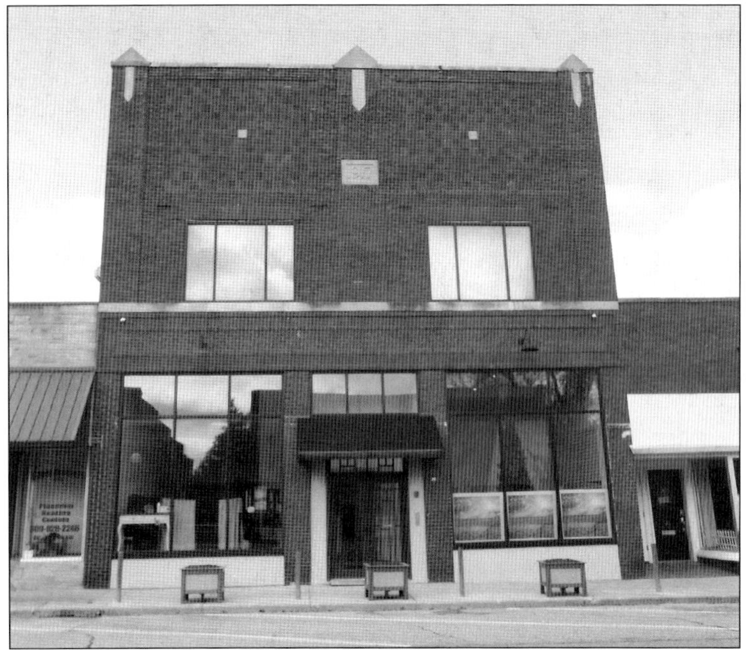

Grocers occupied 212 South Main Street from the early 1870s until the fire of 1894. From 1917, when the current structure was built, until 1959, it housed Hammer Grocery. From 1962 until 1974, it was occupied by K&S Furniture before it moved to 202 South Main Street. Later businesses included Schrock Cabinets and the Victory Christian Center. (AC.)

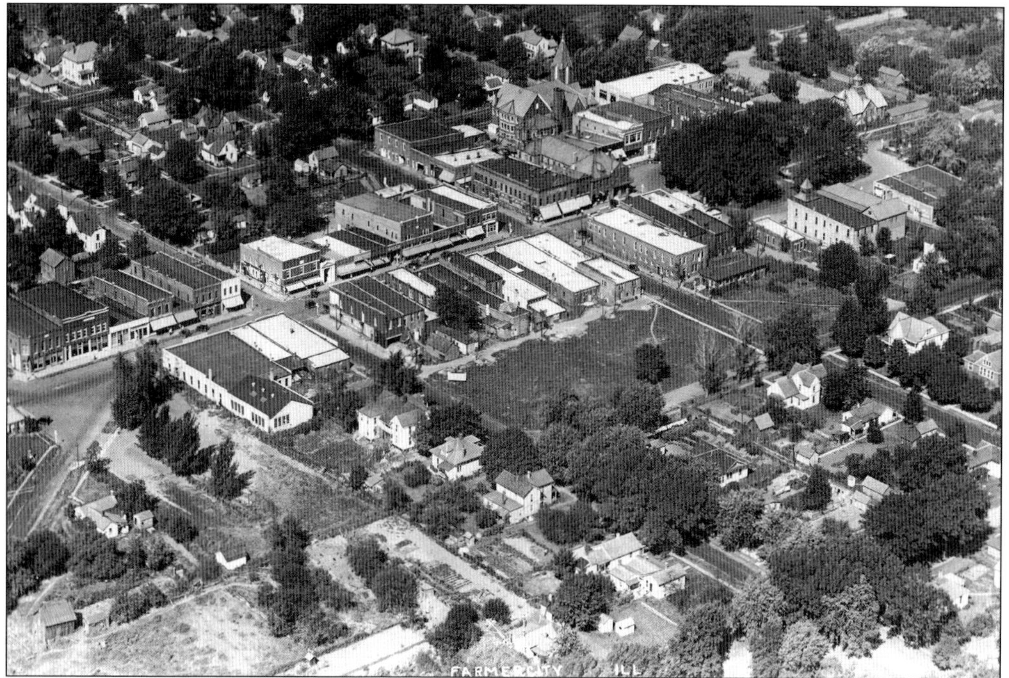

By the style of the vehicles on Main Street, this photograph was probably taken in the 1920s. At that time, W.H. Gould Jewelers and Optometrist occupied the building at 214 South Main Street. The second Weedman bank sits south of the tree-filled square at the far right. The Methodist church steeple rises at the top center. (FCGHS.)

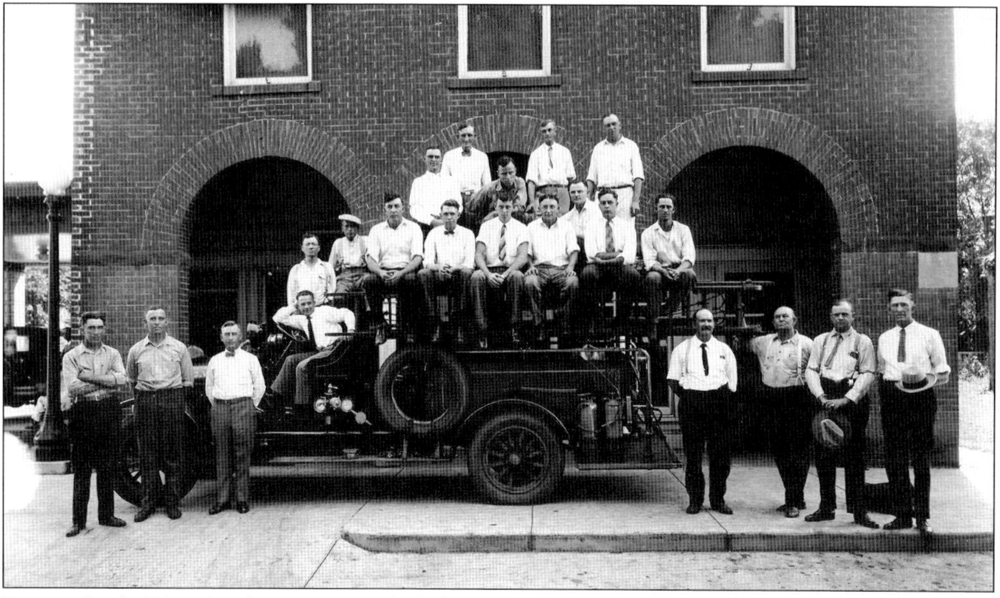

Farmer City's 1920s fire department included, from left to right, (first row) ? Holmes, Tink McMurphy, Carl Derr, John Kopp, John Shell, Ted Weedman, and Oliver Guthridge; (second row) Lafayette Cox (in driver's seat), Frank Jones, Guy Wence, Berle Morgan, John Johnson, Leon Rous, Dale Reeser, Clarence Smith, Ernie Ownes, and Irwin Call; (third row) unidentified, Dwight Roth, Homer Vance, and Claude Reeser. (FCGHS.)

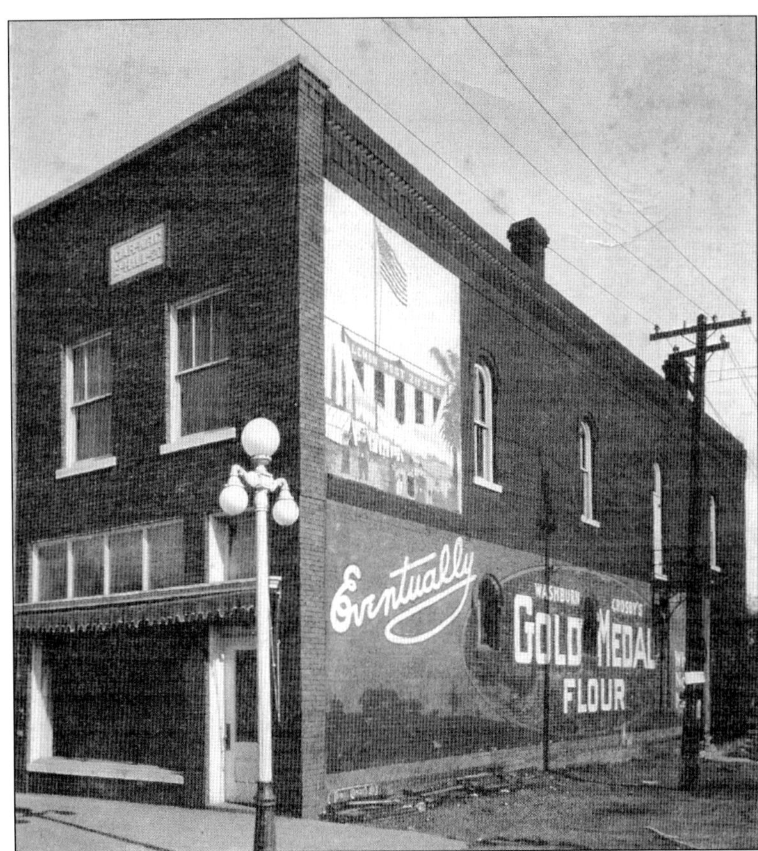

The McLain Hotel was located at 223 South Main Street from around 1850 until 1879 before the building was used by several businesses until 1920. In 1920, the second floor became home to the local Grand Army of the Republic (GAR), a Civil War Union veterans' organization, and the Women's Relief Corps (WRC), the GAR's auxiliary organization. From 1970 until 1986, it was used by the Gammage Law Firm. (FCGHS.)

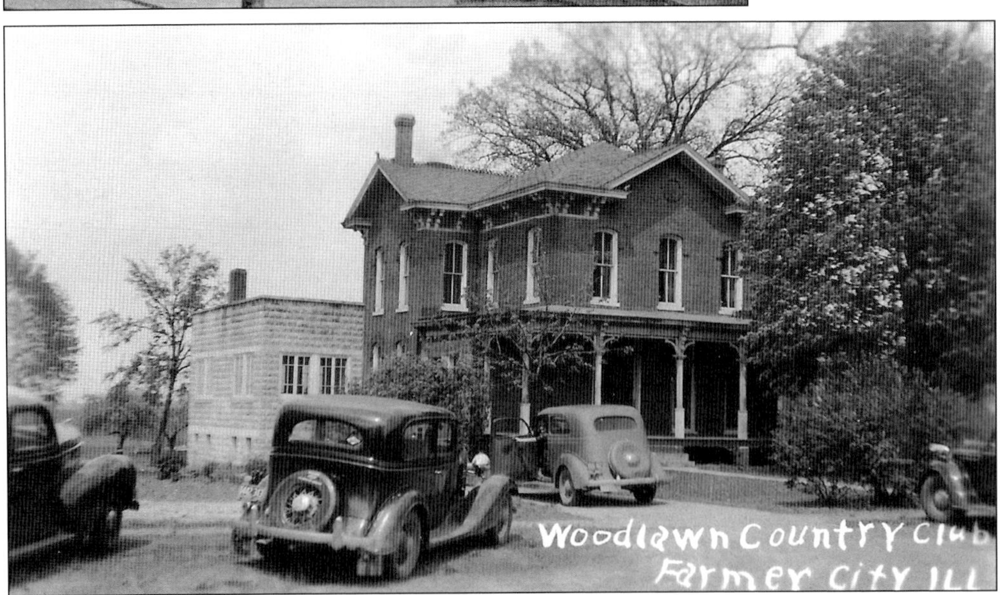

The Woodlawn County Club was founded in March 1922 after organizers purchased 56 acres at the northeast edge of town. The next year, the grounds and clubhouse were ready to use. By 1963, a swimming pool was added, and several years later, grass replaced the sand greens. In 1978, a modern building replaced the club's farmhouse. (FCGHS.)

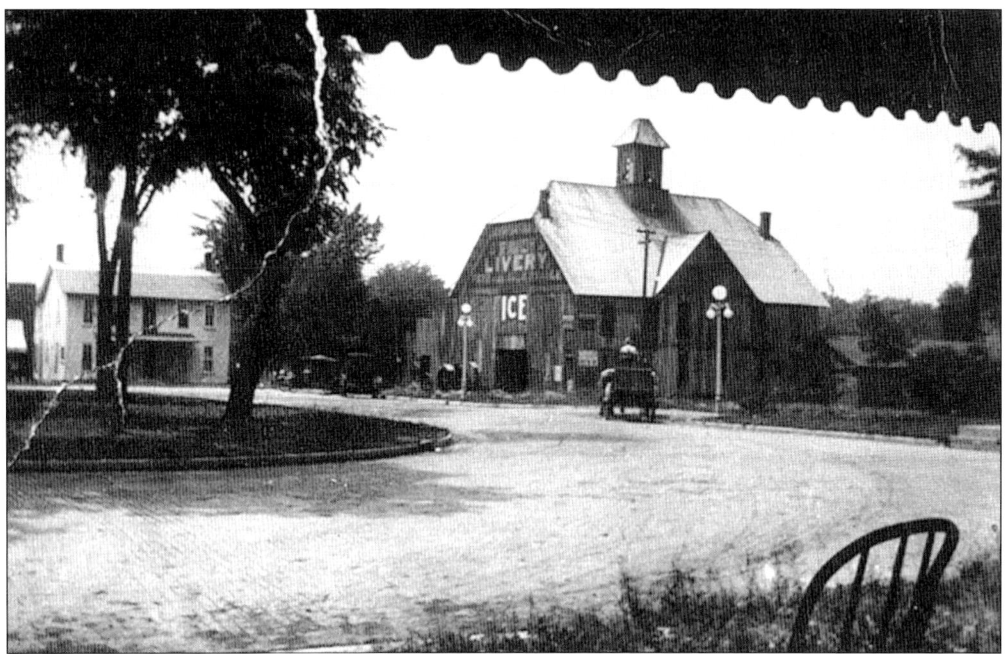

In the 1880s, the Farmer City Horse Breeders Association erected their Park Livery Feed and Stable on the northwest corner of the square, facing the park. In time, it became an icehouse and then storage space for surplus farm machinery. Eventually abandoned, it was demolished in May 1923. (LA.)

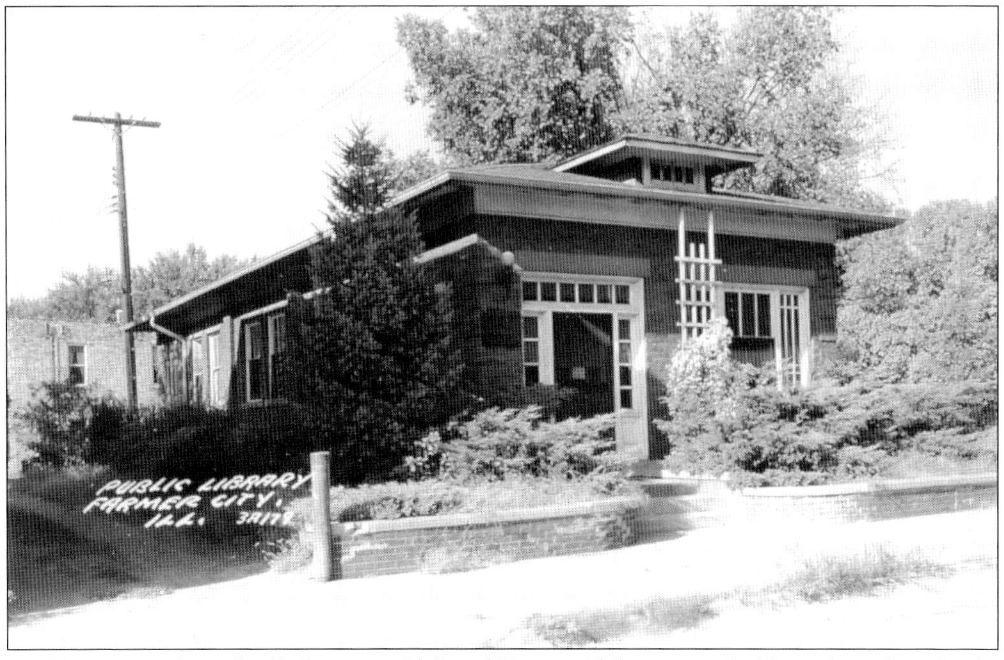

In 1897, women from the Shakespeare Club and History Club organized a library by making books available through the newspaper's office. After 1904, city hall's upstairs front room became the library. In 1927, through donations, the Farmer City Library Association purchased the East Green Street post office building, later enlarging the library in 1981. (FCGHS.)

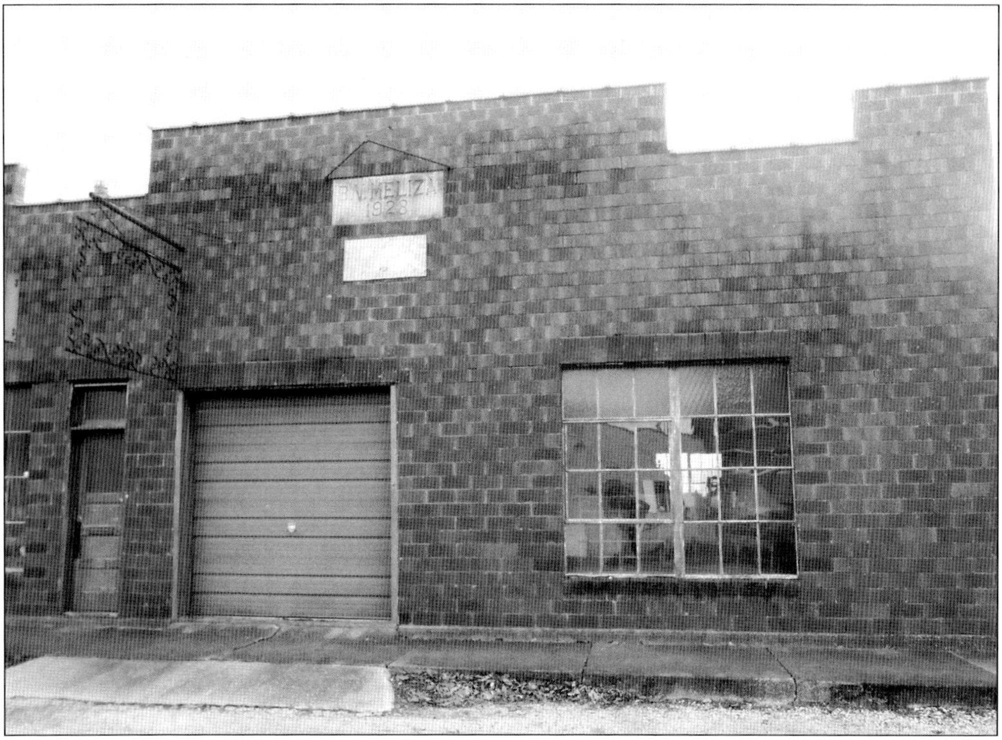

A blacksmith shop opened at 111 West Green Street around 1892. In 1928, Broe Meliza constructed a shell around the structure, creating the Bilt Rite Factory. In addition to horseshoeing, blacksmithing, welding, and repair work, he provided custom-made Model A truck bodies and beds. In 1998, artisan blacksmiths Mark and Mindy Gardner opened Flood Plain Forge for unique metal work. (AC.)

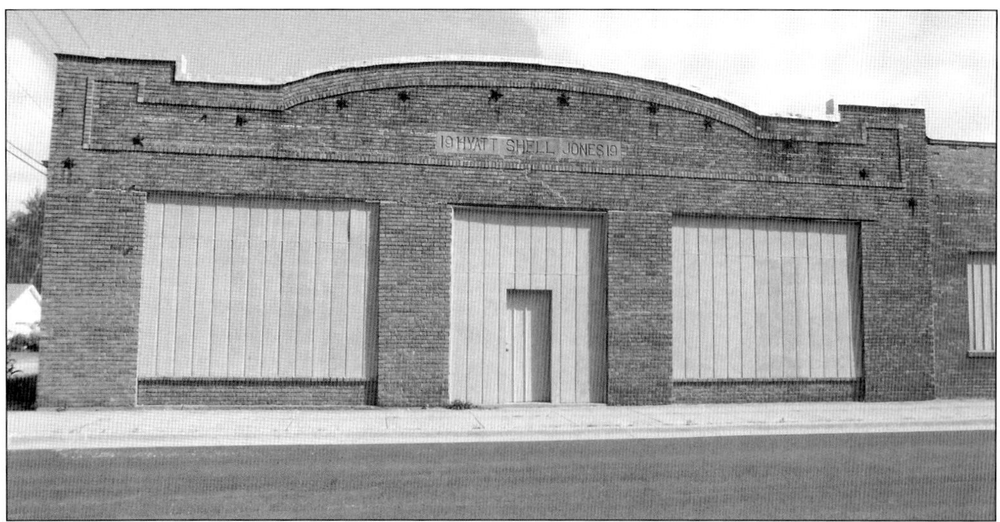

The Hyatt, Shell, and Jones garage and John Deere implement business were once located at 103 North Main Street. But by November 1915, construction began on a new fireproof garage at West Market and North Williams Streets. In 1929, W.G. Shell took over the building's west side, selling Chevrolets. (AC.)

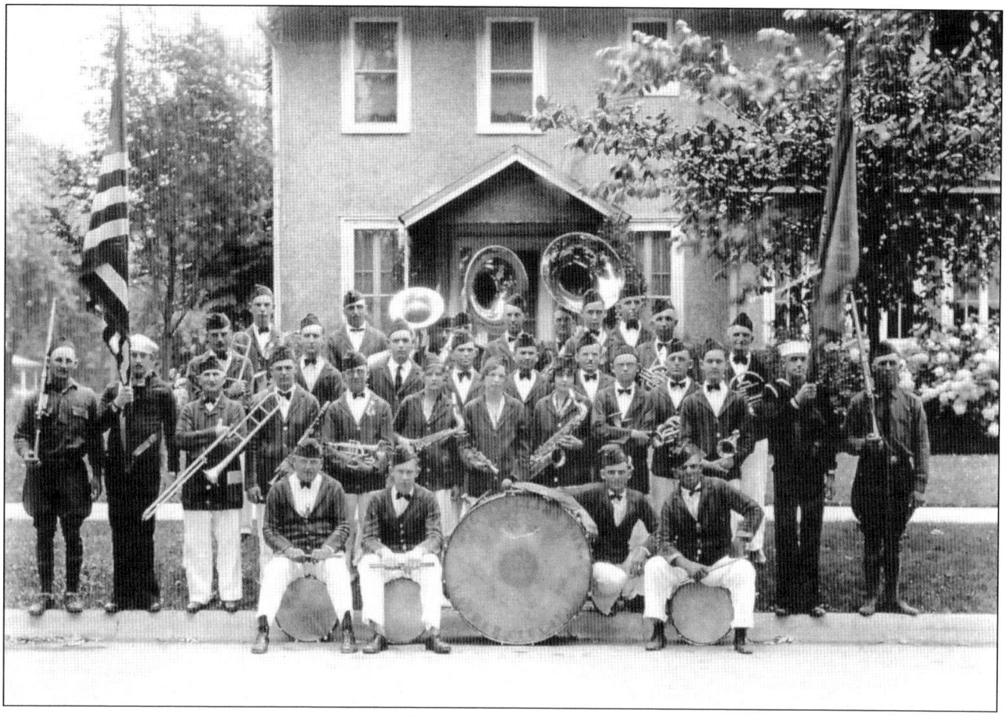

Members of the American Legion Joe Williams Post 55 Band pose in 1929 in front of 116 North James Street. Named after a local man in 1919 who died during World War I, the post was the first DeWitt County Legion post to be chartered. Several people in the photograph had also belonged to the old Farmer City Band. (FCGHS.)

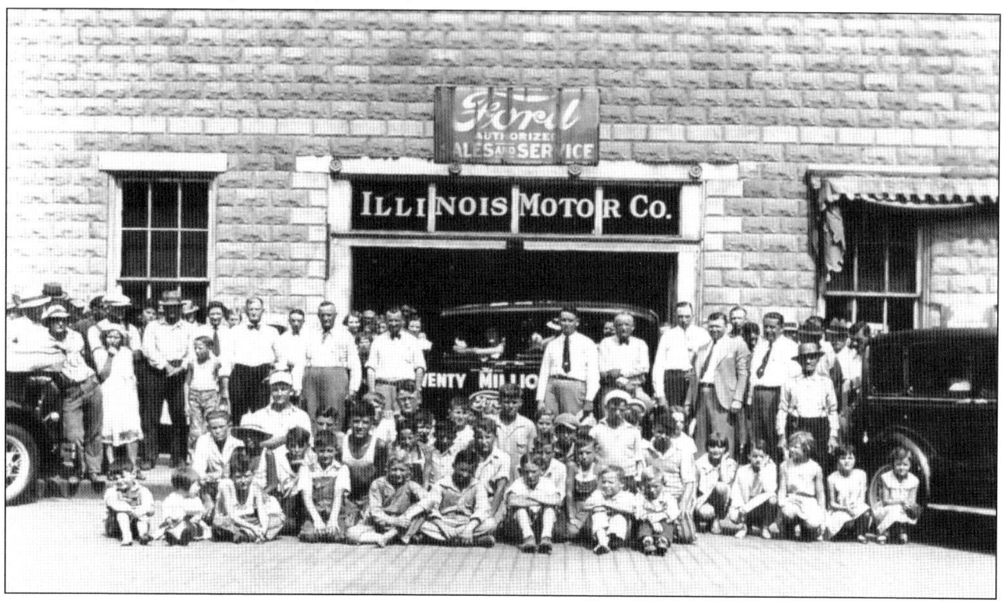

In July 1931, the Ford dealership displayed the 20 millionth Ford car, part of a countrywide tour along with 15 of the latest car models. One car came with a radio and loudspeaker, and another included a moving picture machine. When the tour completed, the special car was placed at Ford's village near Dearborn, Michigan. (FCGHS.)

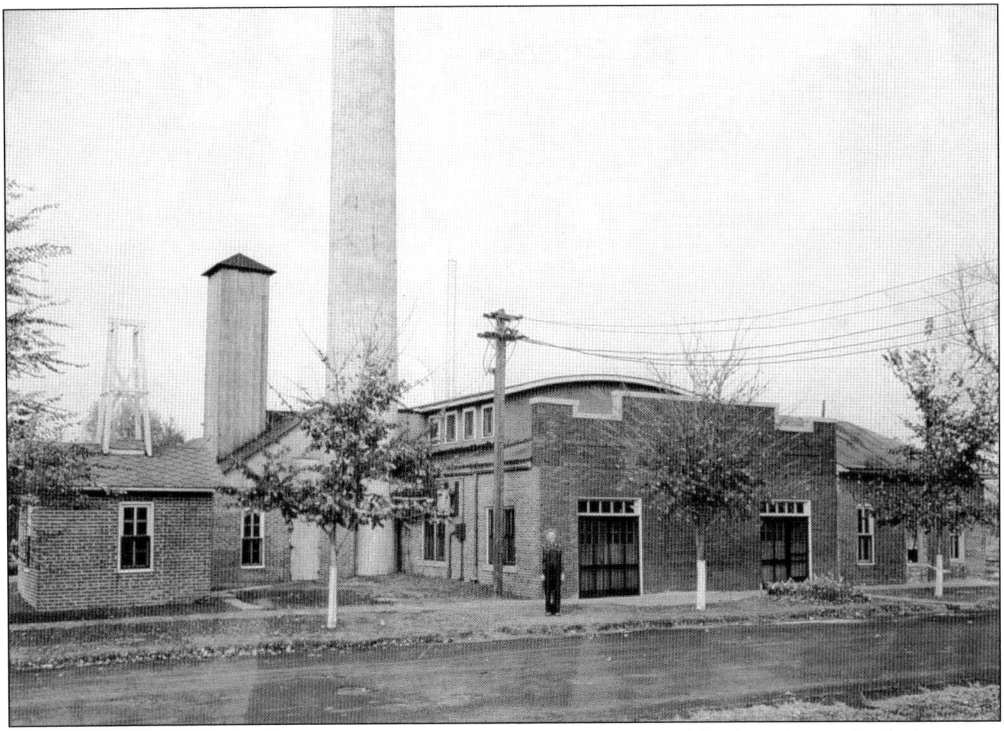

Abraham Evans built Farmer City's first electric light plant, steam-operated, in 1888. The city purchased it in 1895. Roy Neal stands in front of the plant in 1935, the year it changed completely to diesel. Multiple structural changes and additions occurred over decades. In 1983, the city began purchasing power from the Illinois Power Company. (LA.)

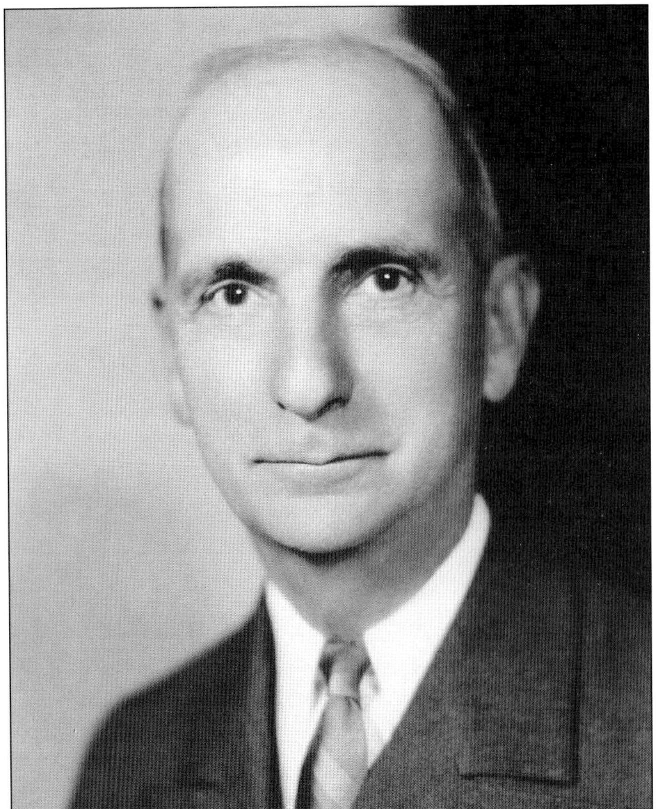

Lott Herrick graduated from Farmer City High School in 1888 and from the University of Illinois in 1892 with a bachelor of arts degree. After obtaining his law degree from the University of Michigan in 1894, he practiced in Farmer City, later becoming a county judge from 1902 until 1904. From 1933 until his 1937 death, he served on the Illinois Supreme Court. (FCGHS.)

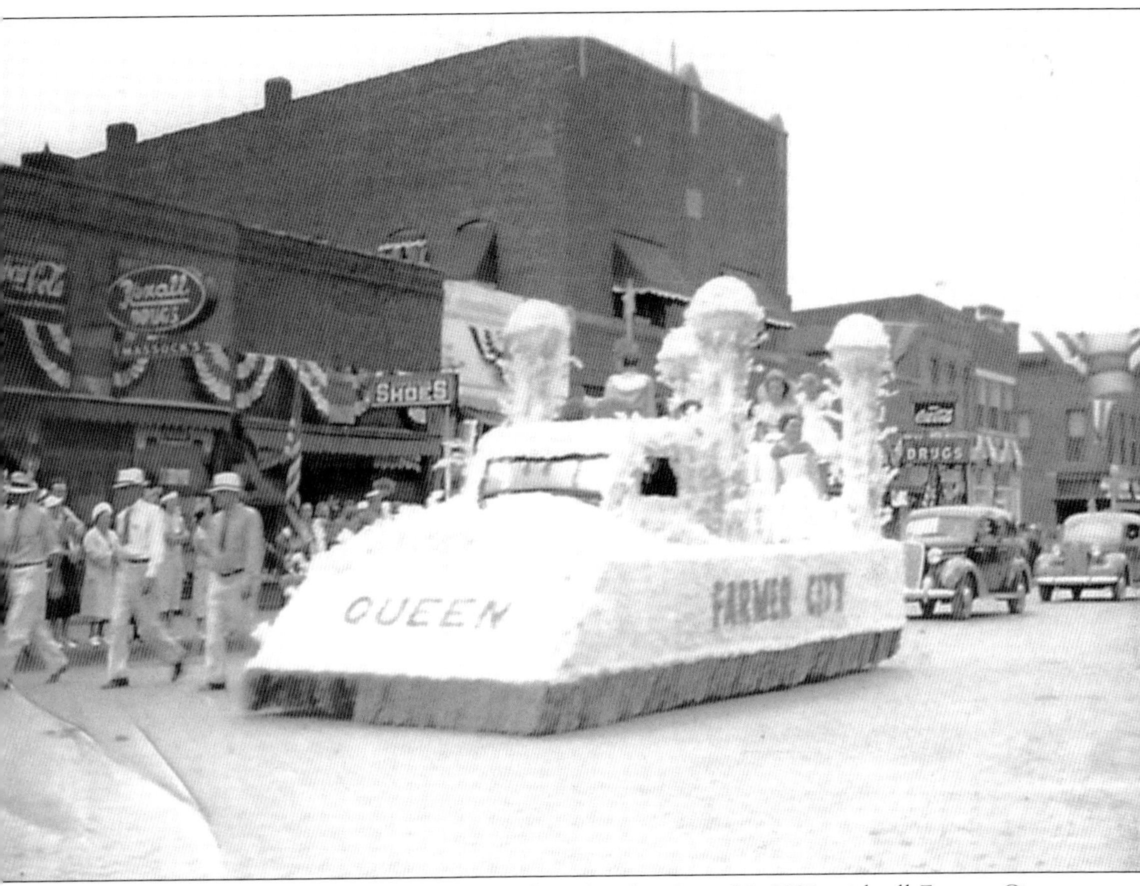

Farmer City's four-day centennial commenced on Sunday, June 26, 1937, with all Farmer City churches holding special services. At 7:30 that evening, the town band gave a concert at the fairgrounds, followed by speeches and a community sing. Evelyn Curtis, 16-year-old Miss Farmer City, was crowned queen of the court of honor during the grand opening. Others in the court included Betty Jo Wash as Miss Columbia and eight attendants-of-honor. Floats filled afternoon and evening parades. A historical pageant was presented on each night. On Monday, after a pet parade through Main Street, prizes were awarded for best decorated bicycle, pet, and children in novelty costumes. The fairgrounds hosted entertainment every evening, including displays of town relics and, on Tuesday, late-night fireworks. The celebrations concluded on Wednesday night with a torchlight parade, entertainment, and prizes for best decorated cars. (FCGHS.)

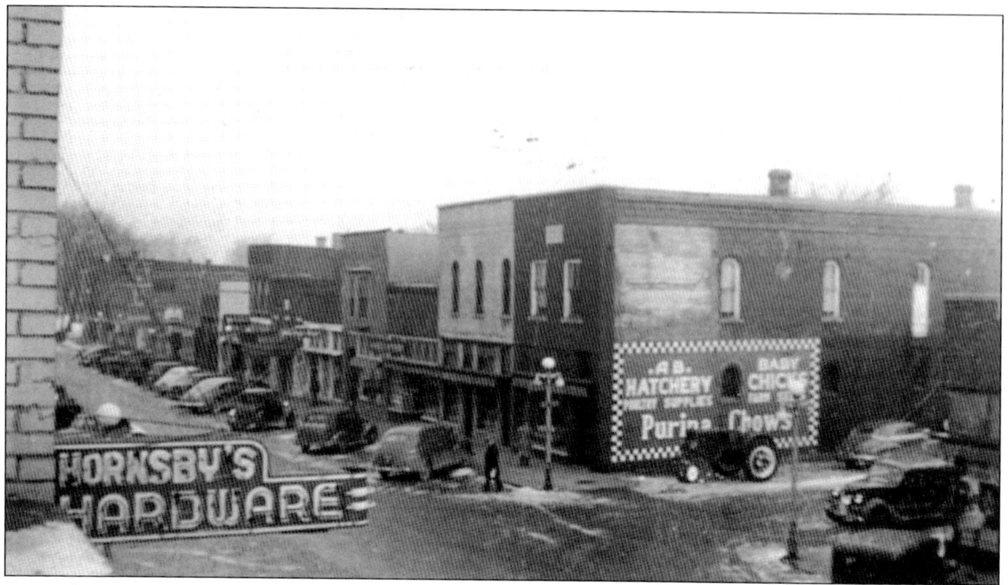

Hornsby Hardware opened in 1941 in the Collier building at 304 South Main Street. The hardware department was upstairs, and a small department store selling items from 5¢ to $1 was downstairs. In time, an appliance section was added. By 1985, the hardware store was replaced by Lambs Variety. (FCGHS.)

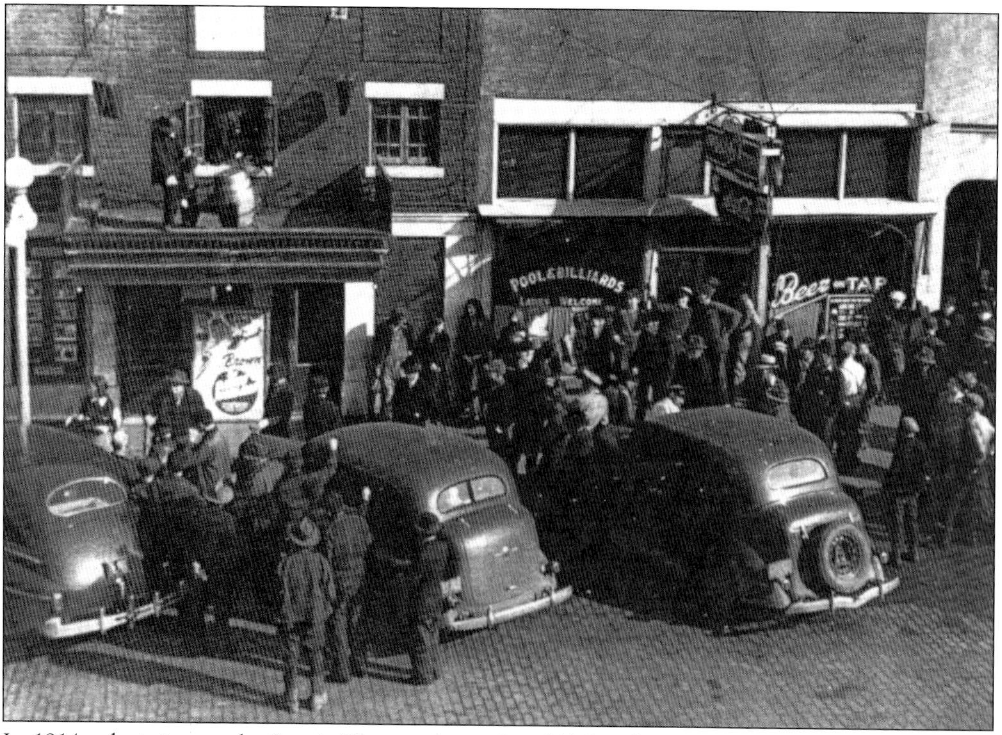

In 1914, admission to the Scenic Theater, located at 211 South Main Street, was 5¢. The owners sold it to John Kendall that same year. In 1917, he renamed it the Kendall Theatre (photographed around 1943) and hired a piano player to accompany vaudeville acts and silent films. The family closed it in 1968. The building was demolished in 2007. (FCGHS.)

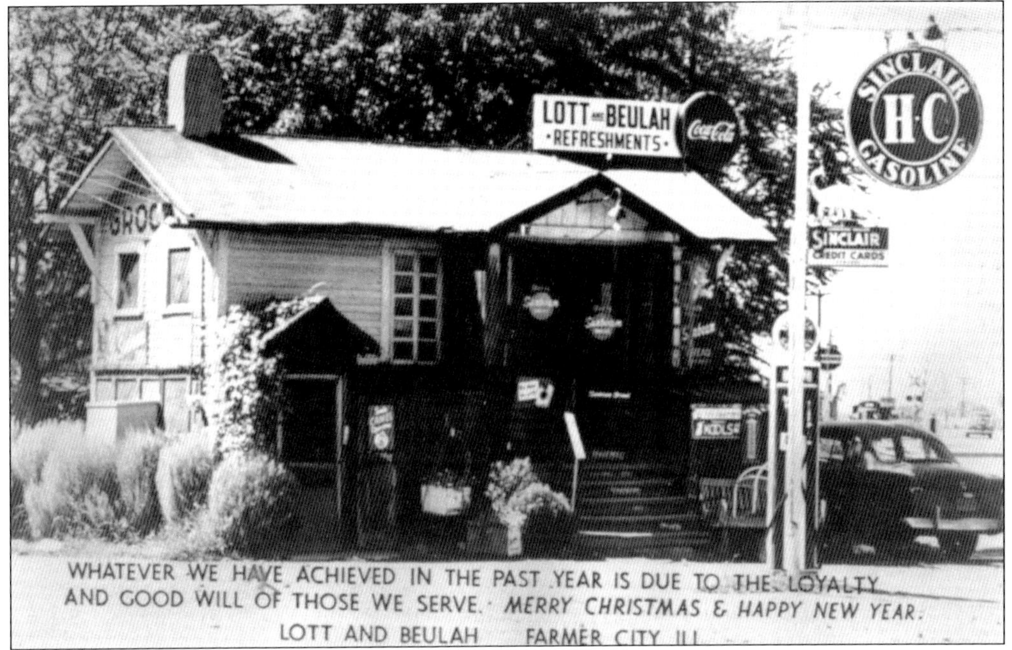

From at least 1940, Lott and Beulah Merrifield ran their North End Grocery at 902 North Main Street. A Sinclair gas station was also on the premises. In 1955, after his wife's death, Merrifield sold the stock and fixtures and purchased a resort at Williams Bay on Lake Geneva, Wisconsin. Both are buried at Maple Grove Cemetery. (FCGHS.)

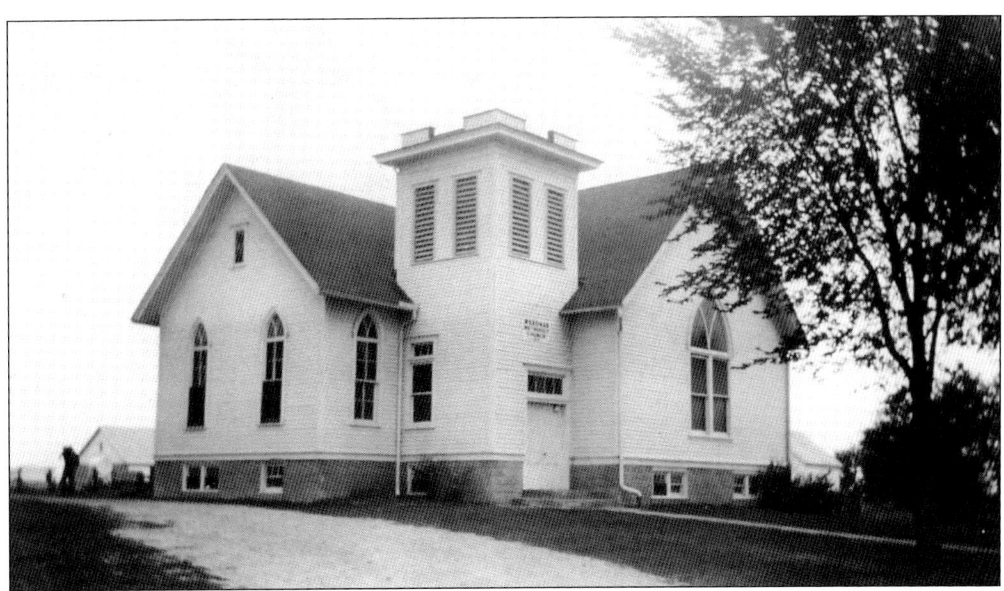

Constructed in 1879, the Weedman Methodist Church is in the unincorporated community of Weedman (partly in DeWitt County), about four miles northeast of Farmer City. In 1899, the church bought the property next to it for a parsonage. A Sunday school room was added in 1914. Many renovations took place over the next decades, including adding stained-glass windows. (FCGHS.)

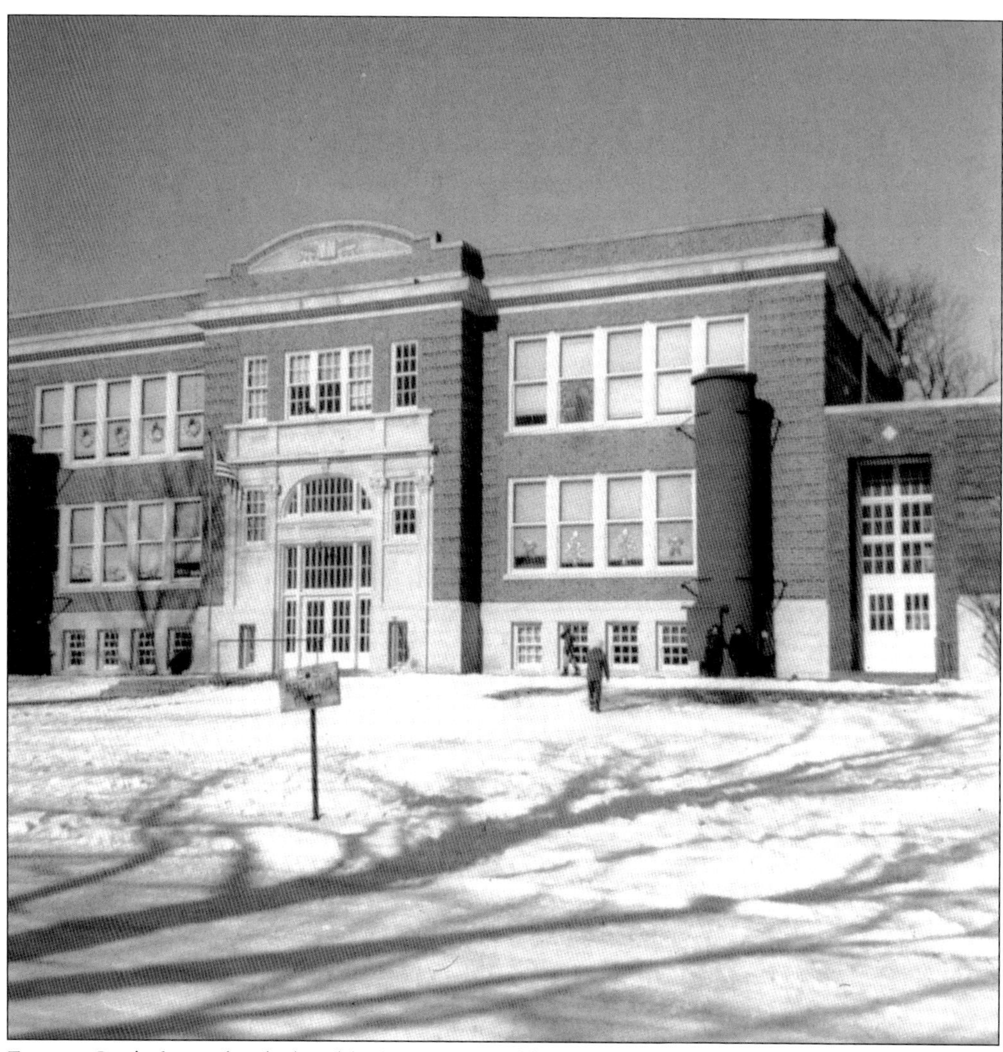

Farmer City's first school, dated before 1870 and located near present-day Green and William Streets, was replaced by a brick schoolhouse in 1873. The eight rooms included elementary and high school grades, with a room for the superintendent. A new grade school, Franklin, was built in 1911, with an addition completed in 1937. The school was heated from excess steam generated by machinery at the light plant two blocks away. This undated photograph by Don Scott shows the 1911 Franklin Grade School, complete with fire escape chutes that were eventually closed down. By 1948, all elementary school children through grade seven were attending Franklin. The school was closed in 1991. In 1994, the city council accepted the only bid submitted—$16,850—for the property. The 1911 portion of the school was demolished in 1995, leaving the gymnasium section. (LA.)

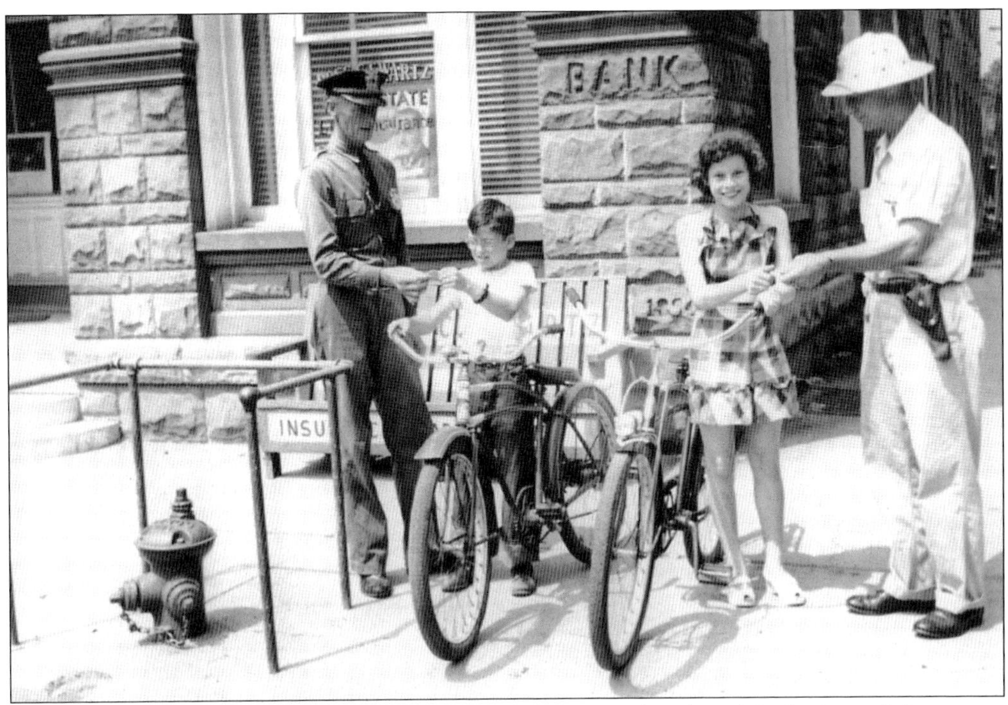

In July 1949, the town's Bicycle Safety Program was sponsored and paid for by Swartz's Insurance Agency, located inside the former Weedman National Bank building (see the word "BANK" etched in the stone corner). Chief of Police O.W. Reinke (left) and Officer Keith Flint (right) give silver dollars to Mary Wilson and Lyndon Short for being the most courteous and safe bike riders that week. (FCGHS.)

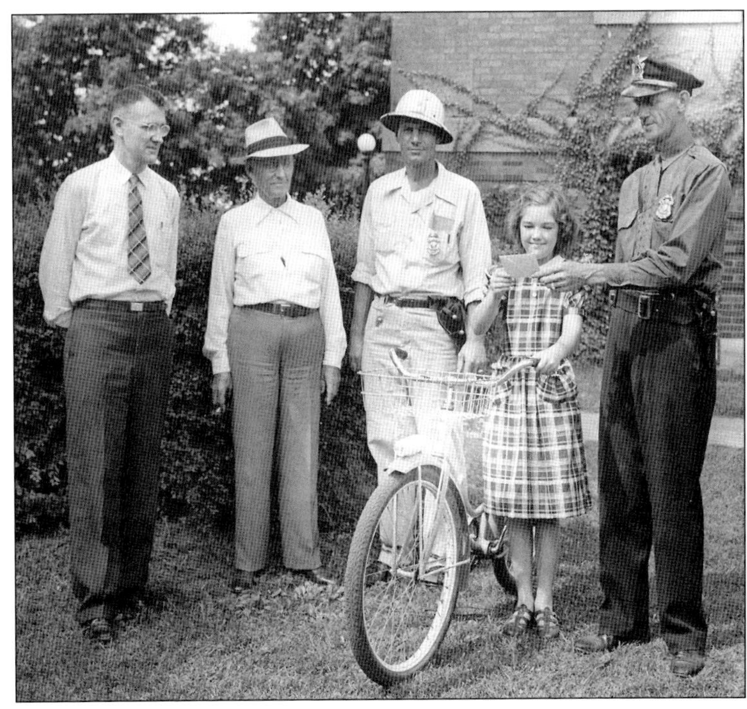

Over each of 11 weeks during the summer of 1949, two youngsters received silver dollars for being the most courteous and safest bike riders. In September, 11-year-old Sylvia Savage was selected from all the summer's recipients to win the grand prize of $5. The people photographed are, from left to right, two unidentified, Officer Keith Flint, Sylvia Savage, and Chief of Police Reinke. (FCGHS.)

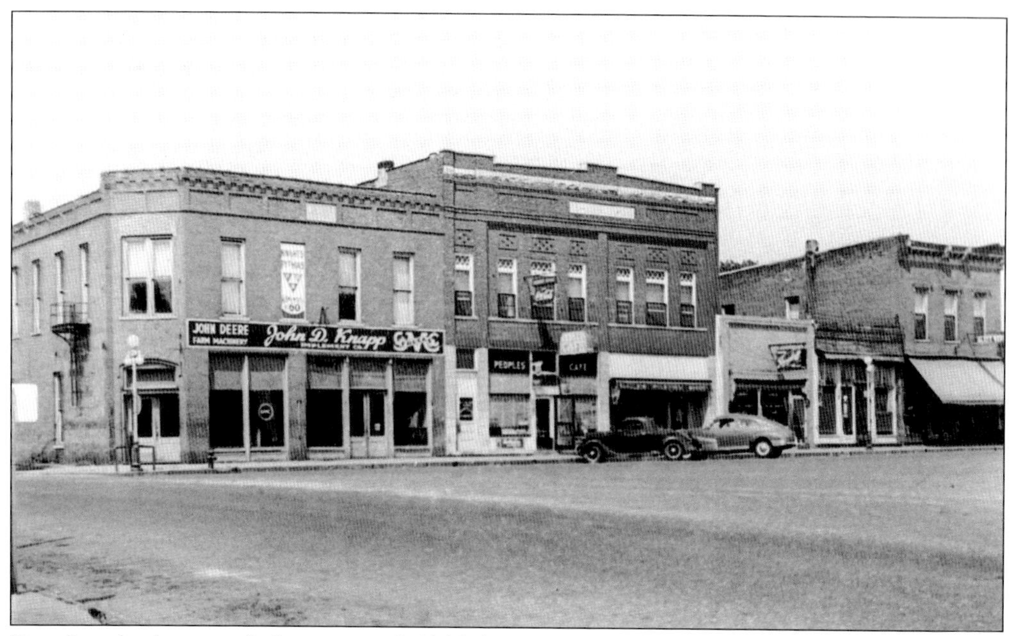

Don Scott's photograph from around 1945 shows 320 South Main Street with the Knights of Pythias Hall on the top floor and Knapp's Implement Company below. Constructed in 1894, the building served as Farmer City's high school from 1911 to 1912. The capstone of the building at 318 South Main Street notes it as the IORM (Improved Order of Red Men) hall. Built in 1905, it later became the People's Café. (LA.)

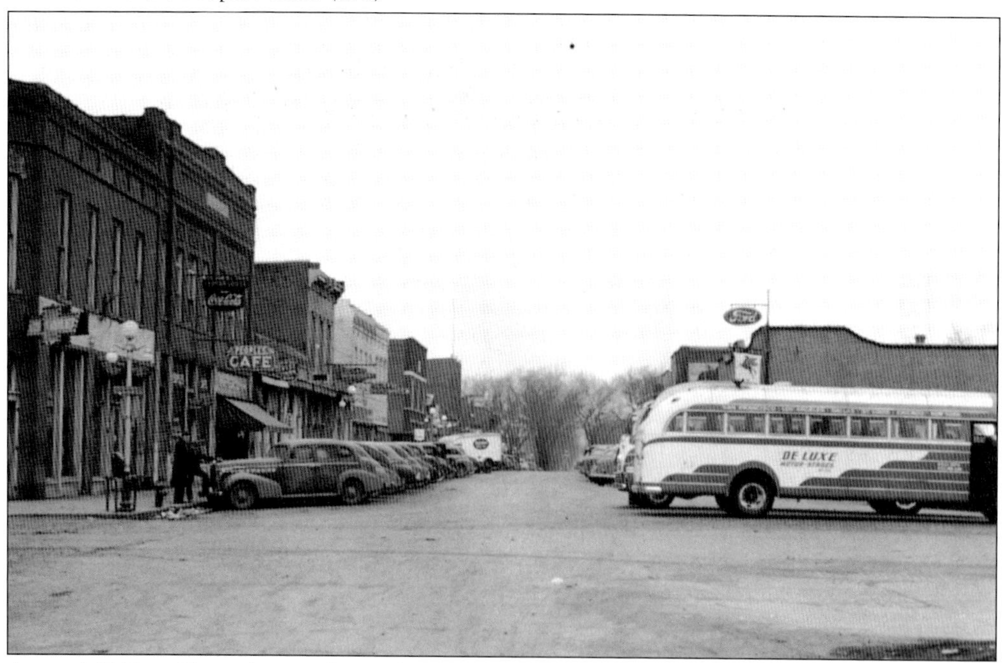

Around 1948, a Chevrolet sign hung above the entrance of 320 South Main Street. At 318 South Main Street, fountain drinks at the People's Café (1931–1986) included Coca-Cola. Hornsby's Hardware stood farther north. A Ford dealership sign advertised its location across the street. Since the 1970s, various banks have occupied the Ford site. (FCGHS.)

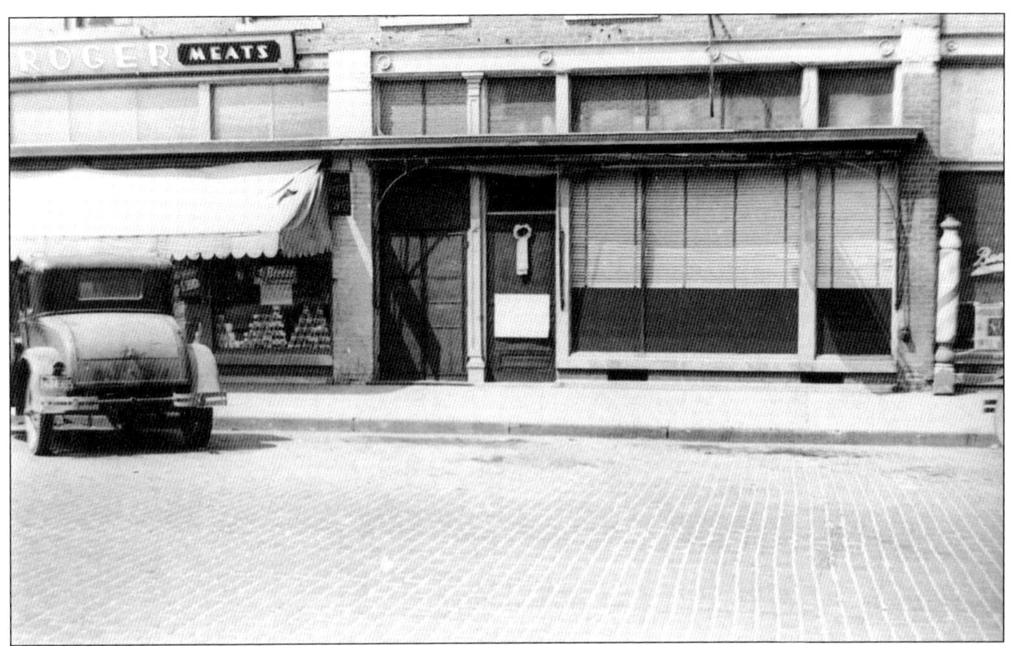

The Kroger Grocery store was established in 1927 in the Gould and Young Building at 120 South Main Street. It was closed in 1956 when the Kroger Company began focusing its business in larger towns, but the former manager, Earl Rich, and his wife set up E&A Dollar Wise Food Store, an independent grocery store, in the same location. (LA.)

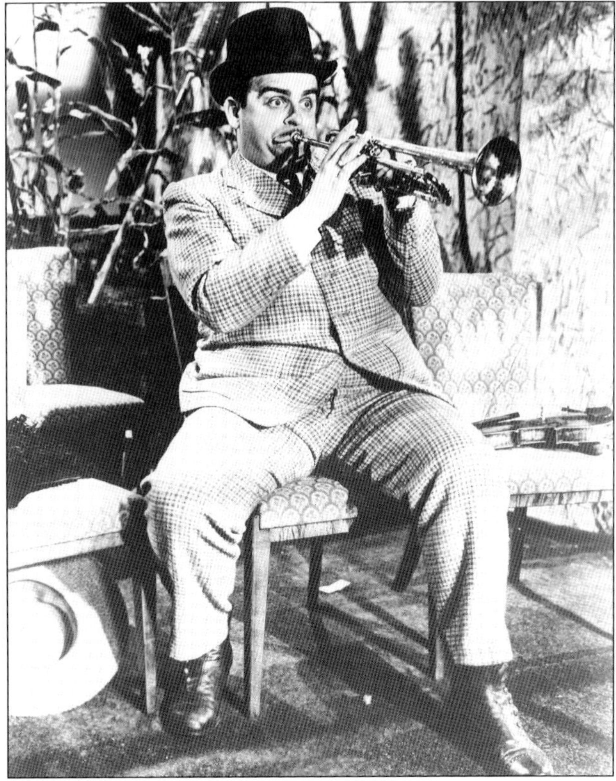

George Rock (1919–1988) learned his trumpet skills in the Moore Township High School Band, later playing for Spike Jones and his band, the City Slickers. He became famous in 1947 for parodying the song "All I Want for Christmas Is My Two Front Teeth" and, in 1952, "I Saw Mommy Kissing Santa Claus." Also an international award-winning sharpshooter, he died in 1988 and is buried in Maple Grove Cemetery. (FCGHS.)

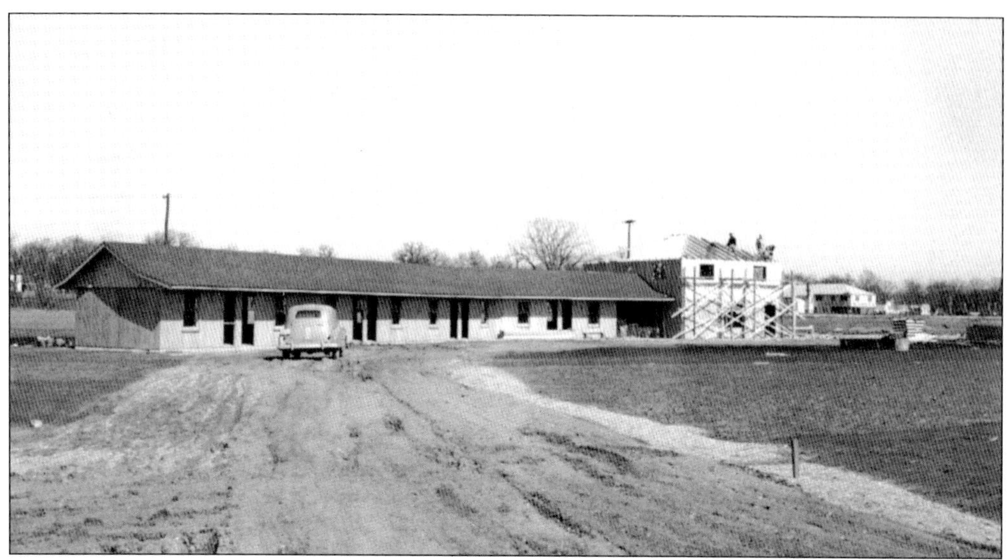

The Elmortel, owned by Ted and Romola Elmore and located near the intersection of Routes 54 and 150, opened for business in May 1951 with eight of 16 units immediately available and the rest finished several months later. In 1955, they sold it to Carl Wright whose son Wilford operated it for several years. The motel was still in business in the 1970s. (FCGHS.)

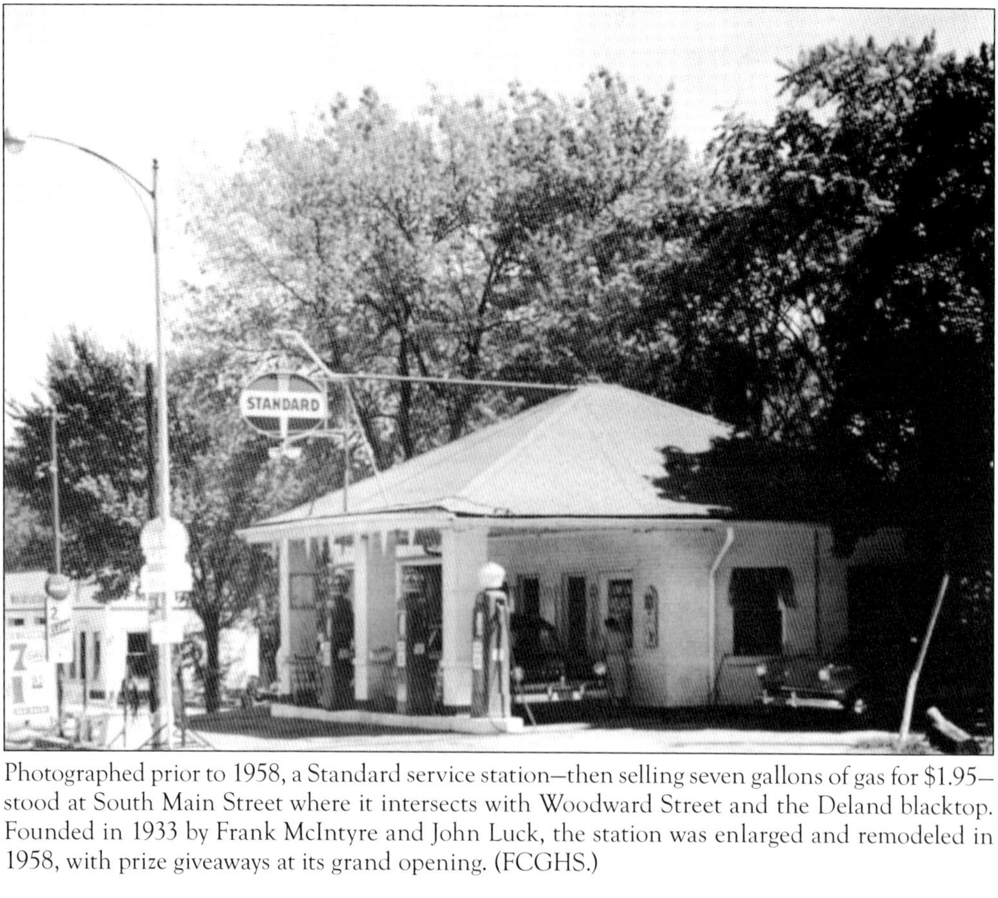

Photographed prior to 1958, a Standard service station—then selling seven gallons of gas for $1.95—stood at South Main Street where it intersects with Woodward Street and the Deland blacktop. Founded in 1933 by Frank McIntyre and John Luck, the station was enlarged and remodeled in 1958, with prize giveaways at its grand opening. (FCGHS.)

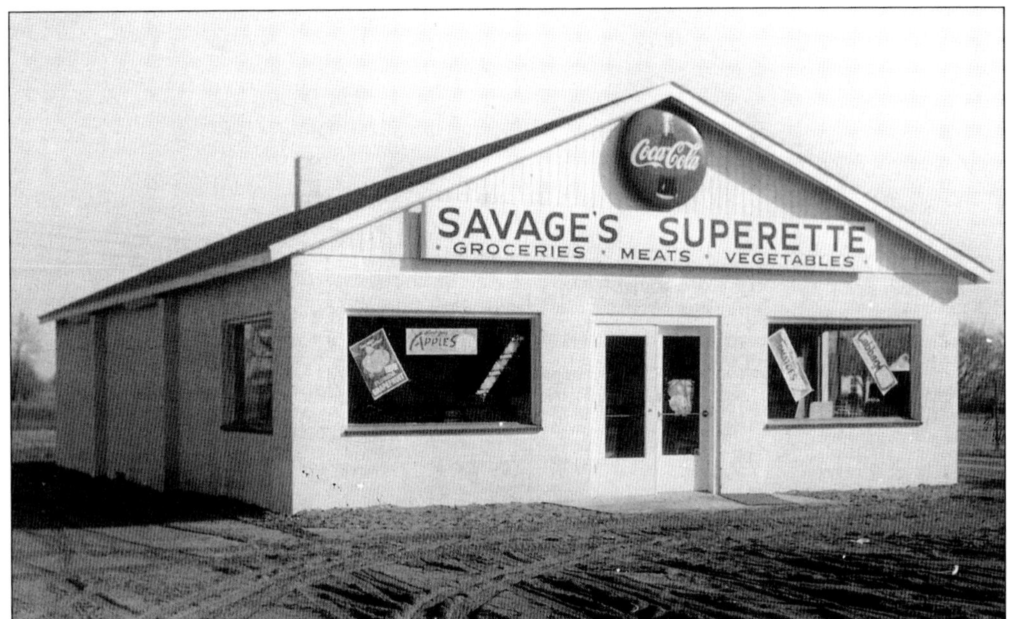

Over 500 well-wishers attended the February 1955 grand opening of Savage's Superette, owned by Ronald and Camille Savage, at the intersection of Route 150 and Richardson Street. The concrete structure was ultramodern with fluorescent lighting and the best in refrigeration. Jerry and Violet Trinkle of Mahomet purchased it in August 1962 with plans to open another supermarket. (FCGHS.)

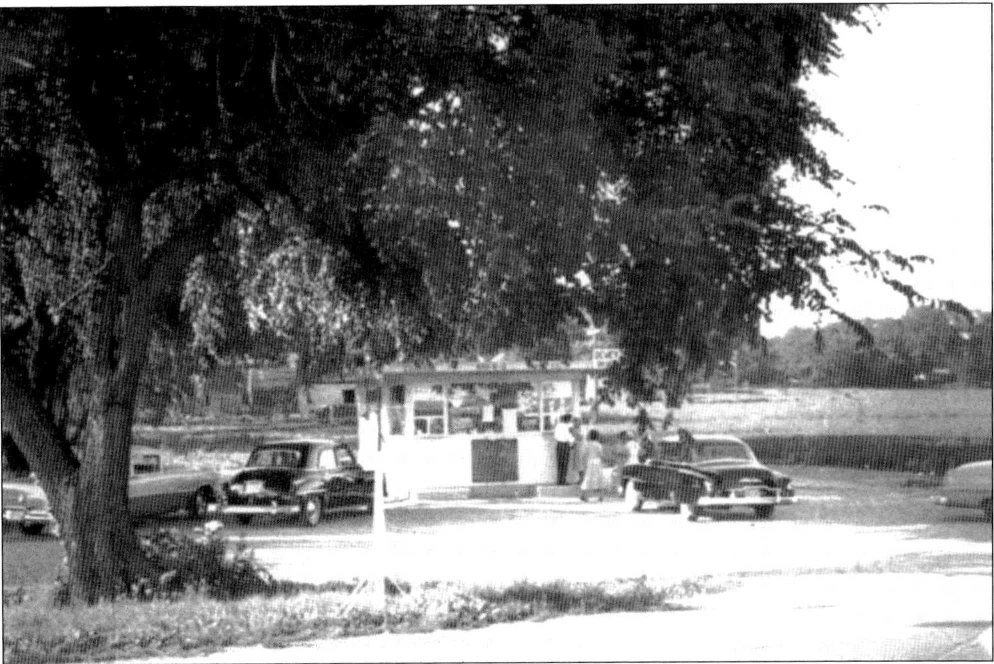
In 1956, Dewey Gronau, a teacher and principal at the Moore High School and Farmer City–Mansfield High School for 21 years, opened Dewey's Drive-In on Route 54 with his wife, Betty. By the 1960s, they would also operate a snack shop at the Farmer City Fair. The drive-in was sold in 2000. (FCGHS.)

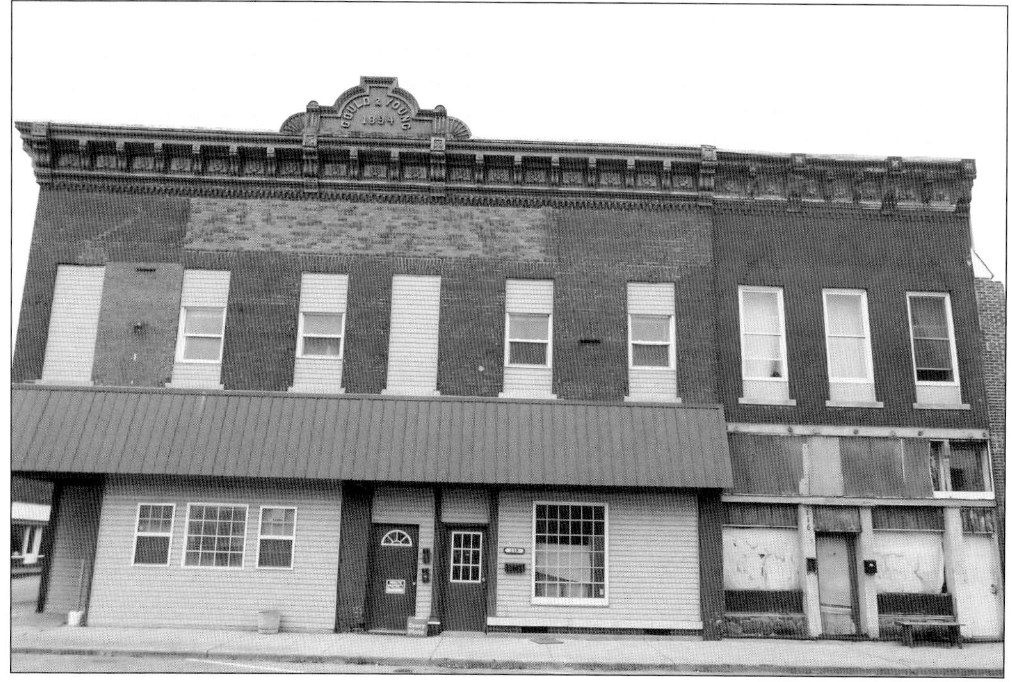

John Gould and Walter S. Young constructed another building at 120 South Main Street after the disastrous 1894 fire destroyed their first one. Around that time, the building's ground floor housed the Fair Store, owned by V.N. Hinkle. The building to the north was erected by John Haffner. At one time, a similar capstone etched with "J. Haffner, 1894" topped his building. (AC.)

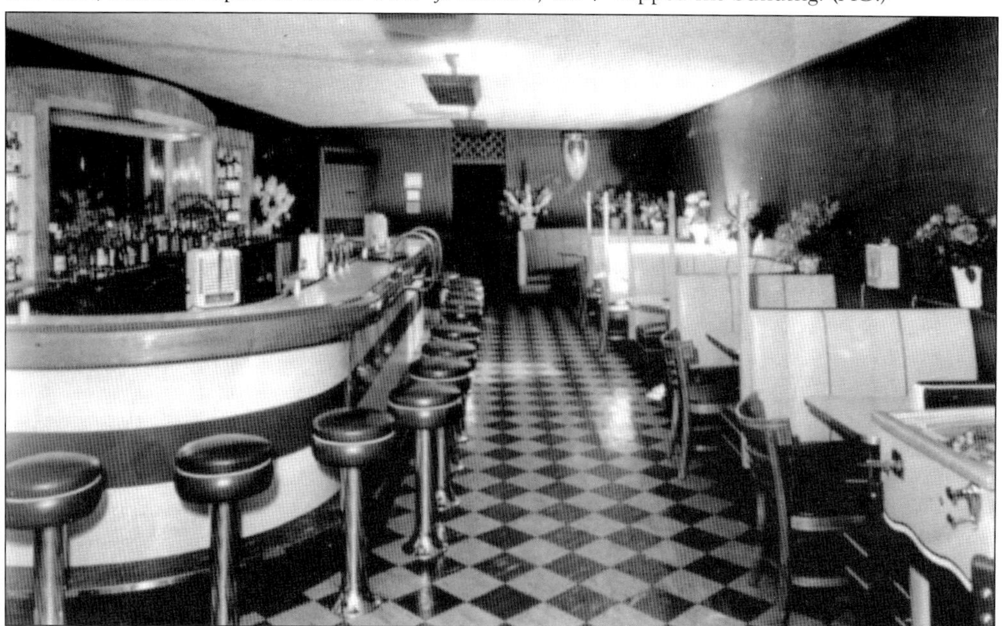

Farmer City's Bob McKinley Jr. and Champaign's James Kane opened their Diamond Horseshoe Tavern at 314 South Main Street, previously occupied by the Blue Room Café, in April 1948. It enticed patrons by advertising that the tavern had air-conditioning. A new owner, Marion Rudisill, ran the bar from 1971 until 1981. (FCGHS.)

Four

From Weldon to Weldon Springs

The Weldon area's first land entry was filed in 1835 by Andrew Pue, but the first actual township resident, Cicero Twist, did not arrive until 1850. The blacksmith was followed around the same time by three brothers named Nixon. Eventually, the township was named in honor of the Nixon family.

By 1872, the town was laid out next to the railroad, platted, and named after the railroad's attorney and Bloomington judge Lawrence Weldon. The men involved in this project were Col. Thomas Snell, James Alexander, James DeLand, and Charles Lisenby.

That same year, Lisenby built the first house, while Snell donated land for the first church. Within seven years, businesses filled the downtown extending to Maple Street. A business district fire in 1879 destroyed almost half of the structures, but new buildings were soon erected.

From the late 1880s through the 1890s, the town offered a bank, an opera house (1898), a light plant (1895), waterworks, and a telephone system (1897). In 1892, the village incorporated, mostly following the ordinances of nearby Clinton. That same year, Weldon's first newspaper began, printed in the back room of the Swigart Bank, later known as the State Bank.

Weldon Springs lies just over the boundary from Nixon Township in Texas Township, west of Weldon and Lane. Some of its topography is due to its owner, Judge Weldon, building a dam with a spillway across a valley, creating an 11-acre lake.

In 1897, fifty people joined together to create the Weldon Springs Association with the purpose of creating a public park. By raising funds through sales of 150 stock shares at $50 per share, they obtained a 50-year lease on 40 acres of land owned by Judge Weldon. In 1936, his son Lincoln Weldon bequeathed the acreage, along with an additional 10 acres, to Clinton to be known as Weldon Springs Park. The State of Illinois bought it in 1948 for a state park.

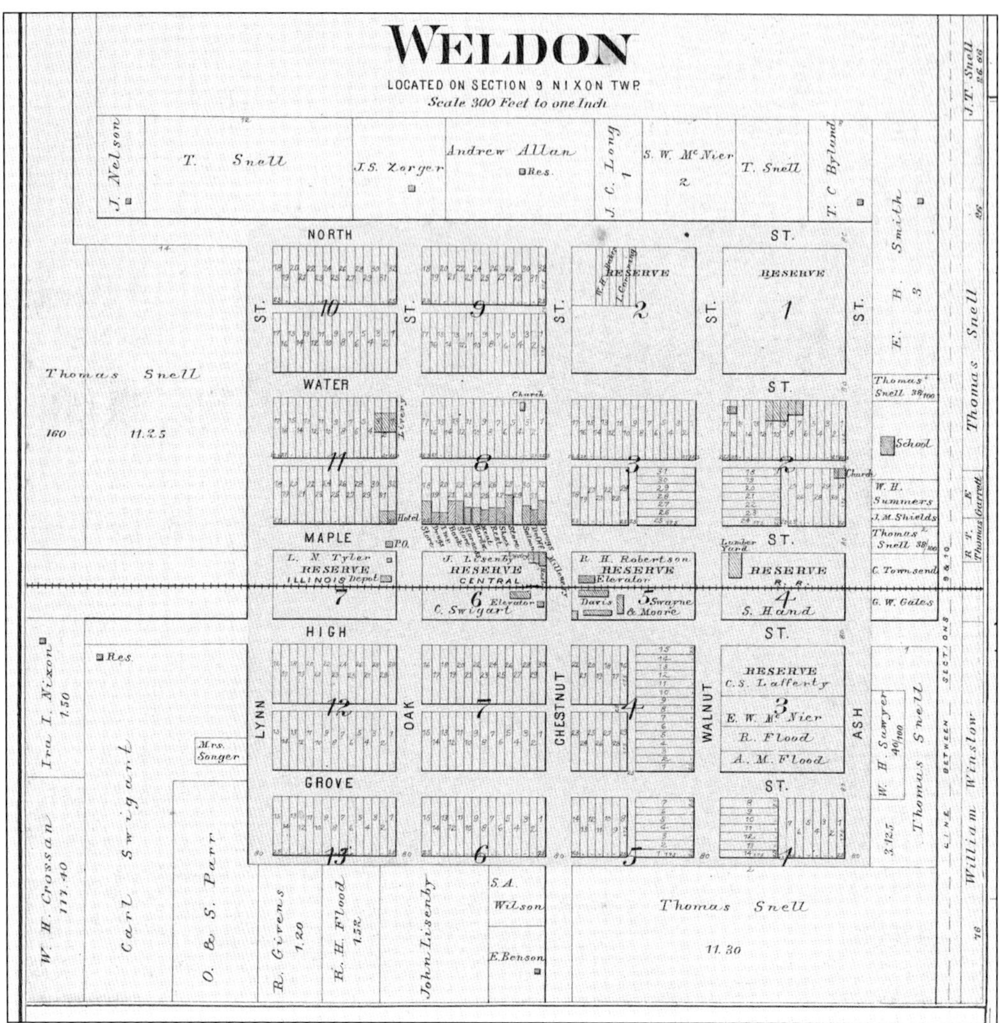

A close-up of the 1894 Weldon plat shows Thomas Snell's name on property throughout Weldon. In 1852, he contracted to build over 400 miles of rail line when the Illinois Central Railroad began construction in the area. During the Civil War, he was a Union colonel. One time, while leading troops through Kentucky, he defied general orders by allowing his men to burn and forage for food. Arrested and jailed, Snell was freed through the help of DeWitt County's Lawrence Weldon and Leonard Swett, a friend to President Lincoln. Later, while businesses were being built along Maple Street, Snell promised to donate a town lot to any religious organization constructing the first church. Baptists, with the most members, assumed they would win, but the Methodists borrowed money to build the proposed church's foundation, thus entitling them to Snell's donation. (LOCGM.)

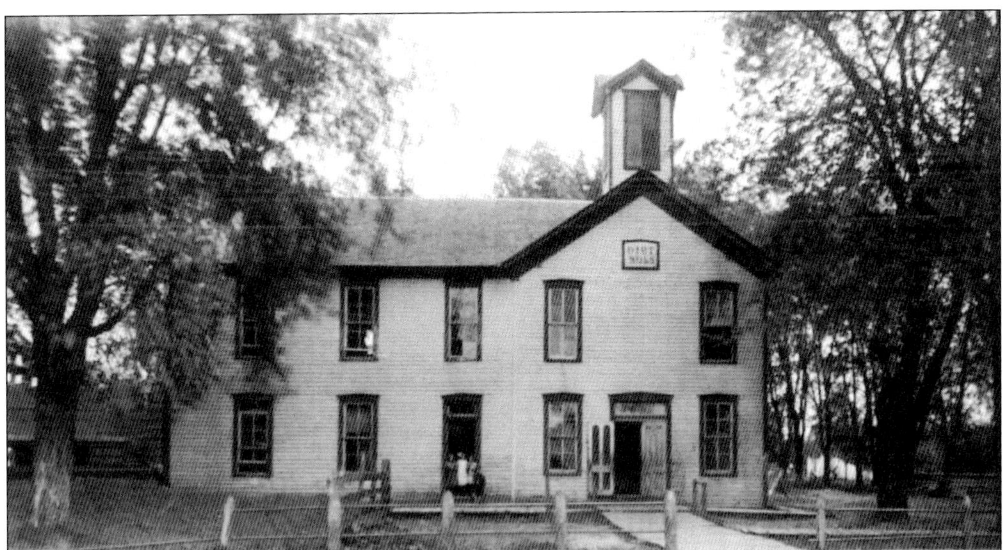

Weldon Grade School, built on the town's east side around 1876, offered elementary classes and a three-year high school. Township high school students were taught on the second floor until 1925. During the 1940s, after many rural schools were consolidated into the Deland-Weldon School District, most school buildings were sold at auction. (WPL.)

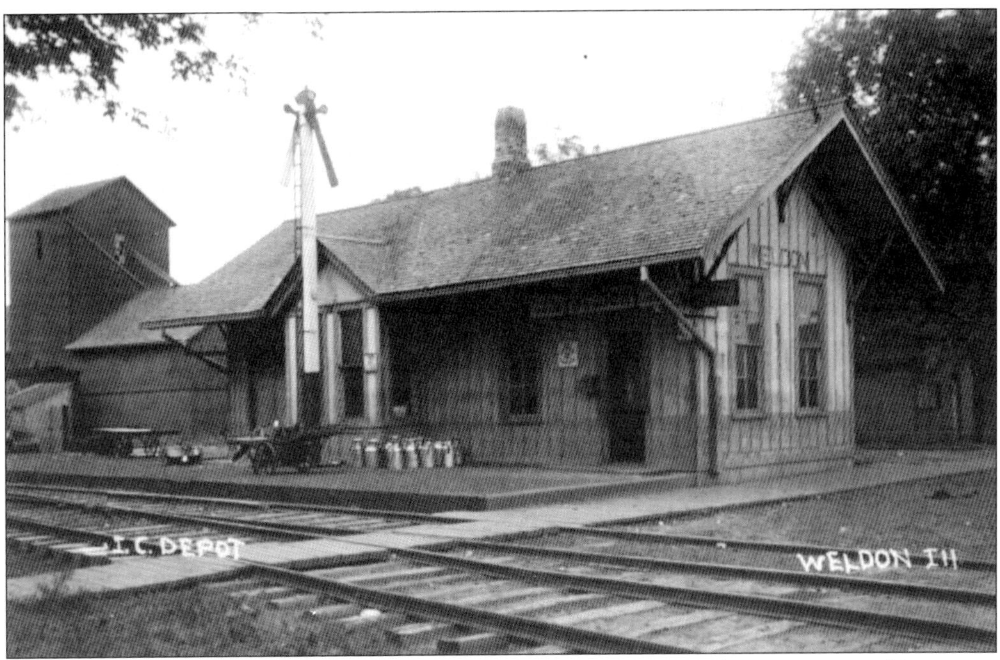

Weldon's train depot was built shortly after the Illinois Central Railroad began running "the Peanut Line," the nickname for the journey from Champaign to Havana. Six days a week, four passenger trains and two freight trains stopped in Weldon. Cargo sometimes included dead bodies being transported for burial. By 1941, only freight trains stopped there. The depot was replaced by the current library. (WPL.)

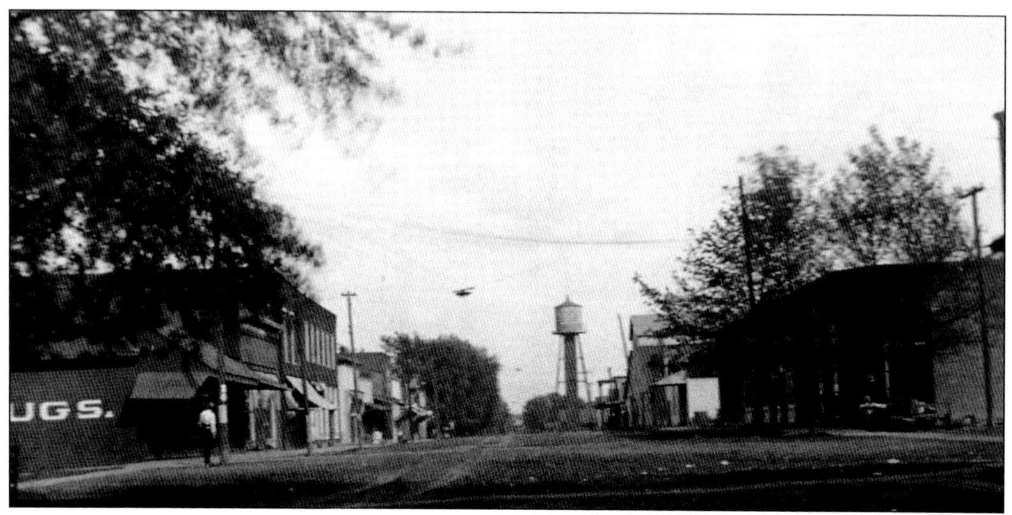

In the late 1800s, Weldon had two hotels, two general stores, a grocer, a confectionary, a millinery shop, a drugstore, two restaurants, two barbershops, a lumber and coal yard, three grain elevators, and two meat markets. The old wooden water tower at the east end of Weldon's Main (now Maple) Street stood since approximately 1895. A new tower was erected around 1925. (WPL.)

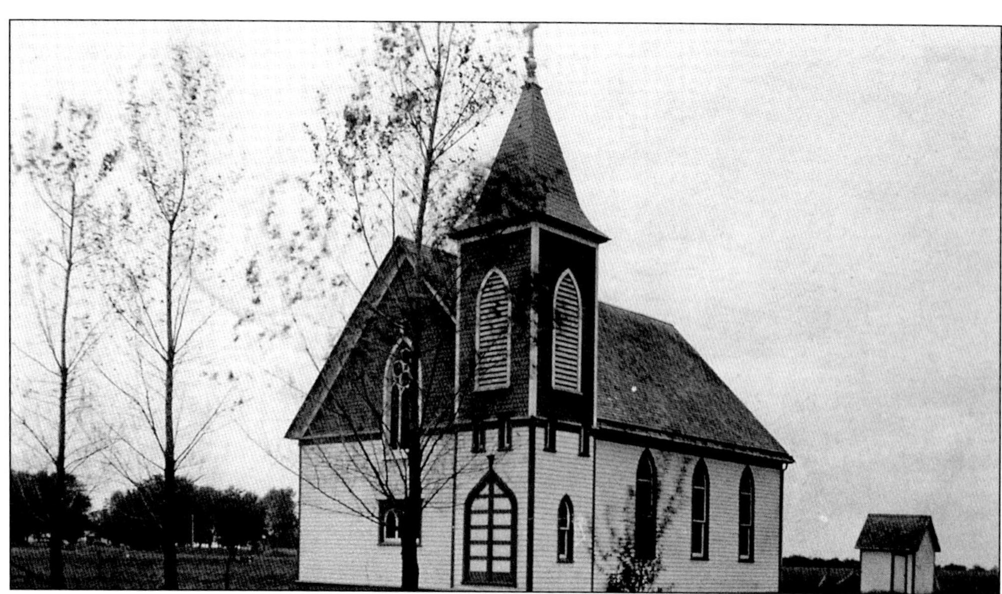

Lacking a Catholic church, many Weldon residents traveled to Wapella for services. Eventually, they worshipped in DeLand's Catholic church and later in residents' homes. Around 1899, residents erected a frame building, St. Michael's Chapel, on Weldon's west side. By 1948, after losing a resident priest, members demolished the church and worshipped elsewhere. (VWPL.)

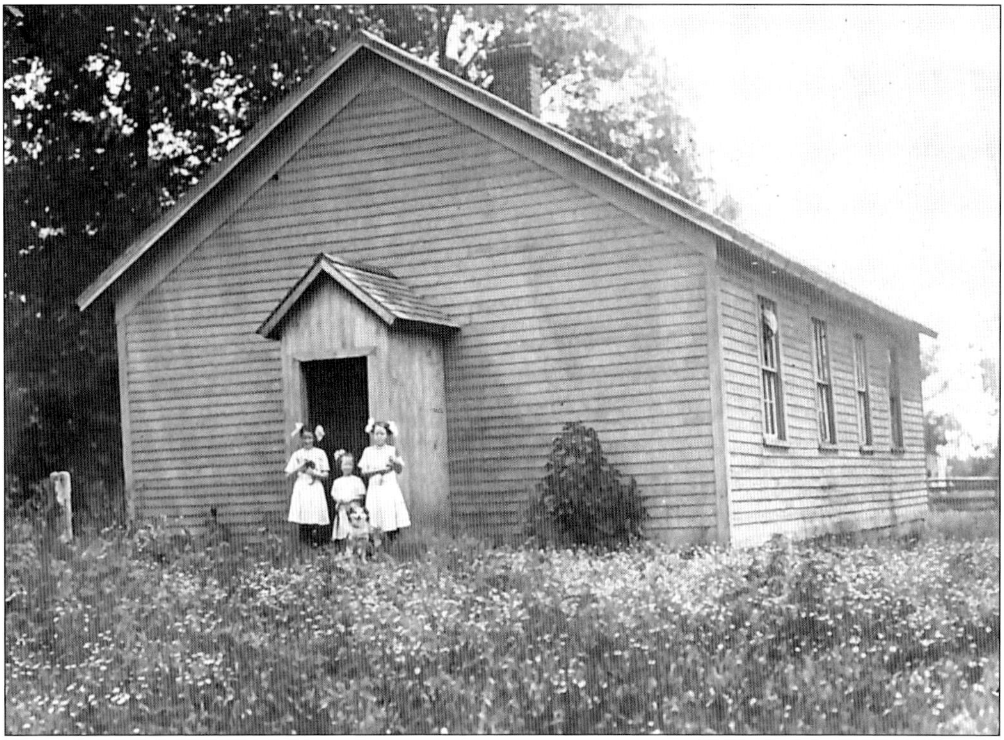

Once part of DeWitt Township and later Harp Township, District 20's Swisher School, northeast of Birkbeck, lay near Salt Creek. The original frame structure (photographed around 1900) was replaced in 1915. With major consolidation of rural schools, the district joined with Farmer City in 1947 and sold the school. It was relocated for use as a garage. (VWPL.)

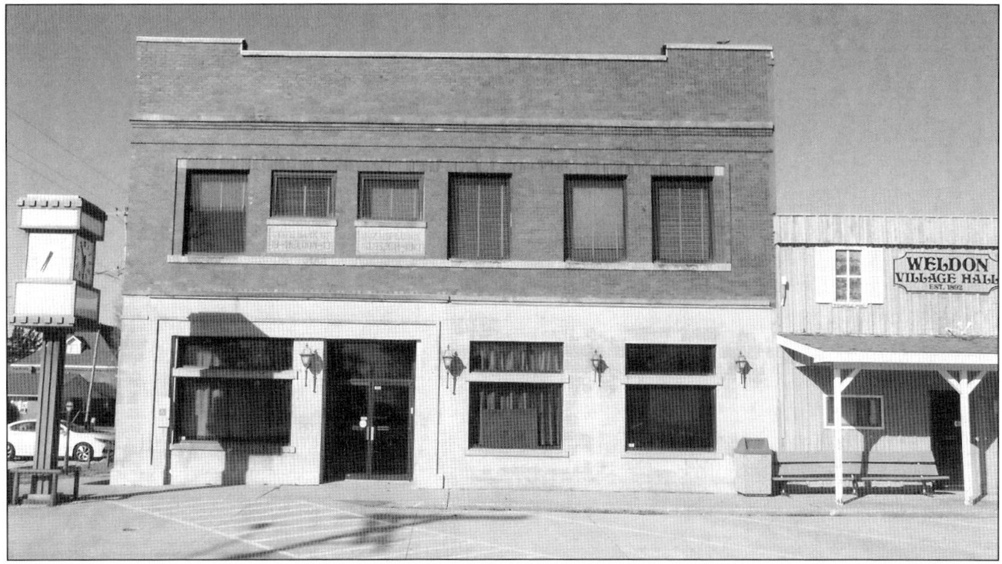

Jacob Swigart's private bank, built around 1887, became the State Bank of Weldon by 1906. After a 1913 fire destroyed the block, the bank rebuilt then closed in 1931. In 1945, the Weldon State Bank opened there, merging over the years with other banks until closure in mid-2021. The right capstone references its connection with Mozart Lodge 96 and the Knights of Pythias. (AC.)

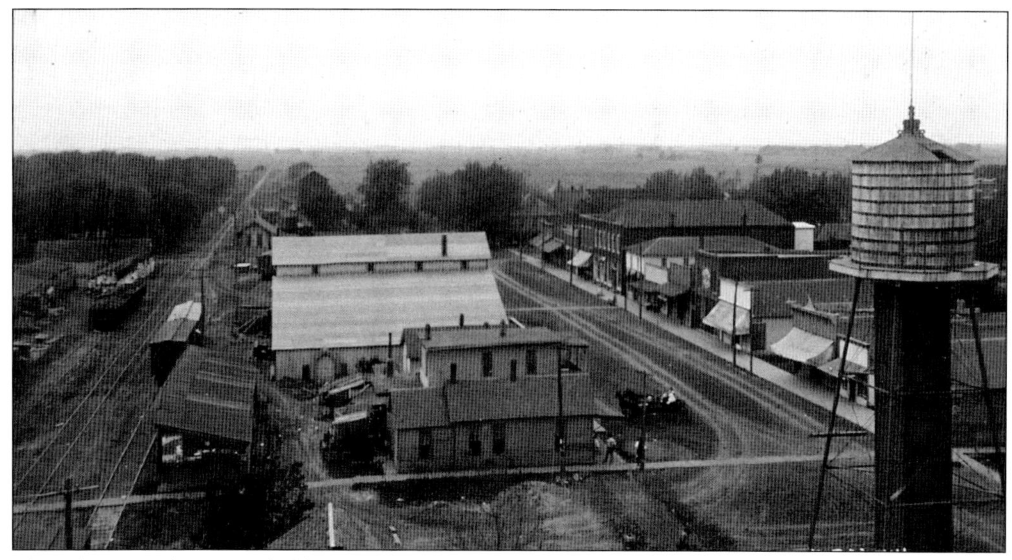

This photograph was probably taken before the August 1913 fire that destroyed businesses on the north side of the main business street. An advertisement for paint hangs on the east side of the shed near the lower left corner. Opposite the men, wagon, and horses, an awning displays "Clothing." Weldon Depot appears in the left background near the third telephone/telegraph pole. (KA.)

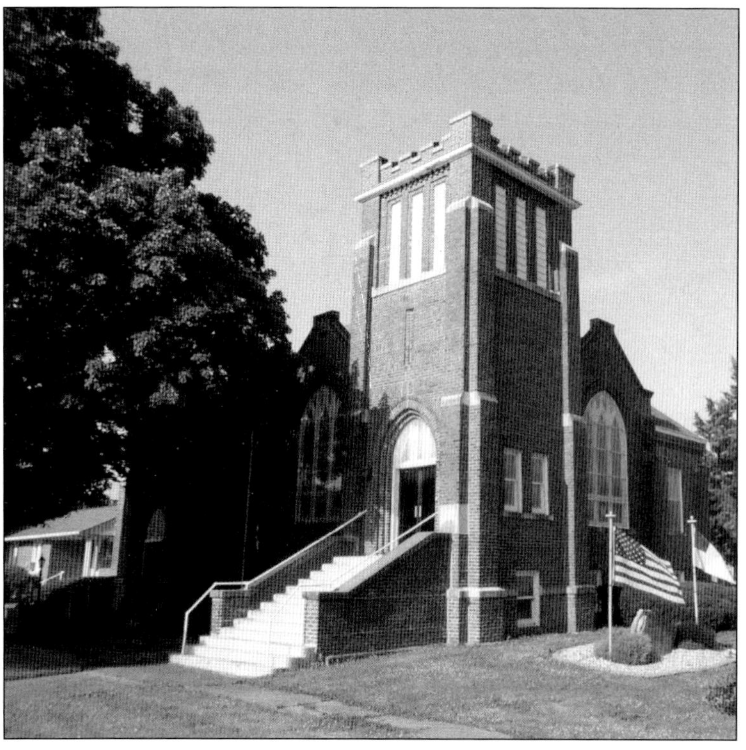

Weldon's Methodist Episcopal church was dedicated in 1874 on land donated by Thomas Snell. Another Methodist church, organized by Methodist Protestants, was built in 1882 in northwest Weldon. A new, Gothic-style Methodist Protestant church (seen here) was erected and dedicated in 1909. By 1938, the two churches federated. The organization became the Weldon United Methodist Church in 1968. (AC.)

An August 1913 fire swept the north side of Weldon's business street, destroying Lodge 922 of the Independent Order of Odd Fellows. In 1919, members erected a new building, later selling a half interest in it to Weldon's Masonic Lodge 746. Clifford Moore's hardware store occupied the site after 1958. Long empty, it was demolished in June 2025. (AC.)

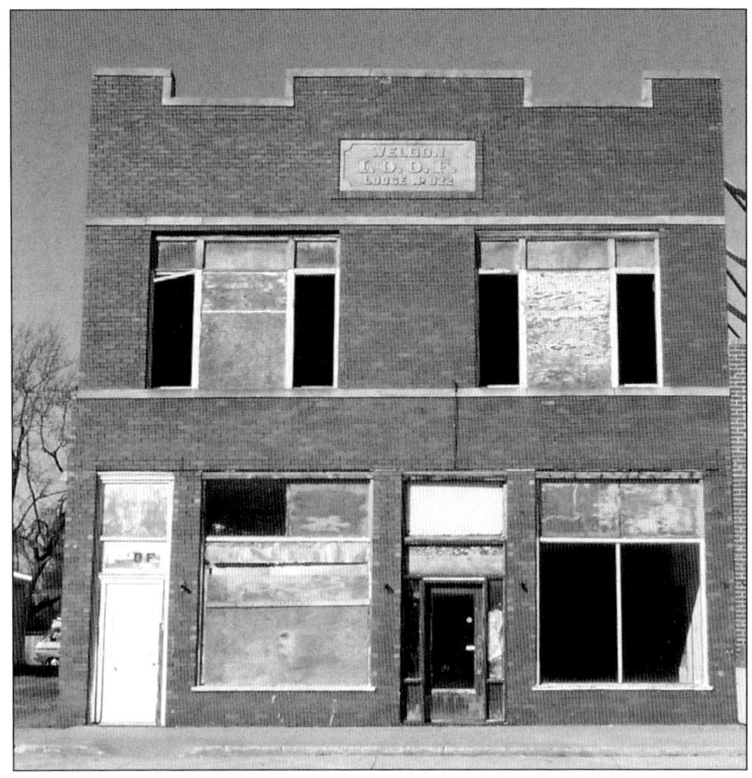

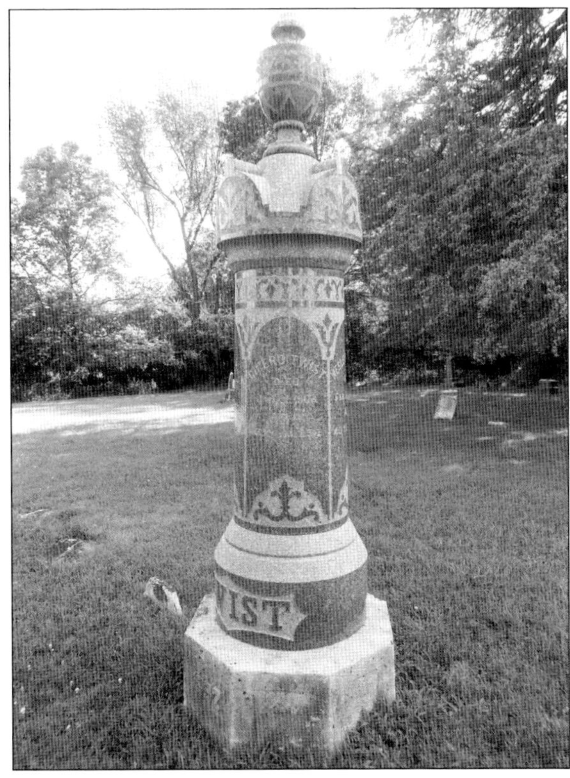

Nixon Township's first settler, Cicero Twist (1819–1903), arrived in the area in 1850. After constructing a log house for his wife and children, he provided classes to nearby children. In 1856, he donated land north of his home for a new school. Twist, his first wife, and three of their children are buried in Lisenby Cemetery in Lane, Illinois. (AC.)

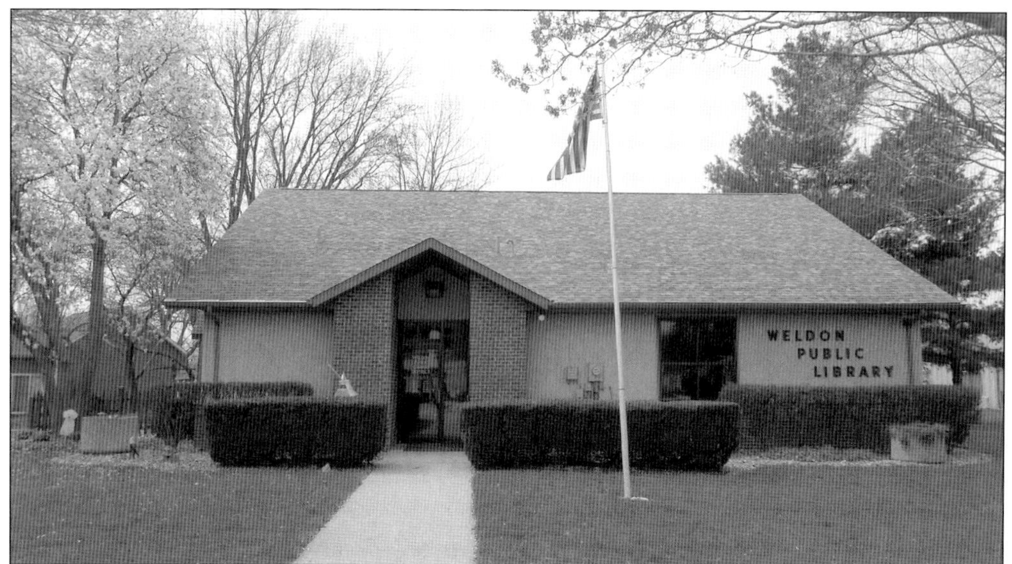

In 1922, Weldon's Women's Club organized books for borrowing (on Saturdays) and placed them on a shelf in Grammer's Grocery. The library's next home was the location of the current post office, then in a building across from the Methodist church. It moved to 495 West Maple Street in 1968. The Lions Club helped a new library open in October 1994 on the site of the former Weldon Depot. (AC.)

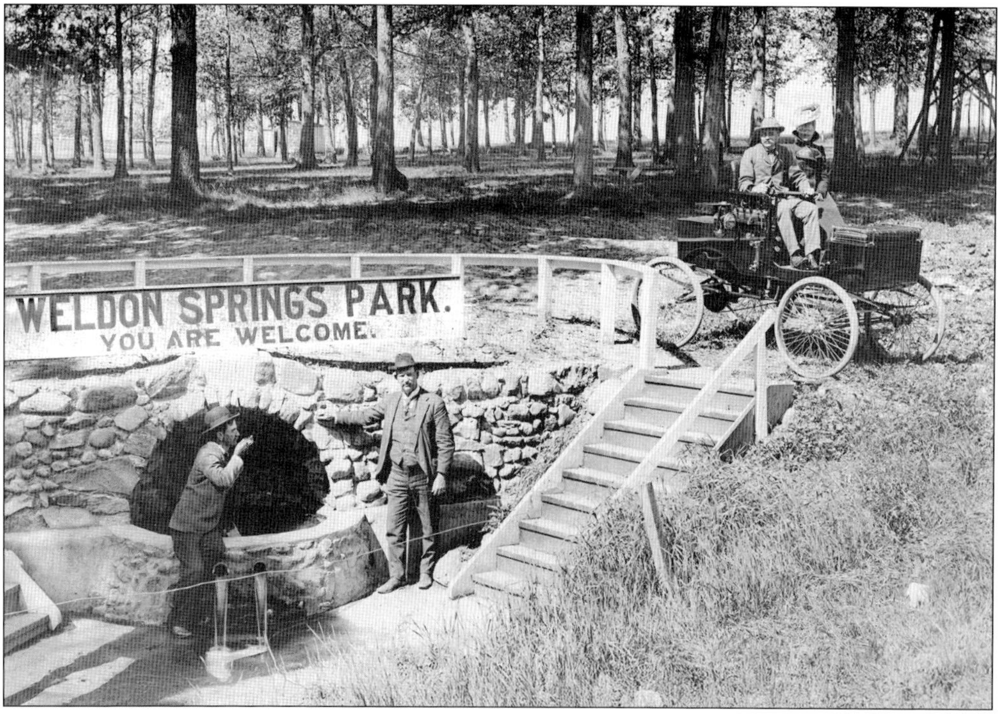

A thick deposit of sand and gravel was left by a glacier covering the Clinton region thousands of years ago. The water emerging at Weldon Springs is the result of rain and snow having drained into the ground over time. Photographed in June 1902, men drink the water while a lady and gentleman observe from their horseless carriage. The area grew from 40 acres to a 550-acre park. (DCM.)

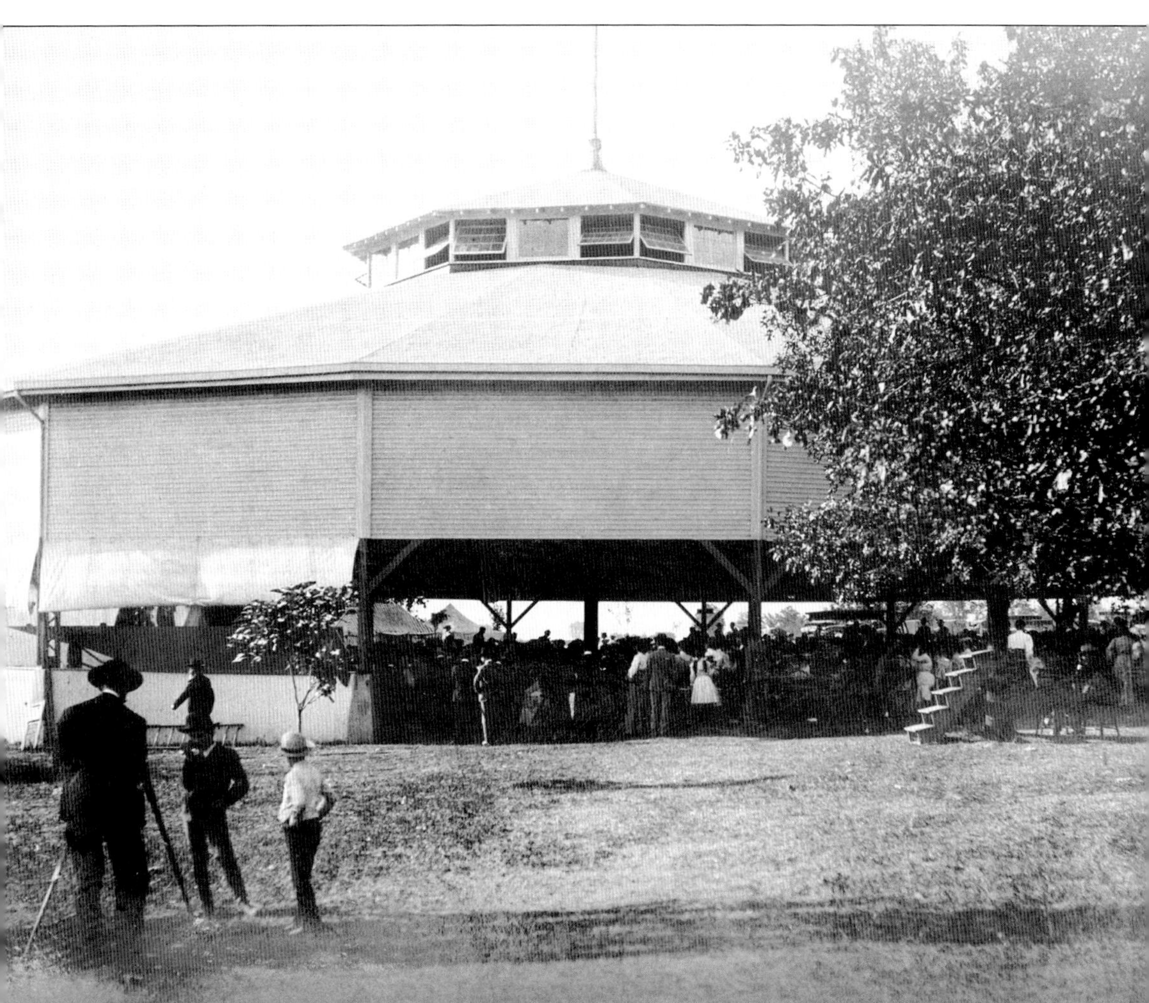

Organized in 1900 and incorporated in 1904, the Weldon Springs Chautauqua Assembly was modeled after Chautauqua, New York, events that provided entertainment, speakers, and classes. From 1901 through 1920, Weldon Springs Chautauquas ran for 10 days every summer. Season tickets cost $1.50. In 1904, the organization determined that an auditorium (seen here) was needed. To reach the $3,000 construction price, it sold $50 subscriptions. By August, the steel building with a diameter of 120 feet was almost complete and could squeeze in about 4,500 people. The next year, the seats were painted sky blue, and in 1906, electricity was installed. As movies and radio offered people more entertainment, Chautauquas grew less appealing. The last Chautauqua was held in the early 1920s, but Weldon Springs continued hosting large church events, including an evangelical speaker in 1945, which brought 2,000 attendees. (DCM.)

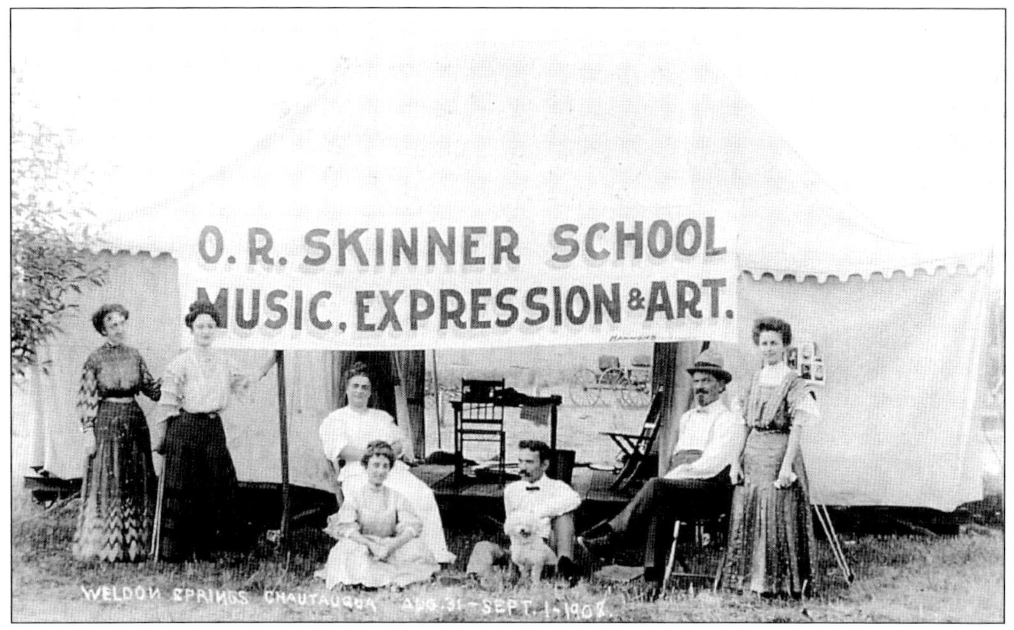

Photographed in 1908, Bloomington's Oliver Ross Skinner School of Music, Expression, and Art presented various cultural programs at Weldon Springs Chautauquas from 1907 until its closure. The 10-week classes included piano, voice, violin, theory, and musical history. Additional classes in art, public speaking, and painting were also among those taught. (AC.)

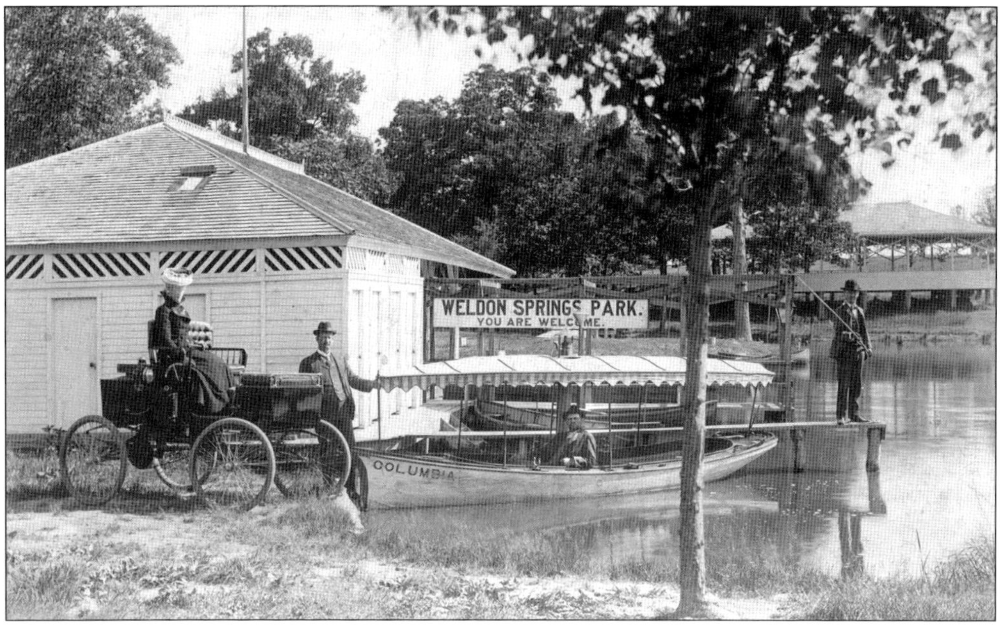

Chautauqua visitors enjoyed Weldon Springs Lake's steam launch, *Columbia*, photographed in 1902. Over the years, political speakers included William Jennings Bryan (four visits); former president William Howard Taft and his vice president, James S. Sherman; Wisconsin senator Robert LaFollette; and six governors. Others included evangelist Billy Sunday, the temperance proponent Carrie Nation, author and activist Helen Keller, and Socialist presidential candidate Eugene V. Debs. (DCM.)

Five

Waynesville and Wapella

In 1826, settlers Prettyman Marvel Jr. (1801–1842) and his wife, Rebecca, established a residence just south of the area known as Big Grove, the first permanent settlement in DeWitt County and six years ahead of Waynesville's founding. The Marvels' daughter Nancy was the first white child born in the county. By 1829, Jeremiah Greenman and his nephew Thomas Dunham had opened the first store there, while Zion and Edom Shugart established a gristmill on Kickapoo Creek. The region was also home to an encampment of Kickapoo Native Americans until they were removed during the 1832 Black Hawk War. That same year, George Isham organized a town called Waynesville near Greenman's and Dunham's store.

When a cholera epidemic swept through the area in 1855, some of the dead were left to be buried along rail fences. By 1872, the town supported three dry goods stores, two grocery stores, and one drugstore (with a doctor's office inside). Ten years later, the town had around 360 inhabitants, almost as many as in 2025.

Settlers arrived in the Wapella area by the late 1820s. In 1854, David Neal, surveyor and vice president of the Illinois Central Railroad, laid out the town, naming it Wapellah after Chief Wapello of the Meskwaki people, who controlled Wisconsin's Fox River area. Approximately 500 people lived in the small town by 1860. Six years later, Wapella was incorporated. In 1925, a newspaper article noted, "Wapella of sixty years ago was a live wire place. The Illinois Central shops and round house were there then, and saloons ran wide open."

The 2020 census showed a similar population but fewer locations for "running wide open." Throughout the years, Wapella was home to at least five churches: the Christian church; Long Point Church; Wapella's Presbyterian church, which was abandoned in 1876; St. Patrick's Catholic Church; and the United Methodist church.

A tornado in 1927 caused destruction in Wapella and the outskirts, but the 1968 tornado caused worse damage. Nearly all homes, businesses, and churches were hit, and some never recovered.

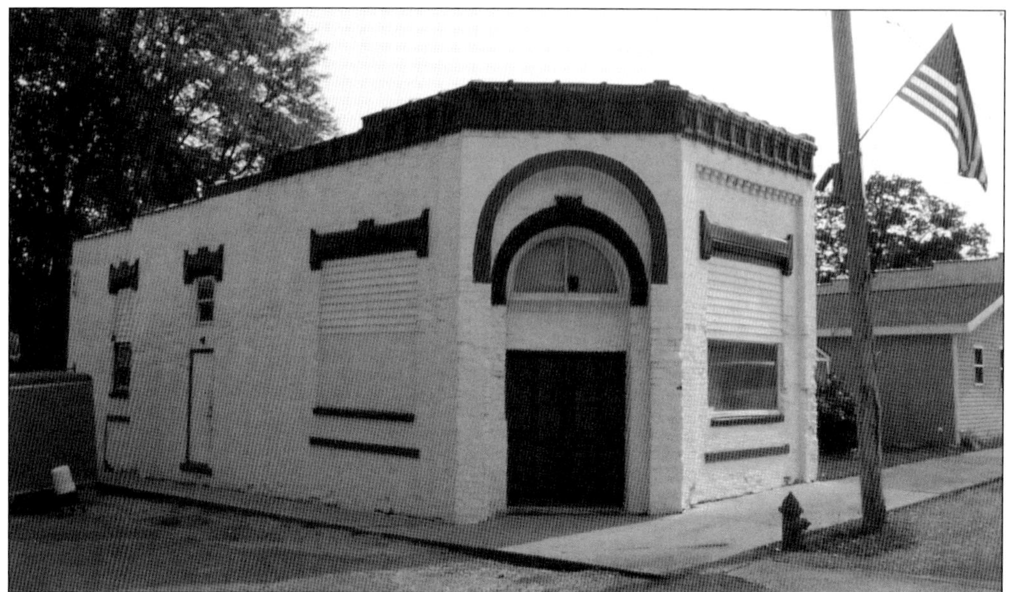

Founded in 1891, the Waynesville State Bank was located at the northeast corner of Isham and Second Streets. After the Great Depression forced the bank's closure in the 1930s, a creamery owner purchased the structure in 1935. In 1966, the Furman-Arnfelt Insurance Agency bought it. It was remodeled after sustaining damage from the May 1968 tornado. (AC.)

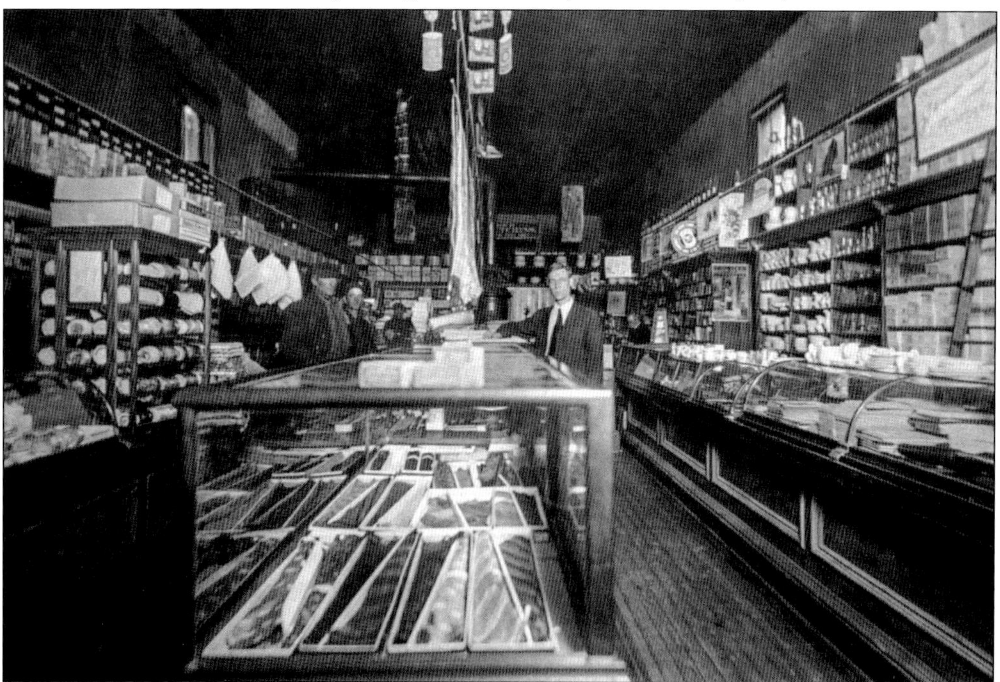

Jeremiah P. Dunham (1814–1897) and his brothers William and Thomas opened a general store in Waynesville in 1851 under the name of J.P. Dunham & Company. After the two brothers left the firm, Jeremiah Dunham's son William became partner. The company's new brick building was constructed at Second and Maltby Streets in 1887, closing around 1915. It became a gas station and repair shop in 1926. (DCM.)

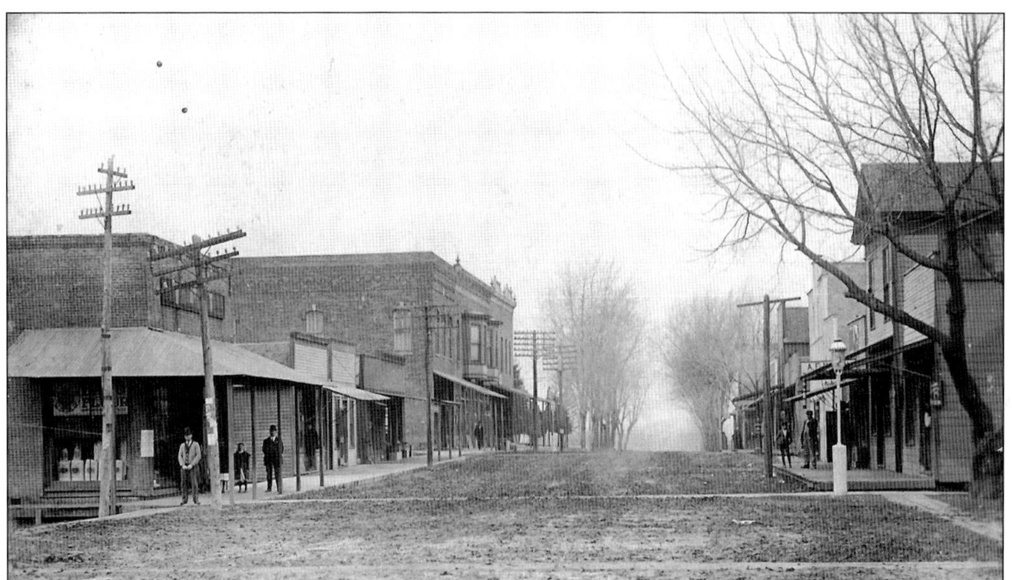

Waynesville's business district appears in this undated photograph. The word "Flour" appears on a sign in the leftmost store window. Businesses included several brick or tile businesses, a carriage and wagon factory, general merchandise stores, a meat market, Harrison's barbershop, boot and shoe repair shops, drugstores, a harness and saddle store, a milliner, physicians, masons, painters, and more. (KA.)

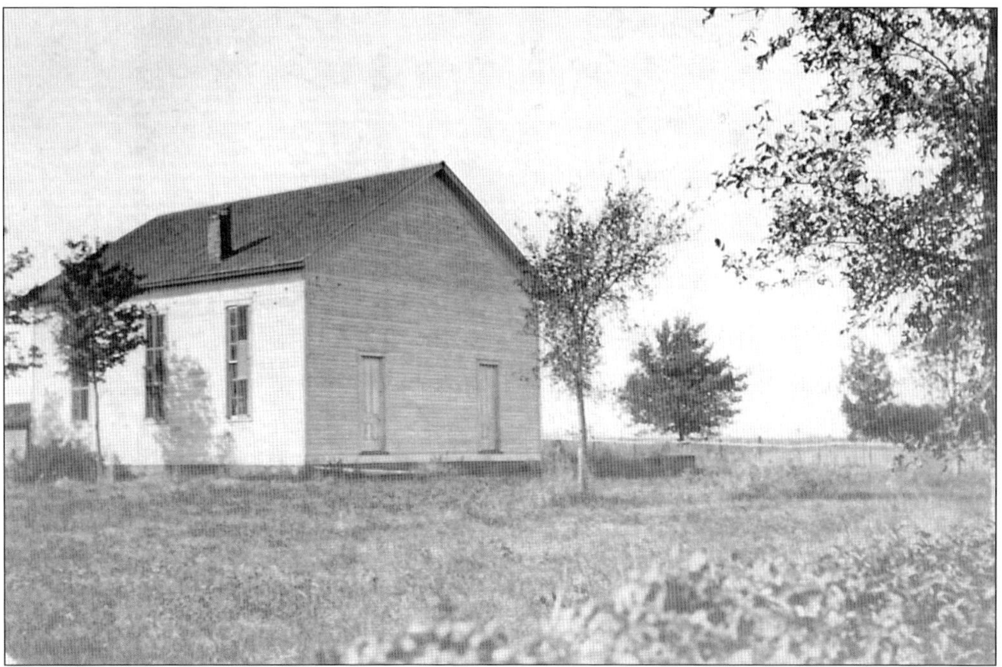

After Elm Grove Presbyterian Church was organized in 1872 in Barnett Township, about 40 members of Waynesville's Presbyterian church (central Illinois's first Presbyterian church, founded in 1836) transferred to Elm Grove. At one time, Elm Grove Church's membership reached about 65, with Waynesville ministers serving both communities. Between 1913 and 1919, the Waynesville church was disbanded and razed. (WTL.)

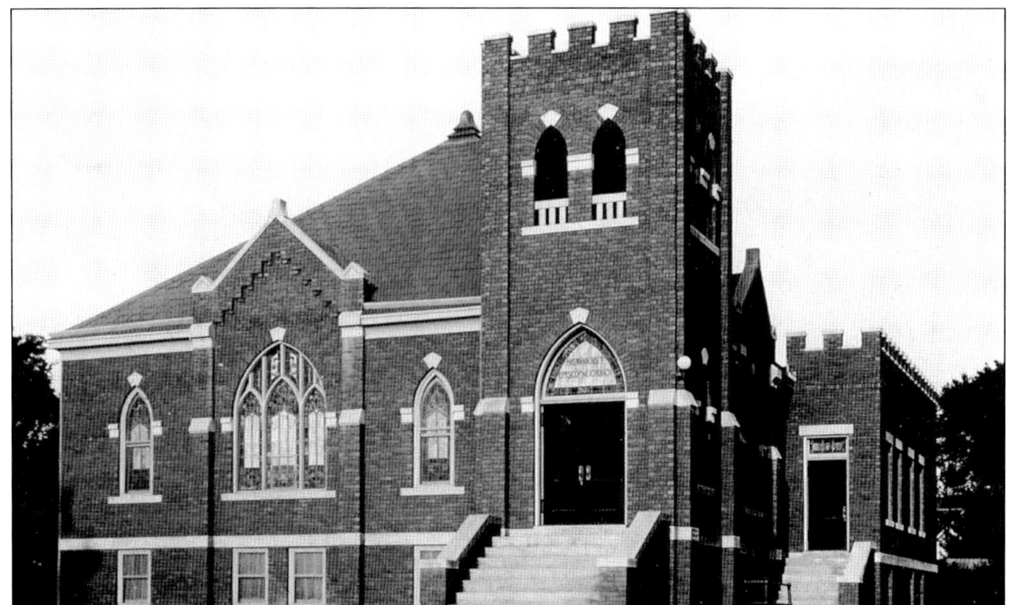

Waynesville's first settlers, Prettyman Marvel and his wife, Rebecca, organized Methodist services in 1826 in their 12-foot-by-16-foot cabin one-half mile southwest of town. By 1839, a frame church was built, replaced in 1849 by a two-story brick structure, then replaced again in 1886 by a frame church. In 1916, after its demolition, the present brick Methodist church was constructed. Members celebrated their 100th anniversary in 1926. (AC.)

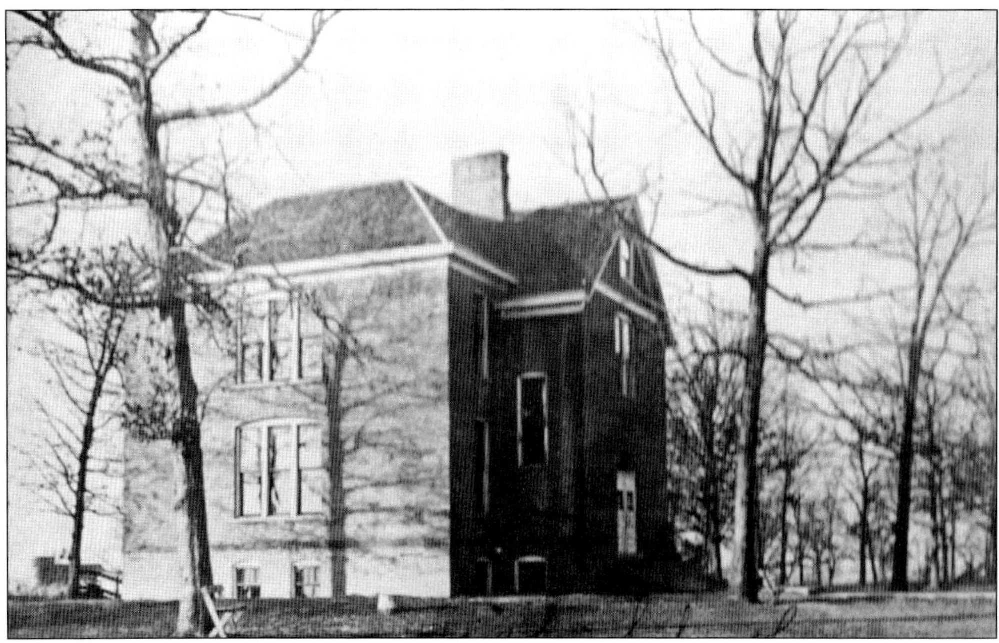

From 1891 to 1892, Waynesville Academy taught students at the opera house before a school was completed at the edge of town. After it closed in 1911, the township leased the building for use as the Waynesville Township High School, Illinois's first township high school. It merged in 1955 with McLean County and housed McLean High School until joining six towns in 1972 as Olympia High School. (AC.)

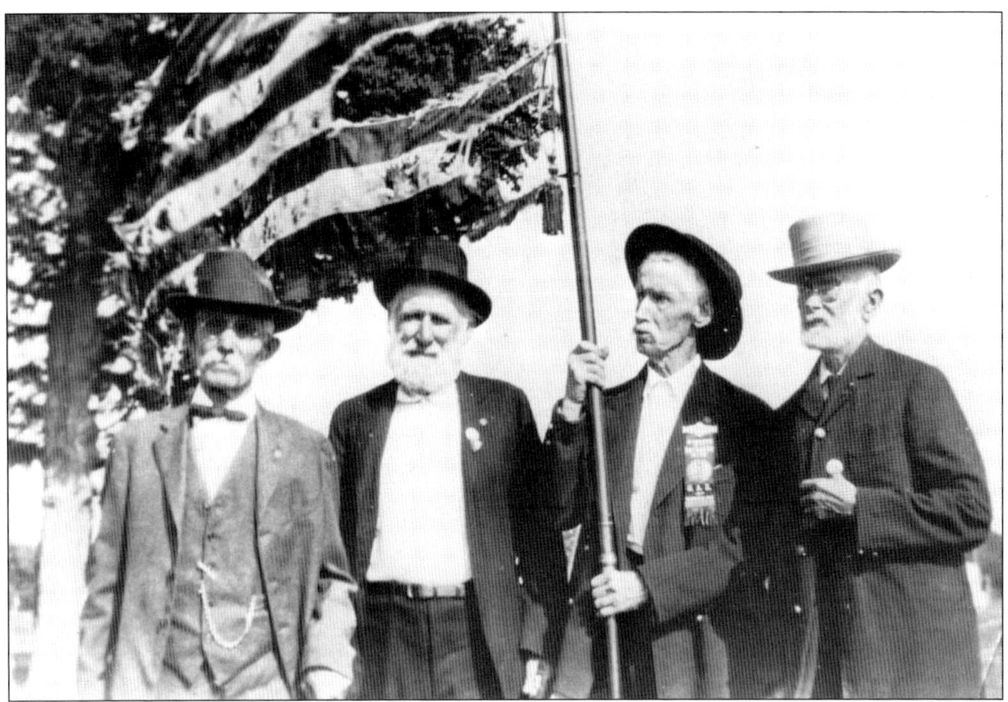

Of the 56 original members of the Waynesville Grand Army of the Republic Frank Sampson Post 298, four of the five surviving Civil War veterans carried their tattered flag and honored fallen comrades on Memorial Day in 1926. The local men included, from left to right, Mervin A. Kephart (1846–1928), Daniel Ellington (1843–1929), Edward Keith Ginnings (1846–1934), and William Mortimer Sampson (1844–1933). (WTL.)

Waynesville's train depot was built shortly after the Illinois Midland Railroad came through in 1874. The line later changed to the Terre Haute & Indianapolis Railroad, then the Vandalia Line, then the Pennsylvania Railroad Company. As vehicles became more plentiful in the 1930s, passenger train usage diminished. In 1963, the depot was razed, and all railroad business was moved to a nearby residence. (WTL.)

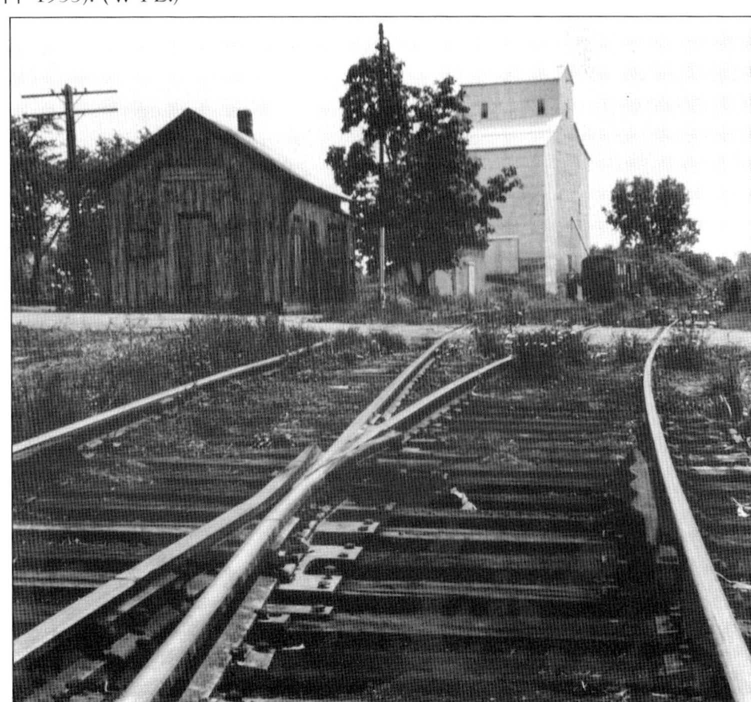

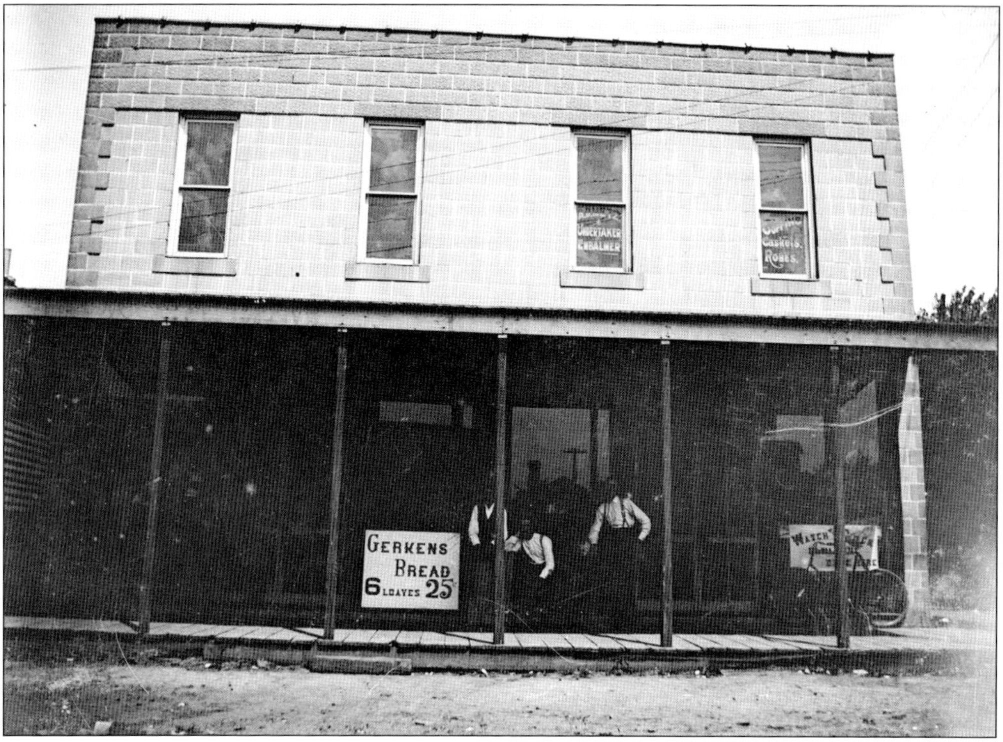

By 1875, Albert Metz's Wapella store was selling schoolbooks, groceries (including oysters), cigars, dishware, and hardware. Later, he added made-to-order walnut coffins. In this photograph, he advertises Gerkens Bread on the ground floor (six loaves for 25¢). His second-story windows mention his work as an undertaker and embalmer as well as advertising caskets. (KD.)

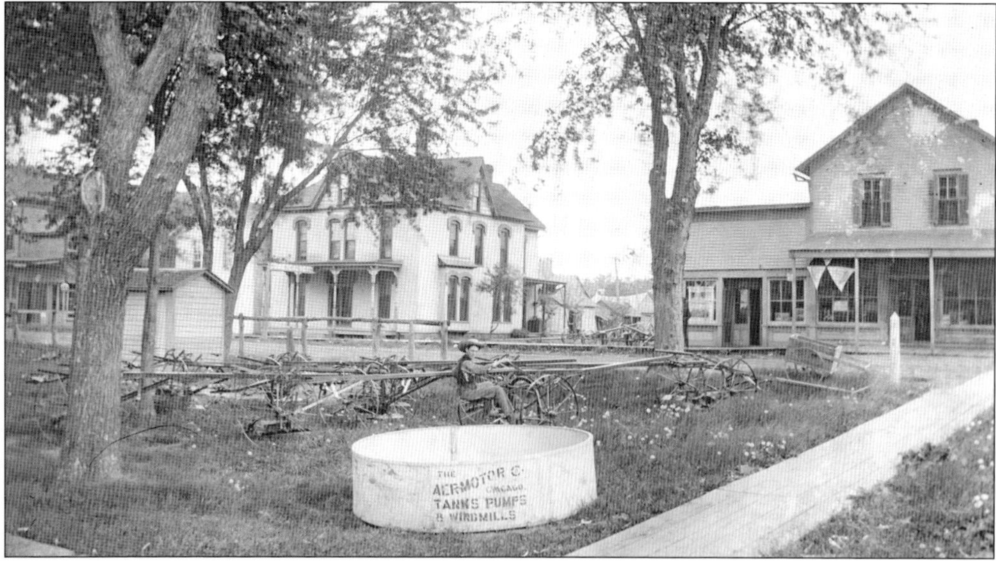

The Corner Café, with a two-room living quarters in the back and five rooms upstairs, appears in the far right background. A young boy sits in the park across the road. Note the wooden sidewalks. By 1953, the café's owner, Lawrence Harmon, also sold bus tickets for a local bus service and handled cleaning for Clinton's Raker Cleaners. The café was open from 6:00 a.m. until midnight. (KD.)

From 1853, various area priests ministered to members of Wapella's St. Patrick Catholic Parish. The first church was constructed in 1857, but the present structure replaced it after it burned in 1882. It was rededicated in 1909 after the steeple tower was added and other changes made. As with many town structures, the church was hit by the May 1968 tornado. (KD.)

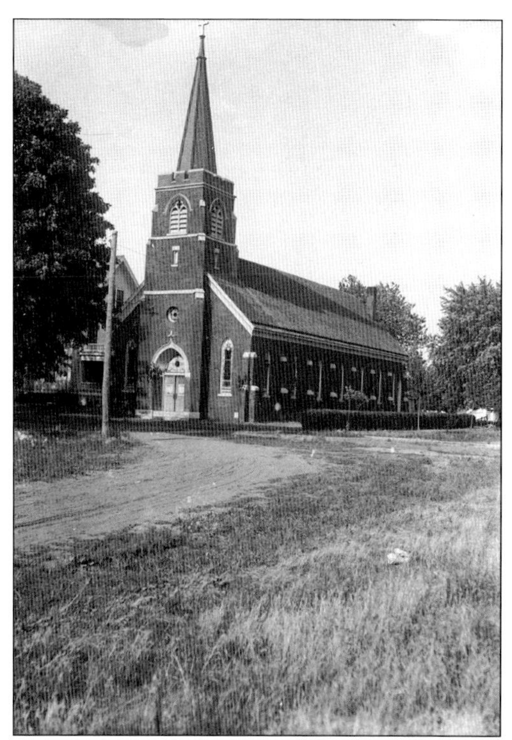

Wapella's train depot appears in this undated photograph. In the 1850s, railroad management considered making the newly platted town a central location between its northern and southern terminals. Thinking that would bring the county seat to Wapella, a hotel was built to hold rail employees and travelers, and a machine shop and roundhouse were built. However, Clinton ended up being the county seat. (KD.)

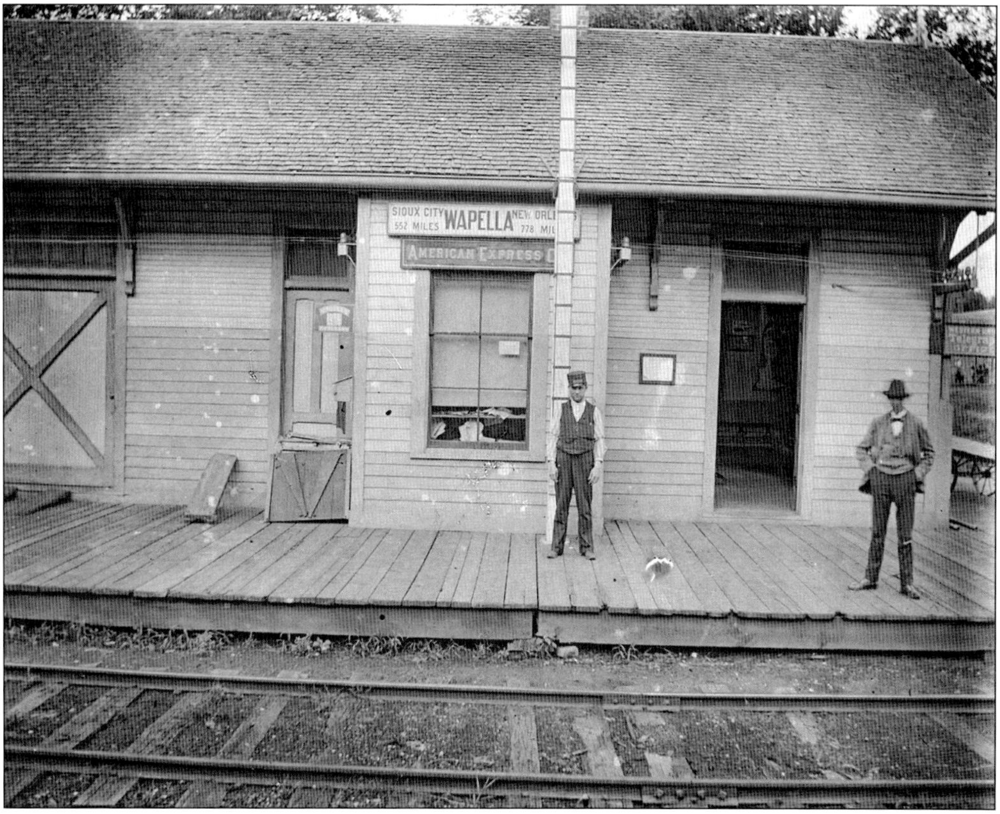

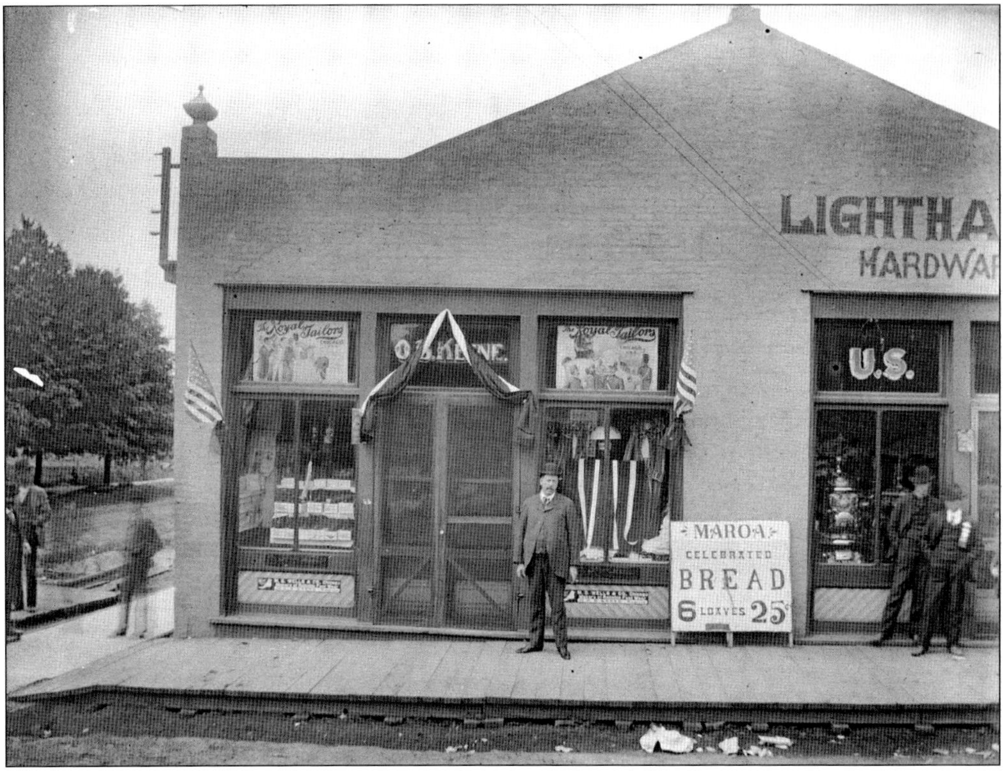

In 1877, John Lighthall operated a barbershop in which he also stocked cigars and offered ice cream. By 1900, he included lunch and snacks. This photograph was taken after Pres. William McKinley's 1901 assassination. The building at the southwest corner of Locust and Main Streets was at one time Lighthall Hardware and eventually Summers Hardware. The name of O.B. Keene (merchant and possible tailor) appears above the left doorway. (KD.)

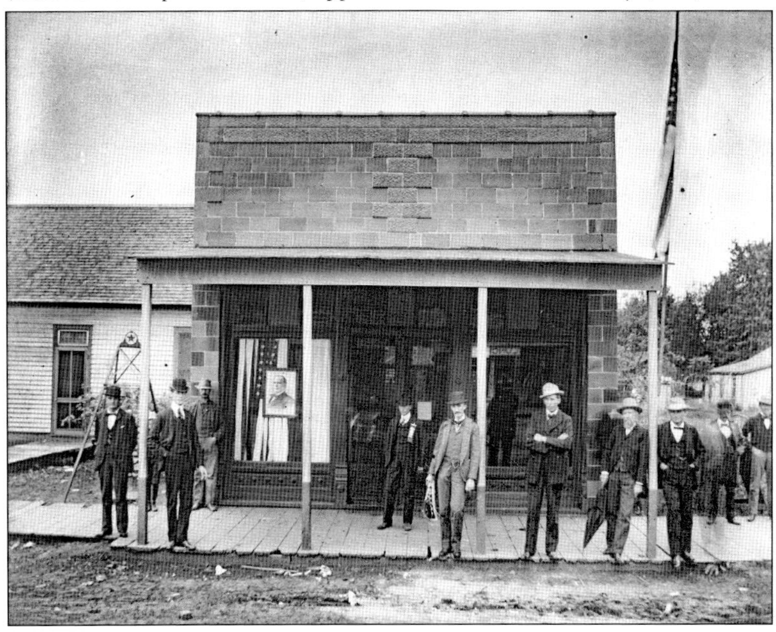

In 1901, men pose outside a store on Wapella's Main Street. Flag bunting drapes behind a photograph of Pres. William McKinley, assassinated in September, soon after the start of his second term. In 1897, this location functioned as the post office and an auction house, both run by John Rolofson. (KD.)

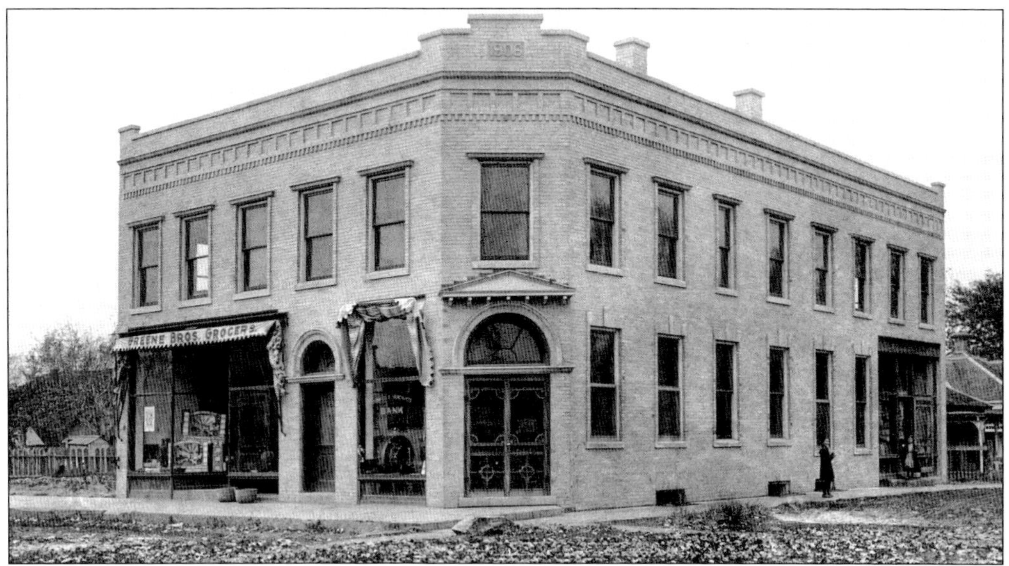

Wapella's Farmers & Merchants Bank, currently occupied by Willow Branch Heirlooms, was constructed at 302 Main Street in 1906 with W.R. Carle as president. Greene Brothers Grocers occupied the building's west side plus 20 feet at the back. The second floor was home to several offices, along with the Seward Nelson Grand Army of the Republic Post 251, organized in 1883. (KD.)

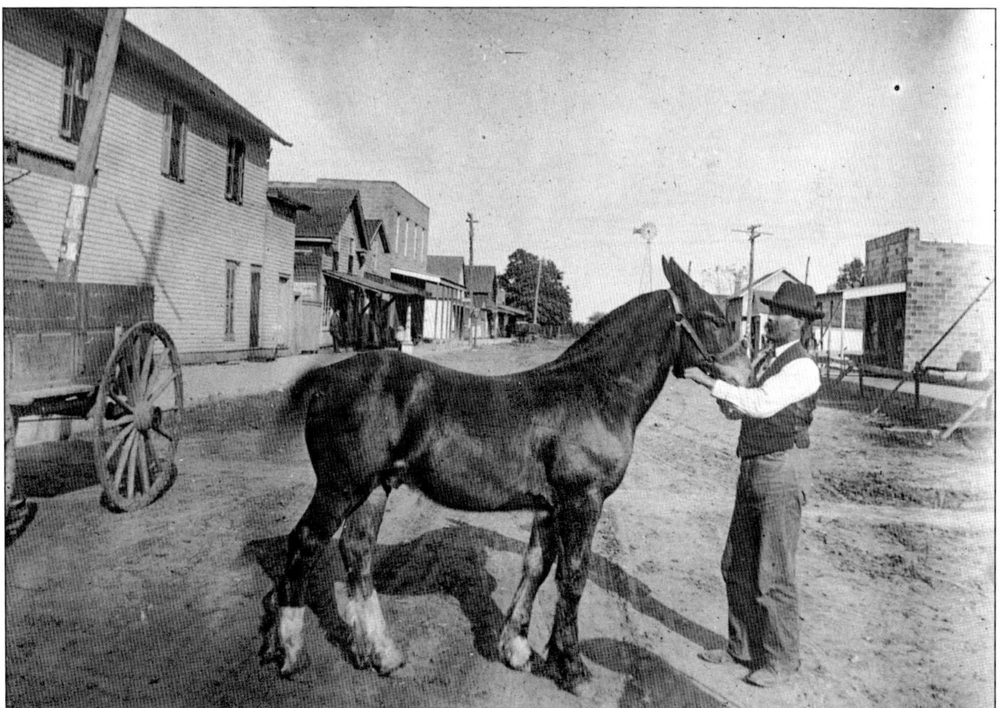

A man and horse stand at the west end of Main Street after 1909 but prior to when the high school was constructed in 1922 (near the background windmill). Buildings identified along the left side of the street are the Corner Café (forefront); Park's Grocery (the first flat-topped building, with four upstairs windows); Miller's Confectionary; and Farmers & Merchants Bank (the structure before the trees). (WVT.)

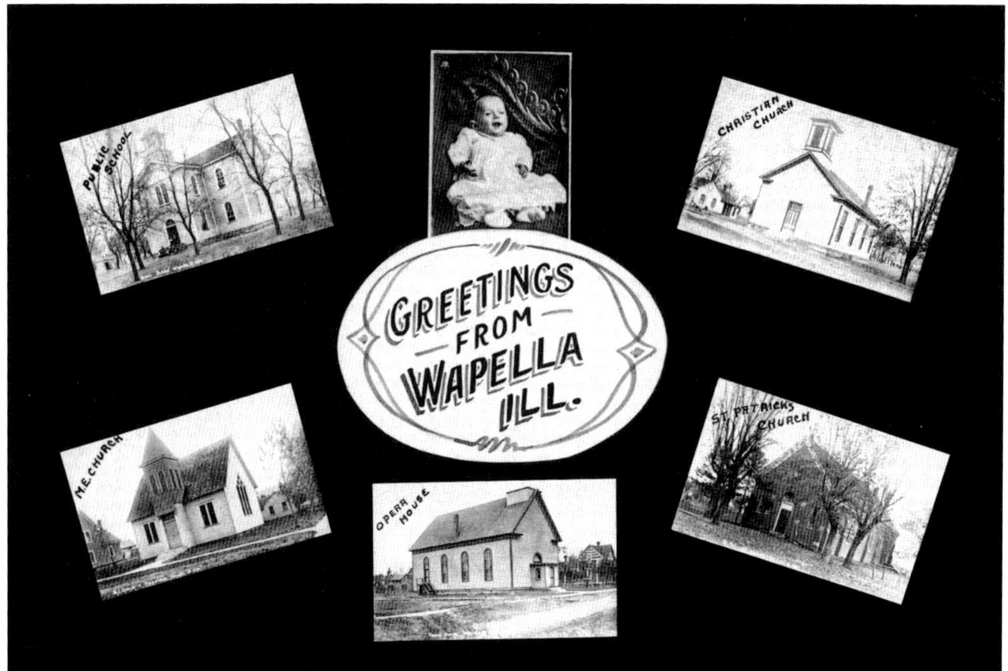

Built in 1868 in north Wapella, the school in this postcard (top left) educated children from grades one through eight plus two years of high school. A brick school replaced it in 1913. The frame Methodist church (bottom left), built in 1858, was destroyed by an 1891 tornado, rebuilt by 1893, and destroyed again during the 1968 tornado. The Christian church (top right) was built in 1868. (KD.)

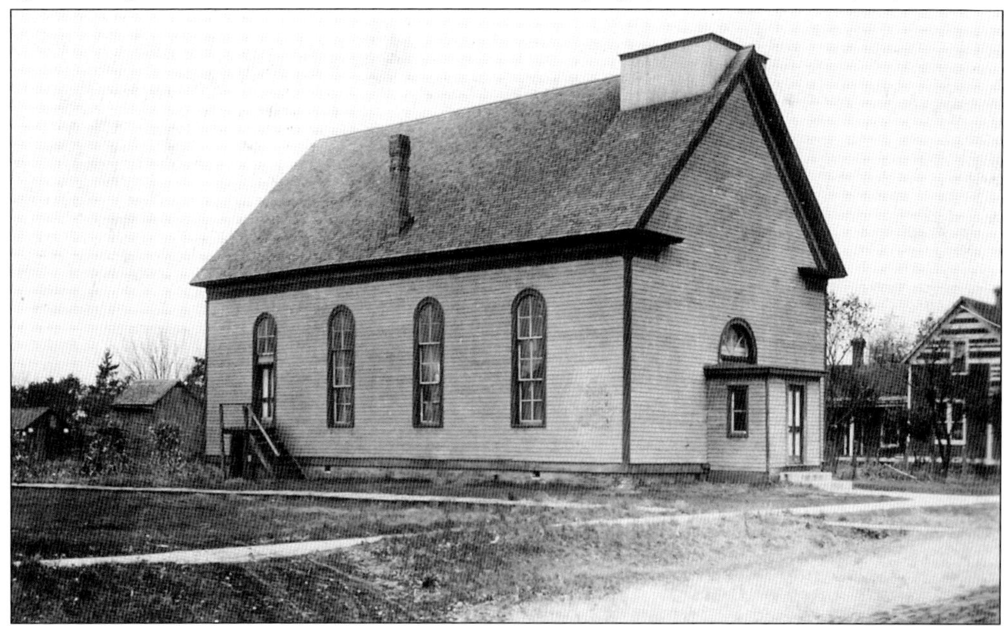

In June 1901, lightning entered the roof of the Alexander Opera House, hitting and splintering a piano leg before passing on to the cellar. Otherwise, damage was minimal. In 1906, the owner sold the structure for $600 to a Mr. Bell, who wanted to build a house there. It was eventually moved closer to the downtown area. Except for roof damage, it withstood the 1968 tornado. (VWPL.)

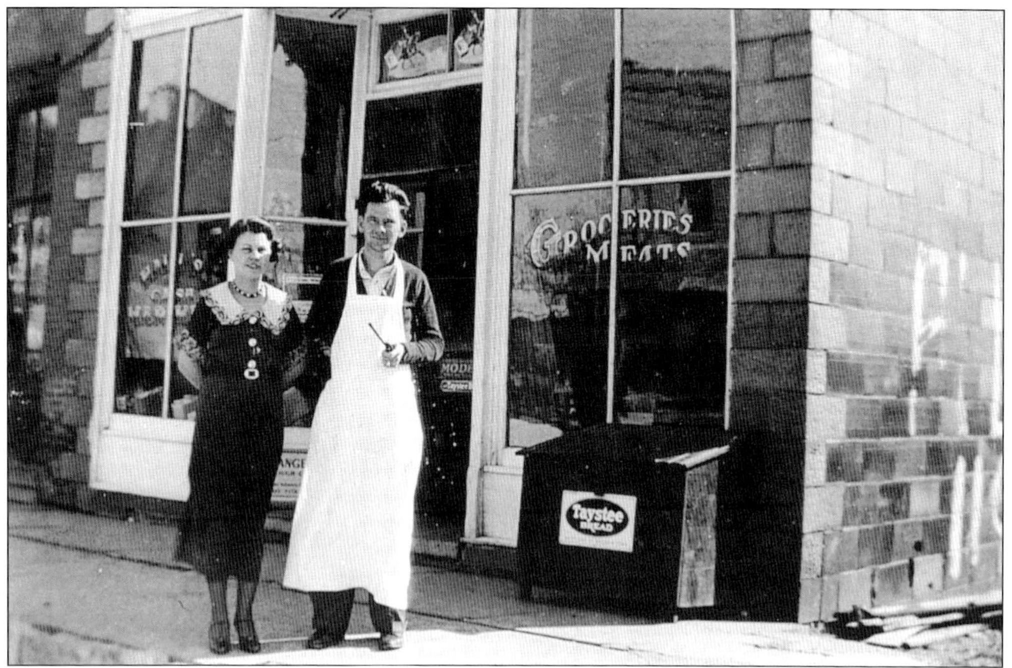

Two unidentified people stand in front of Miller's Café, immediately west of the Lighthall Hardware building, around the late 1940s–1950s. In the 1930s, when free movies were shown on the south side of Main Street, Miller's provided snacks. The Community Fire Protection District buildings at 315 West Main Street now occupy the former location of Miller's and Lighthall's. (WVT.)

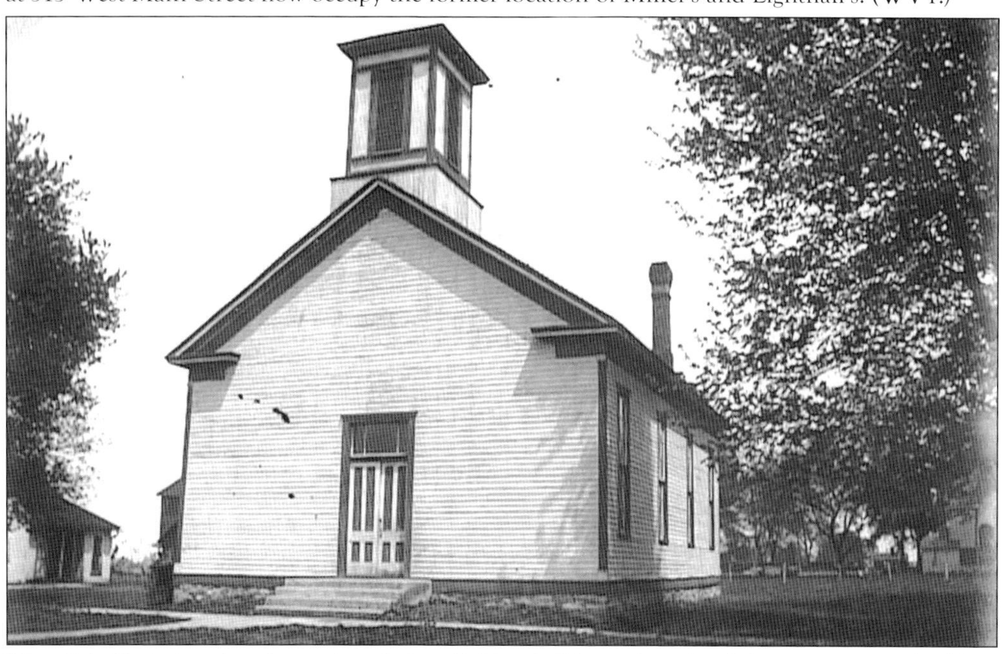

Wapella's Christian church was founded in 1867 with 30 members. In 1868, a permanent building was constructed on Locust Street, three blocks north of Main Street. By 1924, a parsonage had been added next to it. With membership increasing, a new structure was built at Poplar and Main Streets in 1948. Over the decades, more additions were made to the facilities. (KD.)

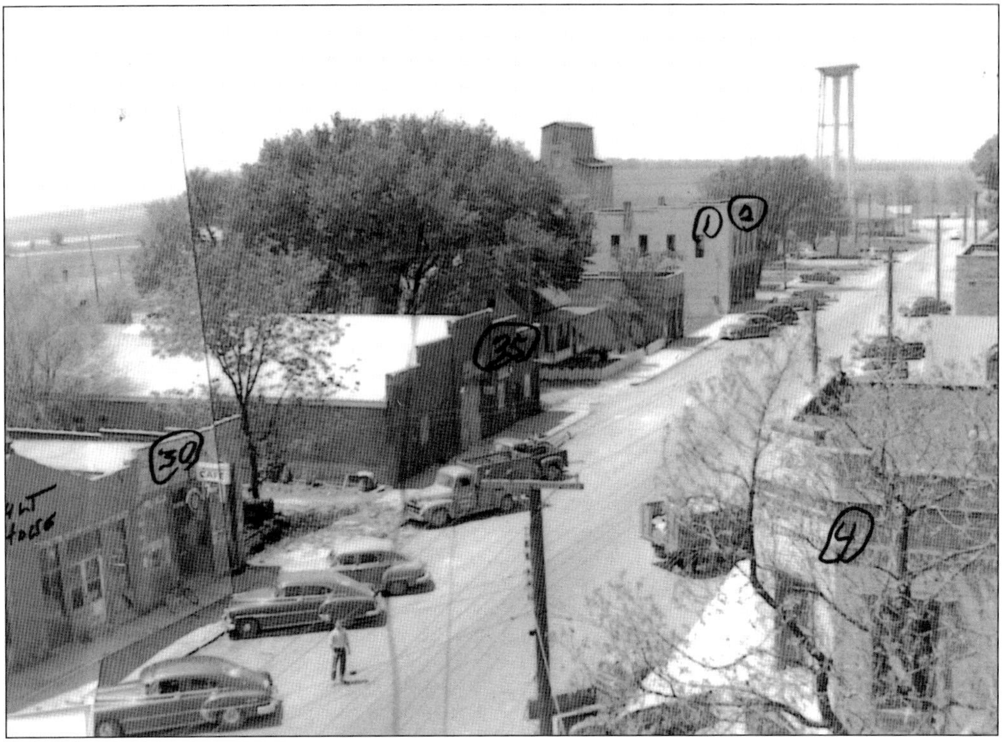

This photograph appears to have been taken around the 1950s. Lighthall Hardware (later Summers Hardware) is to the far left, across from number 4, the Farmers & Merchants Bank. Miller's Café is number 30. Number 35 is Canaday Brothers Garage, while Rabbit's Barber Shop is number 1. Built in 1884, Troxel Brothers grocery store is number 2, run by twin brothers Joe and Jay from 1937 until 1963. (WVT.)

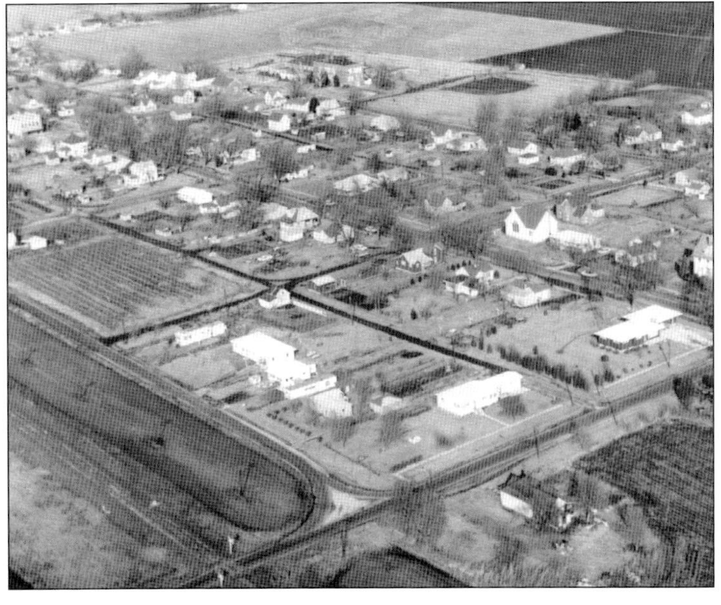

Wapella High School (now Wapella Park) stands in the center background surrounded by open fields in this undated aerial photograph. In 1994, the school closed and was annexed into the Clinton School District. The building was demolished soon after the last graduation ceremony. Two blocks west is the corner of Main and Locust Streets, home to the Farmers & Merchants Bank building. (WVT.)

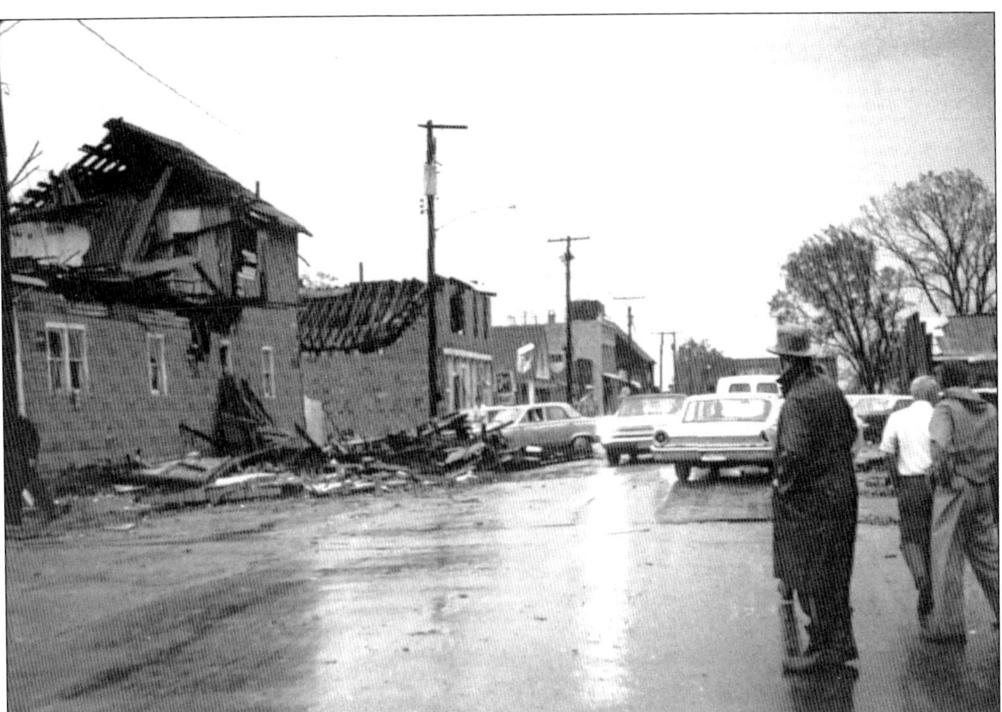

On May 15, 1968, a seven-mile-wide tornado slammed DeWitt County, followed by 10 inches of rain. Wapella was particularly affected, with almost every structure damaged and several destroyed. Two people died in Wapella and two near Farmer City, with 56 more injured countywide. Damages topped $10 million, equal to more than $72 million in today's costs. This photograph looks east down Main Street. (VWPL.)

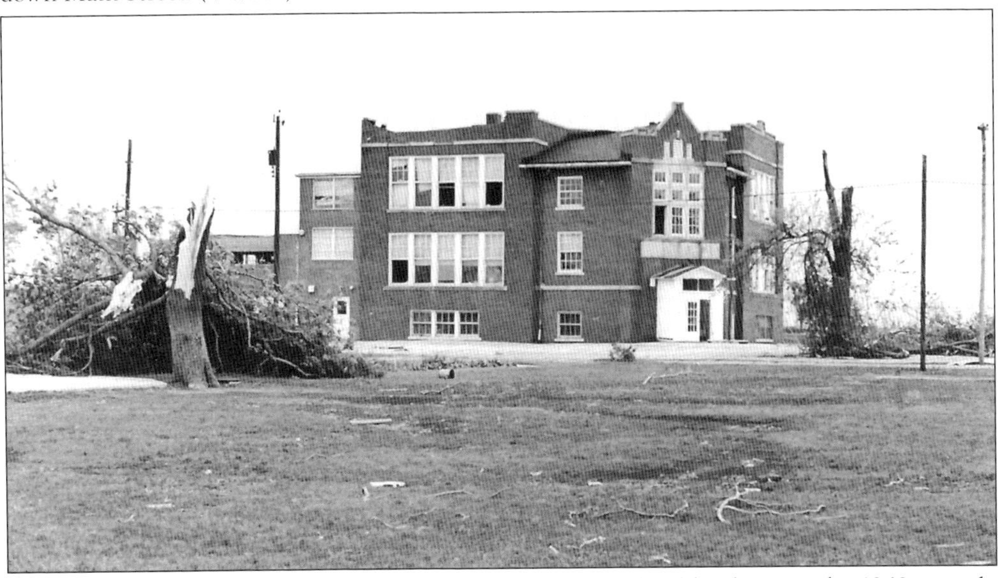

Wapella grade children were fortunate to have already left school by the time the 1968 tornado hit, or injuries in town might have been worse. Although it suffered damage, the grade school was not destroyed. The high school was utilized as a collection point for clothing and meals for the homeless. (VWPL.)

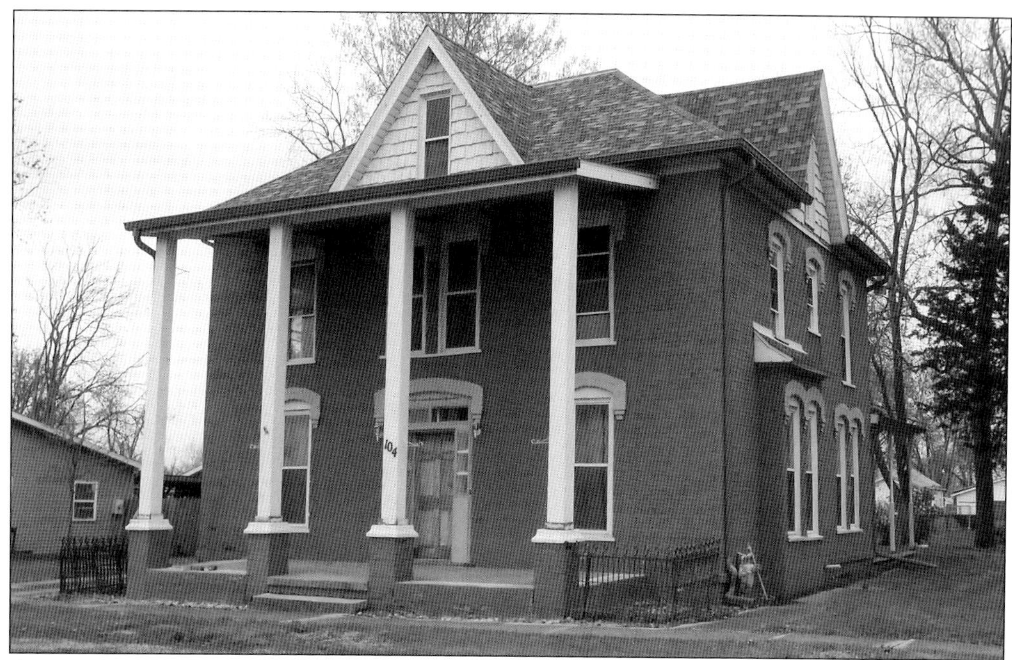

Anticipating that Wapella would be the Illinois Central Railroad's choice for a base of operations, a two-story brick hotel was constructed in 1854 at 104 North Oak Street. After the railroad chose Clinton instead, the Wapella Hotel was used as a general freight house and ticket house. By the 1890s, it became a hotel again. In 1930, Henry Woollen purchased the property from his parents. (AC.)

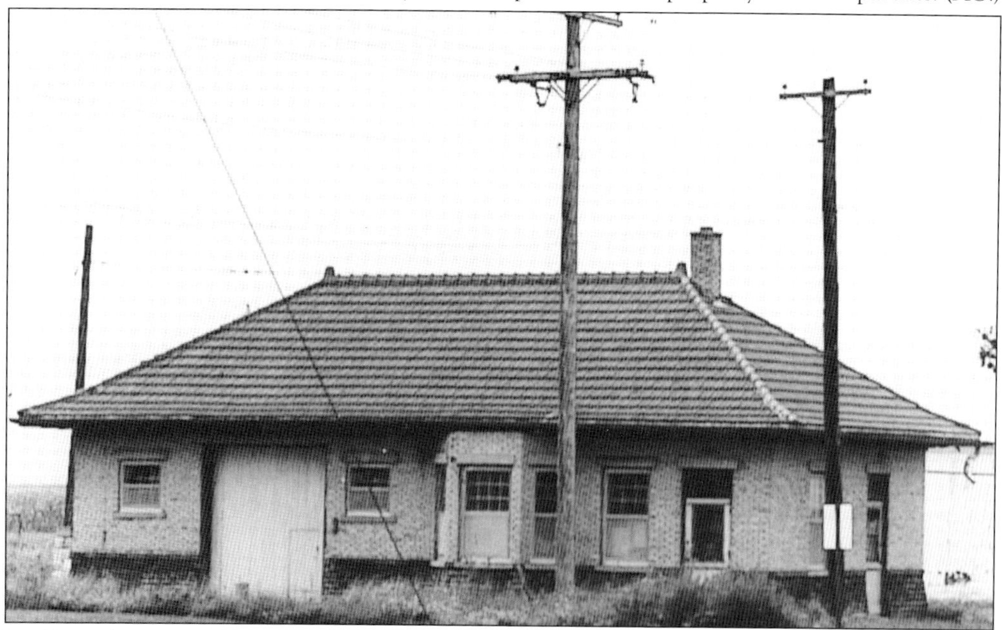

In 1901, the DeWitt Board of Supervisors transacted a 20-year franchise with the Interurban Electrical Railway Company to run an electric railway from Bloomington to Decatur. Stops between Bloomington and Clinton included Hendrix, Randolph, Heyworth, Earls, Bucks, Carle Springs, Wapella, and Ducey. This undated photograph shows Wapella's abandoned interurban station prior to its 2003 demolition and replacement by a gas station. (WVT.)

Six

Kenney and Hallsville

Early Tunbridge Township families included the Butlers, Kenneys, Coppenbargers, Randolphs, Halls, and Fruits. In 1828, a few years after Jacob Coppenbarger arrived and filed the first land entry, his son John joined with blacksmith Jack Henderson to make a set of millstones to be used on the Coppenbarger farm. The stones currently stand outside the Kenney Heritage Museum.

In 1871, the year after the Illinois Central Railroad came to the area, John and Moses Kenney platted the 40-acre town on Kenney family property. They chose to name the town Kenney to honor their father. Incorporated in 1875, the town's initial businesses included a grocery, blacksmith, doctor, and newspaper, the *Kenney Gazette*.

As the town grew, so did fire possibilities. One fire in the business district in 1884 consumed many of the wooden structures. Four years later, after 37 business buildings and several homes were in ashes from a worse fire, brick became the required construction material.

Kenney's population peaked with 800 residents in 1910.

Businesses comprising the first town of Hallsville included general stores, a wagon shop, a school, a blacksmith, at least one doctor, and Old Union Church and Cemetery. The first Old Union Church, a log chapel built in 1838, was moved in 1915 to Kenney, whereupon a new one was constructed. The cemetery is just south of Bungtown Road (an area nickname), several miles north of Kenney, running west from Hallsville Road.

Not wanting to be sidelined when the Illinois Central Railroad ran tracks two miles to the north of the village instead of through it, residents platted a new village in 1871 immediately north in Barnett Township. As noted in an 1872 newspaper, "The town of Hallsville . . . is being removed. Some of the people are moving their houses and goods to the railroad station on the Havana Road, about a mile distant and others are removing to Beason." Sadly, in 1924, most Hallsville business structures were destroyed by fire.

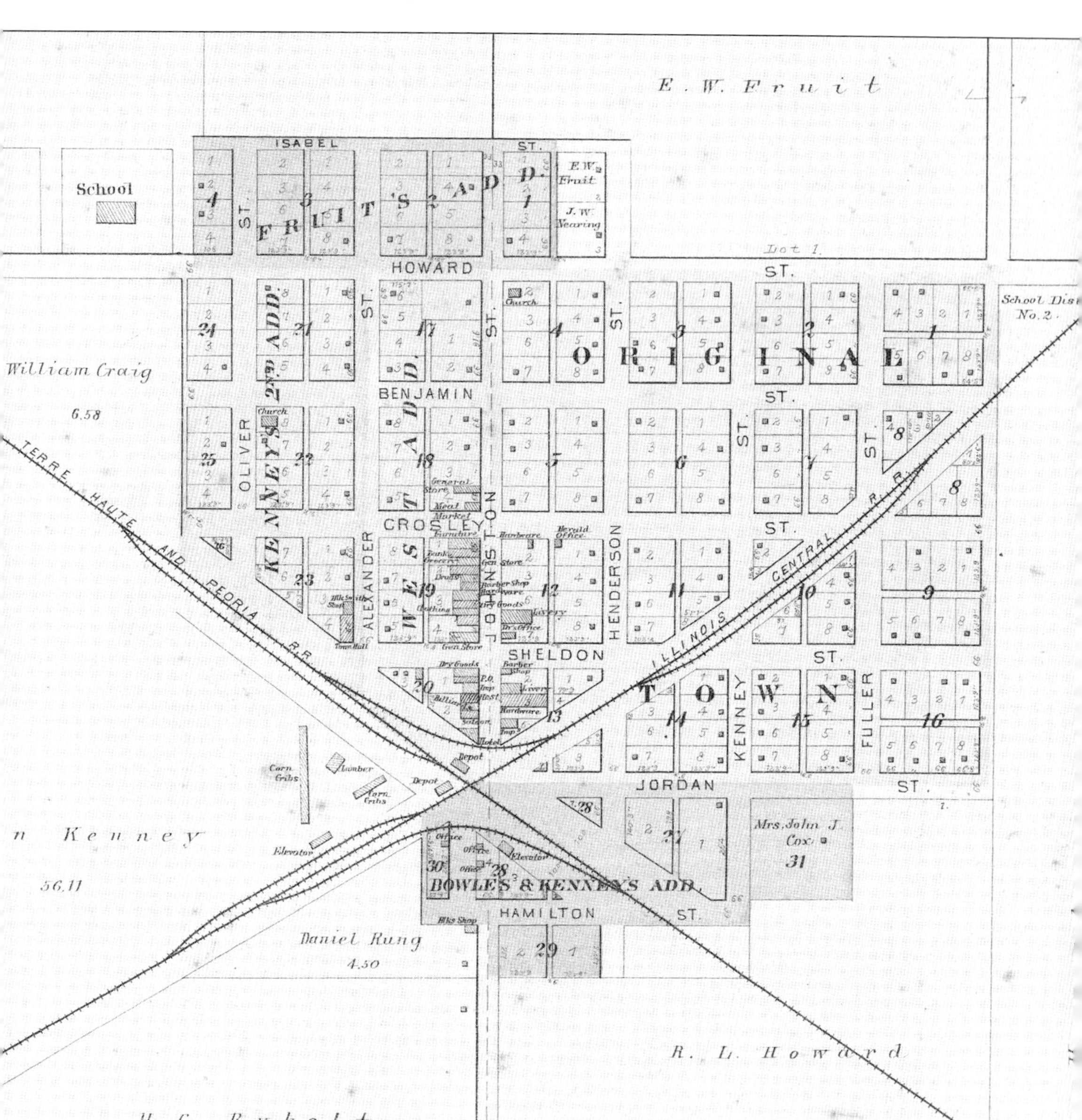

In September 1871, after a rail line crossed diagonally through 40 acres of Kenney family land, leaving two three-cornered tracts, the acres were platted into 16 lots (see the "Original Town" area). Businesses and residences soon sprang up. This close-up view from Kenney's 1894 plat shows block 19 comprising the main business area around Johnston Street, from Crosley Street on the north to the depot on the south. After fires in 1884 and 1888 crippled the town's business section and left some residents homeless, only brick construction was allowed. The town hall sits across the street from the tracks on the southwest corner of Alexander Street. A blacksmith shop was located just north of the town hall. The current Kenney Heritage Museum occupies a spot formerly used by a furniture store, bank, and grocer. Farther south were a pharmacy, clothing store, and general store. (LOCGM.)

Born in Kentucky to James and Amelia Kenney, town founder Moses Kenney (1822–1875) married Martha Walker (1828–1853) in 1850. In 1851, their daughter Laura was born in a home where the Kenney United Methodist Church now stands. She married Joseph Martin Bowles, grandson of Rev. Hugh Bowles, another early area pioneer. Moses Kenney is buried near Martha in Tunbridge Cemetery. (The plaque shown has an incorrect birth year.) (AC.)

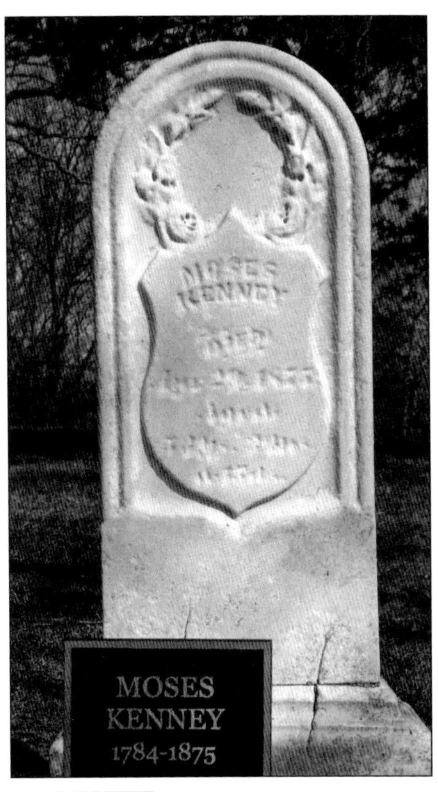

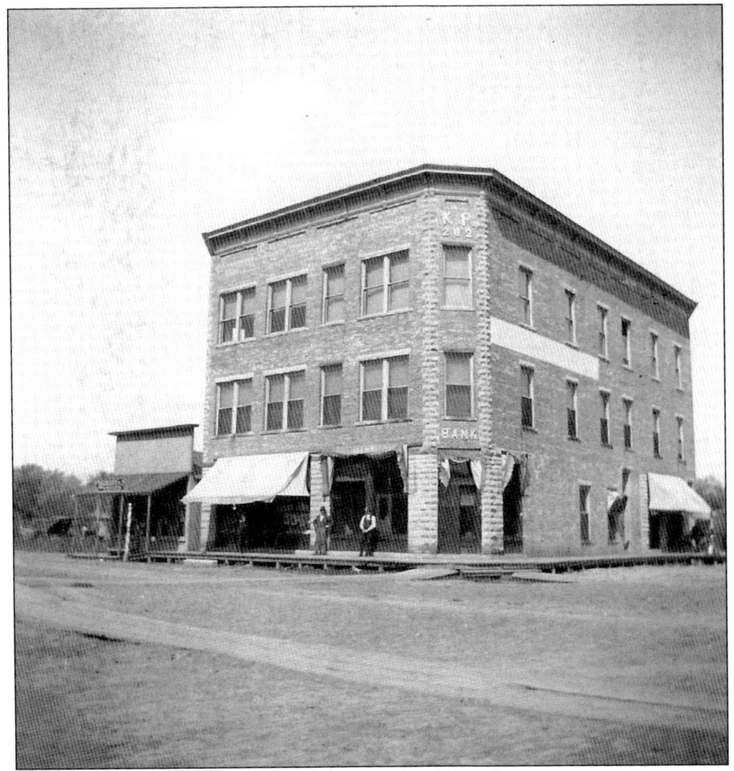

The Bank of Kenney (nicknamed "Suttle's Bank"), founded in 1890 by Henry Clay Suttle and Leonard Kirby Scroggin (Suttle's father-in-law), is photographed to the right of a laundry. In December 1912, the bank became the Farmers State Bank. It merged in 1918 with People's Bank (diagonally across the street), founded in 1898 by G.K. Ingham and Richard Snell. The current fire department occupies the bank's location. (KHAM.)

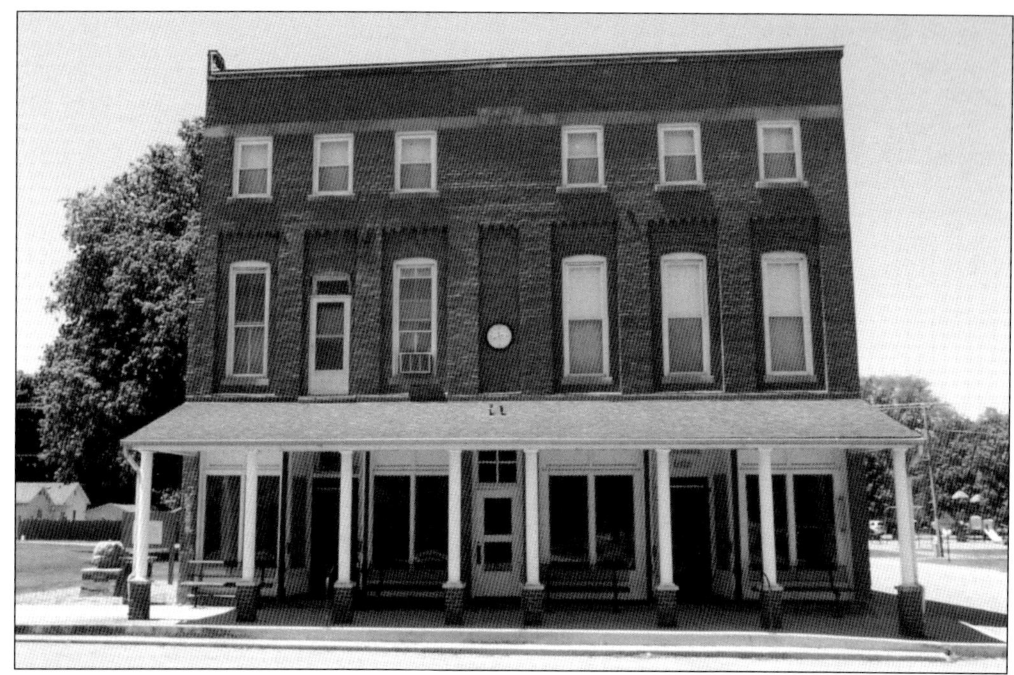

The Kenney Community Center capstone displays "I.O.O.F.," the abbreviation for the Independent Order of Odd Fellows lodge. Chartered in 1874, Lodge 557 met in various locations until 1891, when James Kenney and "Shorty" Wells constructed what became the Odd Fellows' Corner, originally a two-story building. In 1893, the lodge purchased it, adding the adjoining building and a third story to both. (AC.)

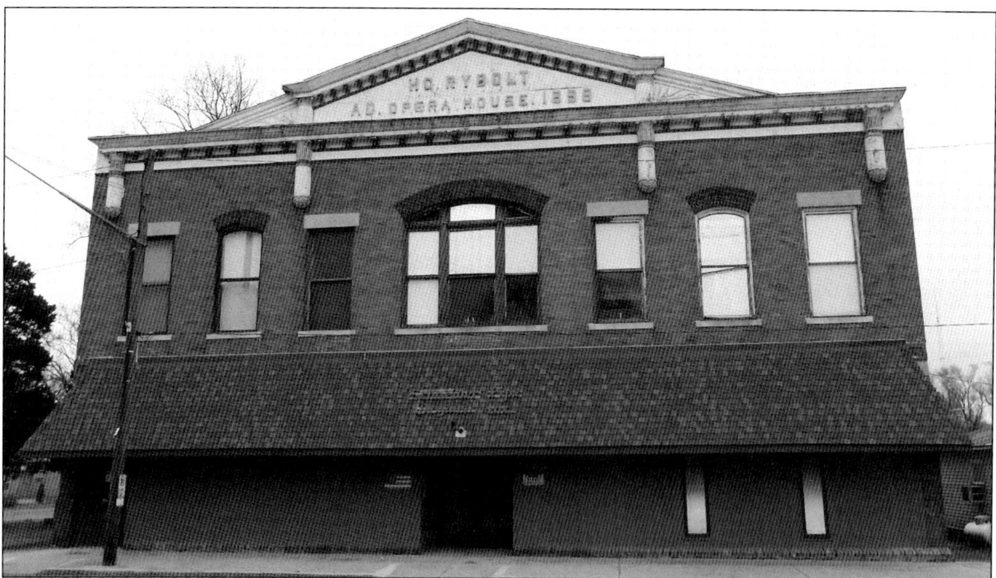

Built in 1898, H.C. Rybolt's Opera House at various times offered musical events, plays, talent shows, and even roller skating. The post office and grade school classes were once located there. In 1907, the Fair Store moved into the building's west portion. After 1940, the building housed the Gratian pipe organ factory and later Schneider Pipe Organs Inc. The owner, Richard Schneider, died in 2023. (AC.)

Constructed over the summer of 1898, Henry Suttle's store was the second building north of the northwest corner of Johnston and Sheldon Streets. In 1907, a pool room occupied part of it, and it was later a restaurant. By the 1920 census, the store was operated by his brother Robert Filmore Suttle and sold dry goods, shoes, and groceries. (VWPL.)

Kenney's Captain Turner Band, in white-trimmed dark blue uniforms, furnished the music for local events starting in the late 1890s and through much of the 1930s. Their music entertained attendees at most of the county's Old Settler Reunions, usually held at Pastime Park. In addition to recreational gatherings and weekly open-air concerts, the band of about 20 men also played at funerals. (KHAM.)

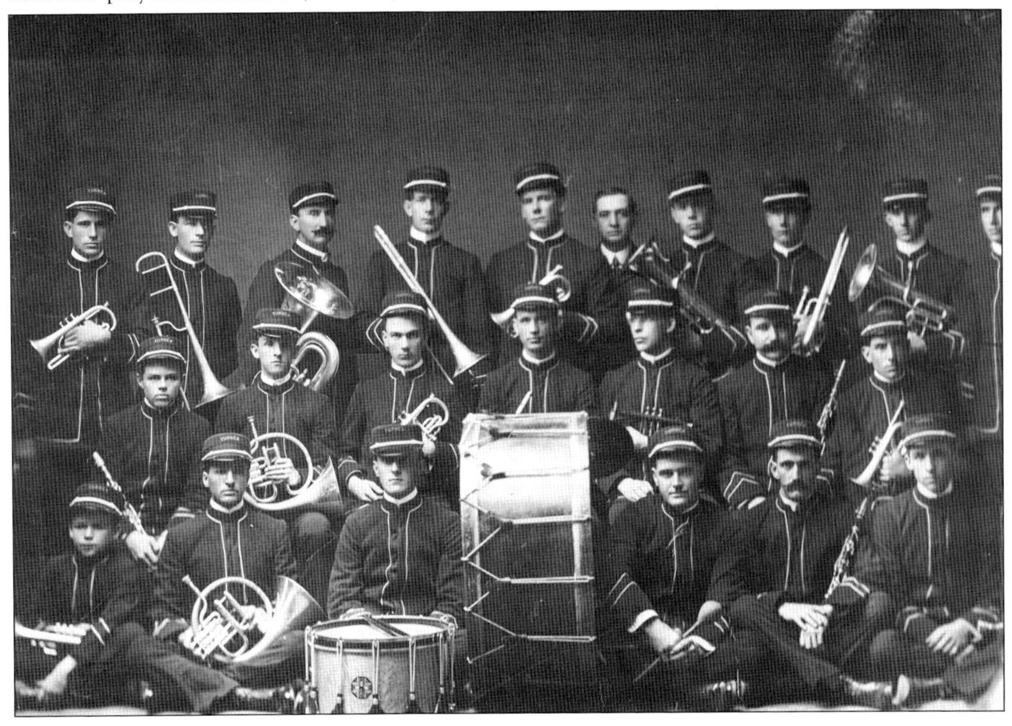

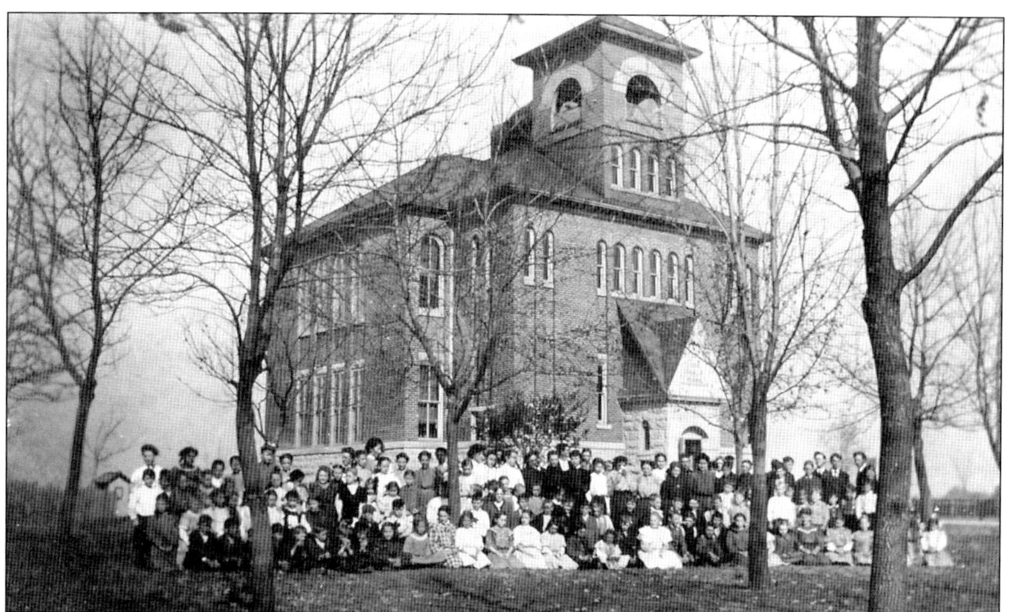

After Kenney's 1880s grade school was destroyed by a January 1894 fire, the replacement on Howard Street was ready by the year's end. Photographed around 1900, the school's eight grades filled four classrooms. In 1952, the Stoutenborough School was moved there from near Rowell to relieve overcrowding. When the grade school closed in the 1950s and utilized the high school, it sold at auction in January 1960 for $1,550. (AC.)

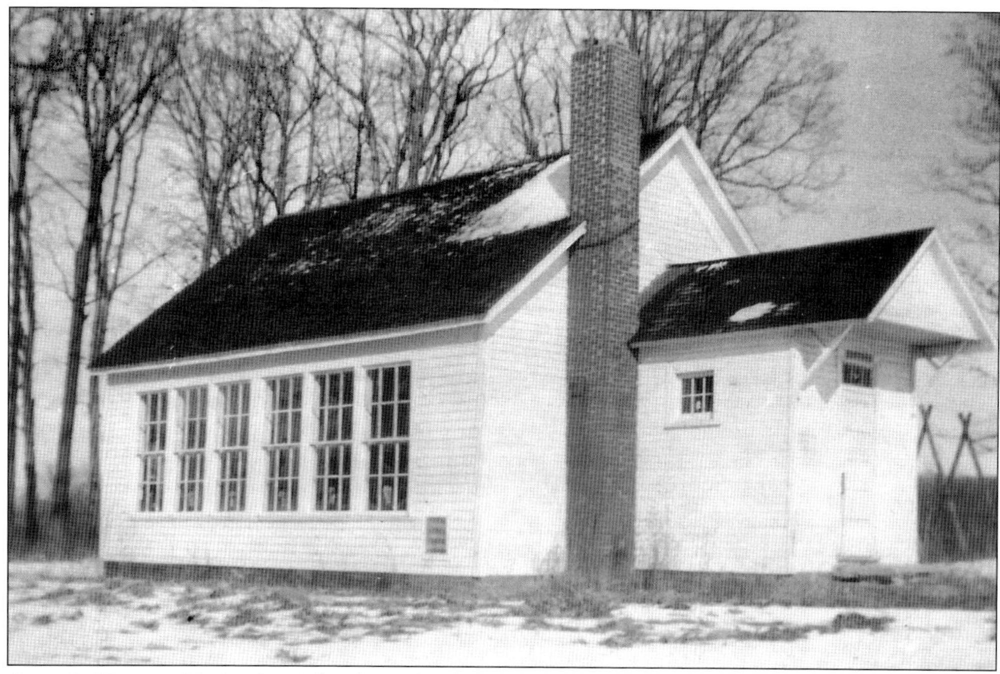

Outside Kenney, Tunbridge School taught children from at least the 1870s until its 1949 closure. By that time, its eight grades had an enrollment of 14 students. Sold at public auction in 1950, it was moved to A.A. Richey's Nob Hill Pony Farm, about four miles west of Clinton on Route 54, where it was used as a tenant house. (VWPL.)

In 1838, Jesse Stout built a water mill along Salt Creek, two miles northeast of Kenney and six miles southwest of Clinton. Nearby was the site of an Indian trading post, the Tunbridge Post Office, and the former community of Franklin. After it fell into disrepair, around 1866, new owner John Morrison rebuilt Tunbridge "Pastime" Mill. In the 1920s, it was finally demolished. (DCM.)

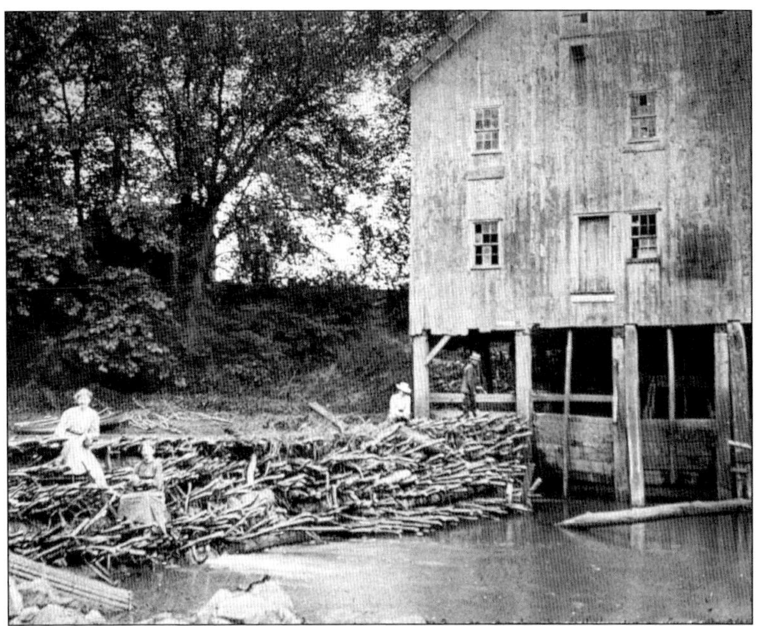

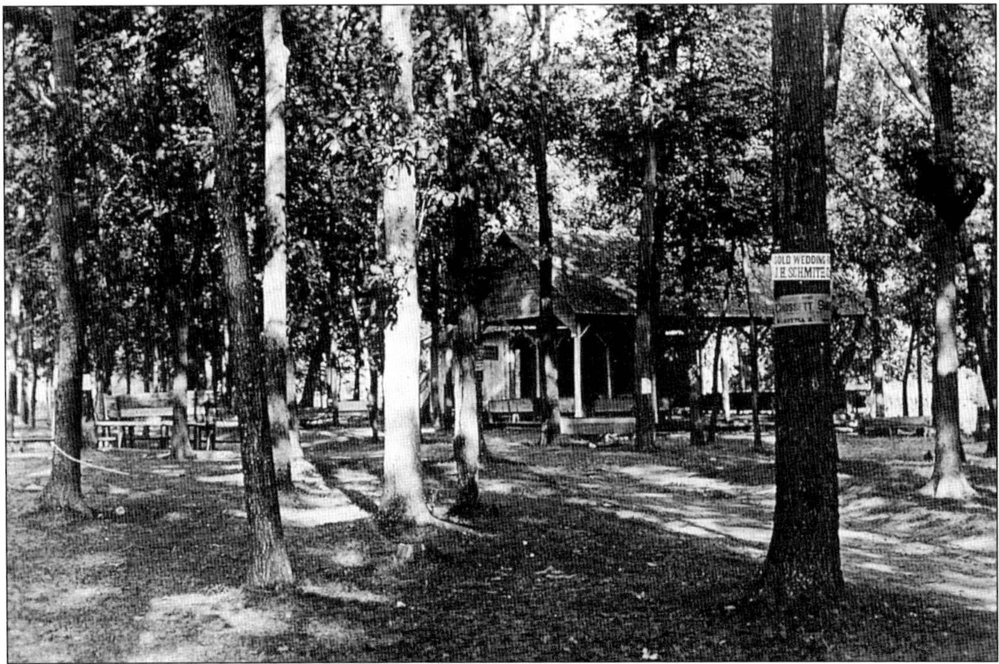

John Morrison built Pastime Park across the creek from his mill by the 1880s. It included picnic huts, a bandstand, a bathing beach, and a dance pavilion, along with a steam-propelled boat called *Wenona* that took passengers upstream for a nickel. The boat would then float back on the creek's current. Starting in August 1887, Old Settler Reunions began gathering there. (VWPL.)

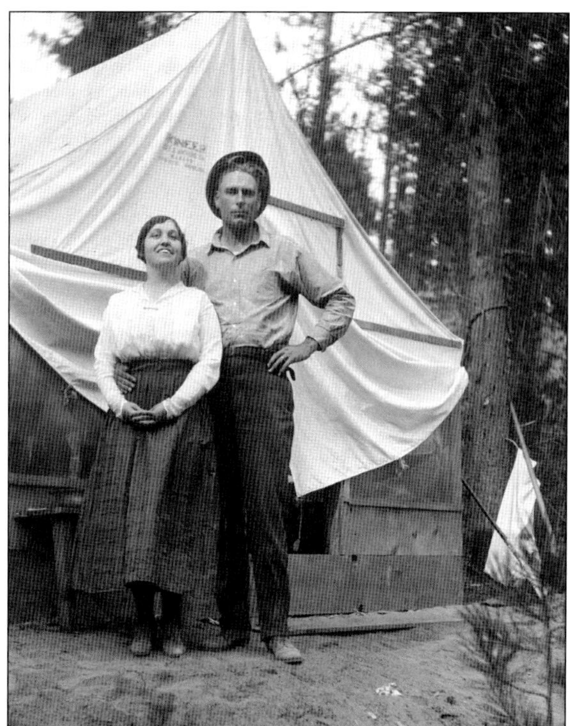

Harry Morrison (1885–1971), John Morrison's grandson, became interested in construction after watching a bridge being built over Salt Creek. In 1912, he cofounded the Morrison-Knudsen Company, constructing such major projects as the Hoover Dam, the San Francisco–Oakland Bay Bridge, the Trans-Alaska Pipeline, and more. Photographed here with his wife, Ann, he was later on the May 3, 1954, cover of *Time* magazine after having changed "the face of the earth." (H-AMP.)

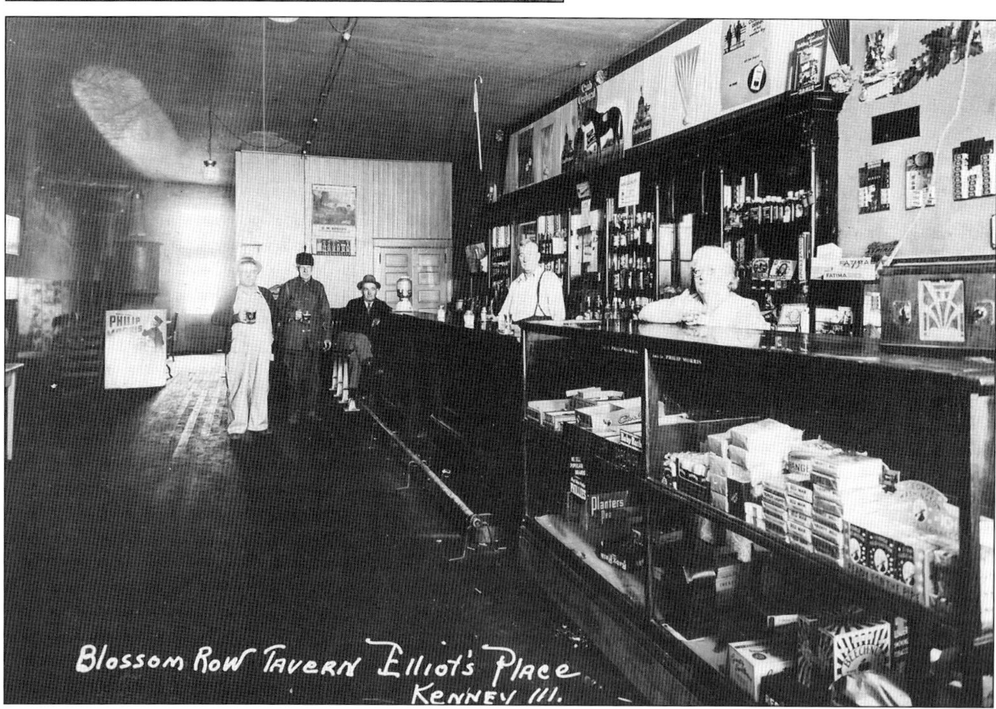

In the 1930s, James A. Elliott (sometimes called "A.J.") and his wife, Dora May, opened a lunchroom in Kenney. Here, they stand behind the counter of Elliott's Tavern while two customers stand with beer-filled mugs. The Elliotts sold snacks, tobacco, and cigarettes. Elliott also ran a service station during the 1930s. (KHAM.)

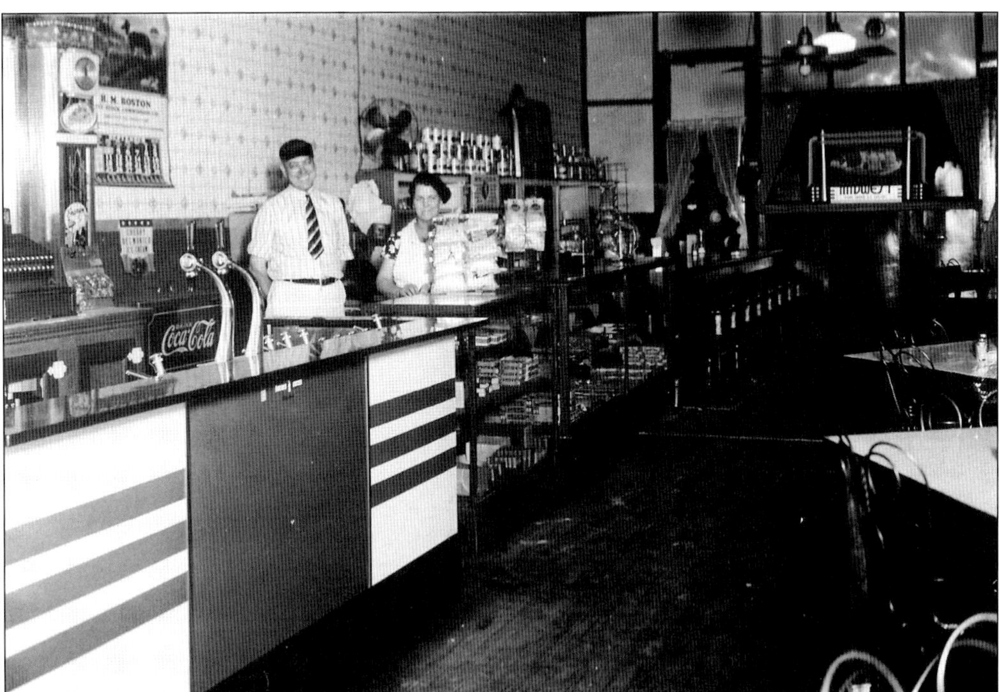

Tracy and Essie Isaac opened Isaac's Café in the late 1920s, sold it in 1937, and began selling Chryslers and Plymouths in Clinton. He eventually returned to running cafés again. Their son Chesley (1917–2005) received a Purple Heart for valor at Pearl Harbor during the December 7, 1941, attack. In the 1960s, Chesley Isaac served on Pres. Lyndon Johnson's Air Force One. (KHAM.)

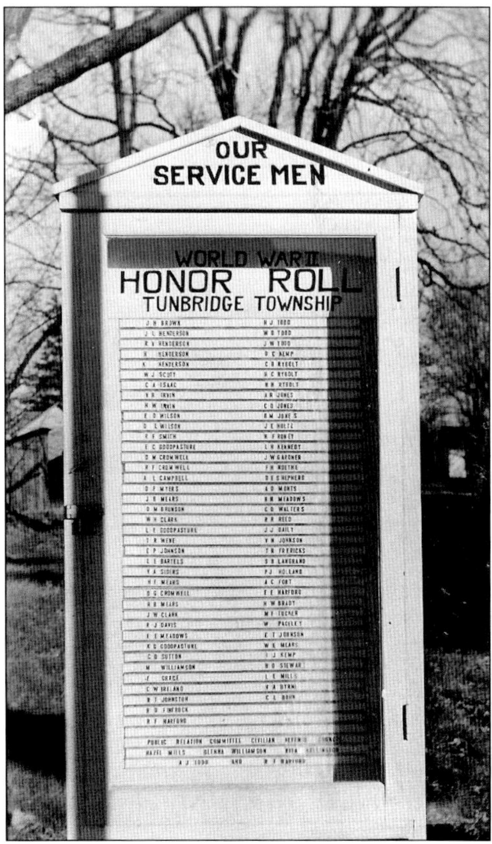

In August 1942, Tunbridge Township erected a flagpole and honor roll monument next to Rybolt's Opera House listing the township's World War II service men. Of the 76 soldiers listed in this photograph, the seventh name in the left column is Chesley Isaac, wounded at Pearl Harbor, son of Tracy and Essie Isaac of Isaac's Café. A new monument sits there now with names from additional wars. (VWPL.)

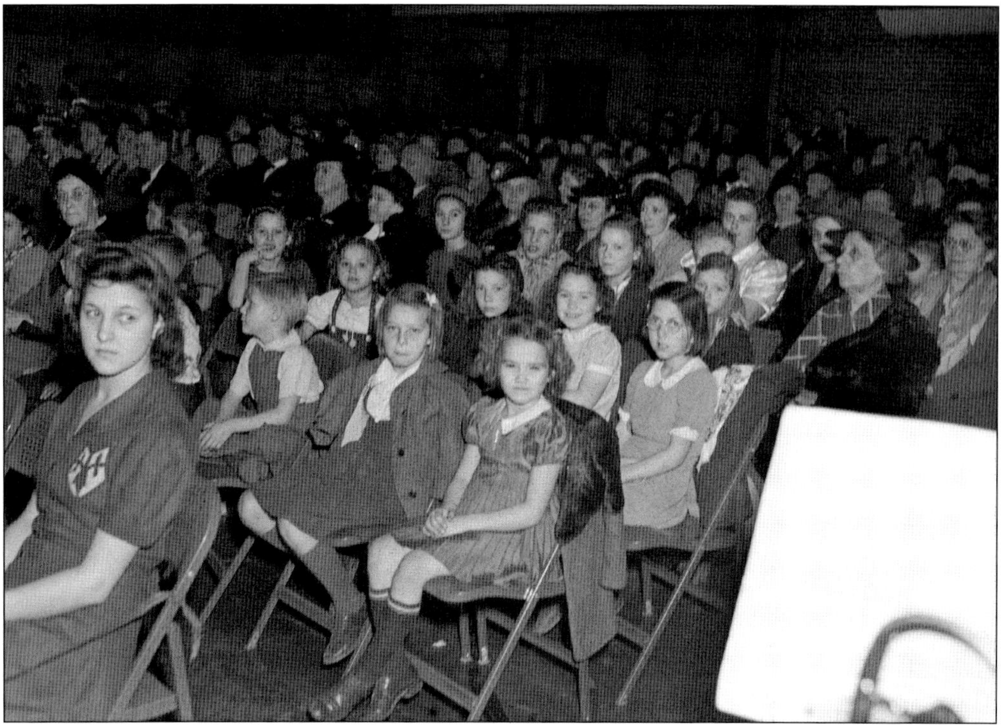

In November 1942, Kenney High School held an assembly to honor Kenney's 100 percent participation in the World War II Victory-Home campaign, the country's first community to achieve this distinction. Nationwide attention noted Kenney's efforts. The village of 100 homes had purchased $100,000 in war bonds, saved fat for making munitions, and salvaged vital goods for the war effort. (MCMH.)

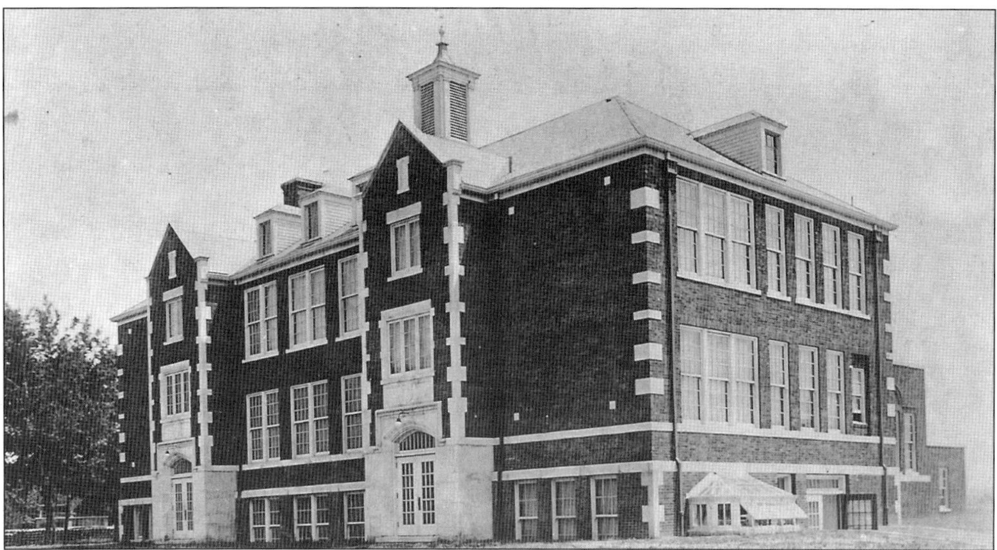

Kenney's three-year high school classes began in 1906, first taught at Rybolt's Opera House. After the new four-year high school on Johnston Street (pictured) opened in 1921, thirteen seniors graduated in 1922. The last graduation occurred in 1955 before the school was annexed into the Clinton School District. The building functioned as a junior high and grade school through 1972 before being purchased that year by a private owner. (KA.)

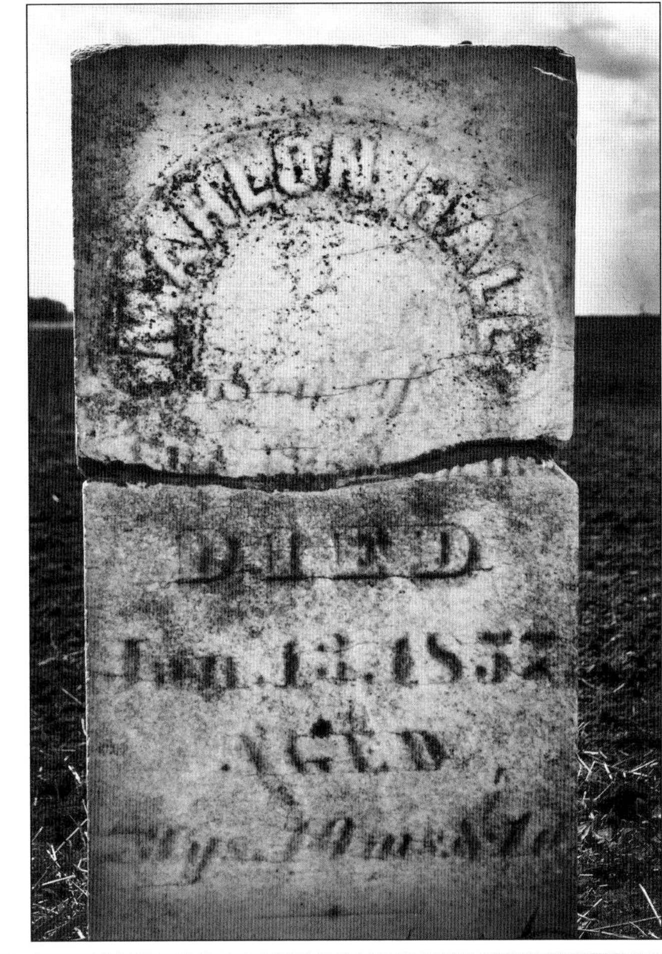

After arriving from Kentucky in 1830, Mahlon Hall (1777–1857) settled in what is now Barnett Township, buying land from the area's first settler, Elisha Butler. He housed the post office, and in 1834, he built Hall Subscription School, the first school west of Clinton and the county's third. His son Darius was the teacher. By 1839, Mahlon Hall was DeWitt County's largest landholder with 1,200 acres. (AC.)

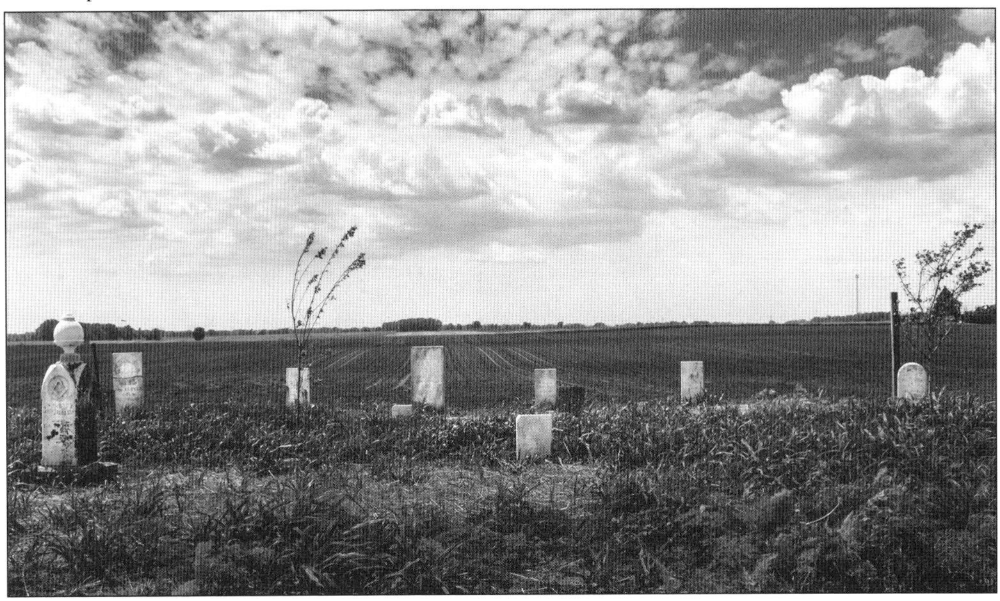

In 1832, Mahlon Hall's daughter Eliza Amos Hall married Jefferson McCarty Hildreth. The following year, Eliza gave birth to triplets. Only living a few hours, the triplets were the first to be buried on land that Hall had set aside that year for a graveyard. Hall Cemetery, currently on private land, is the oldest interment spot in the township's section 33. (AC.)

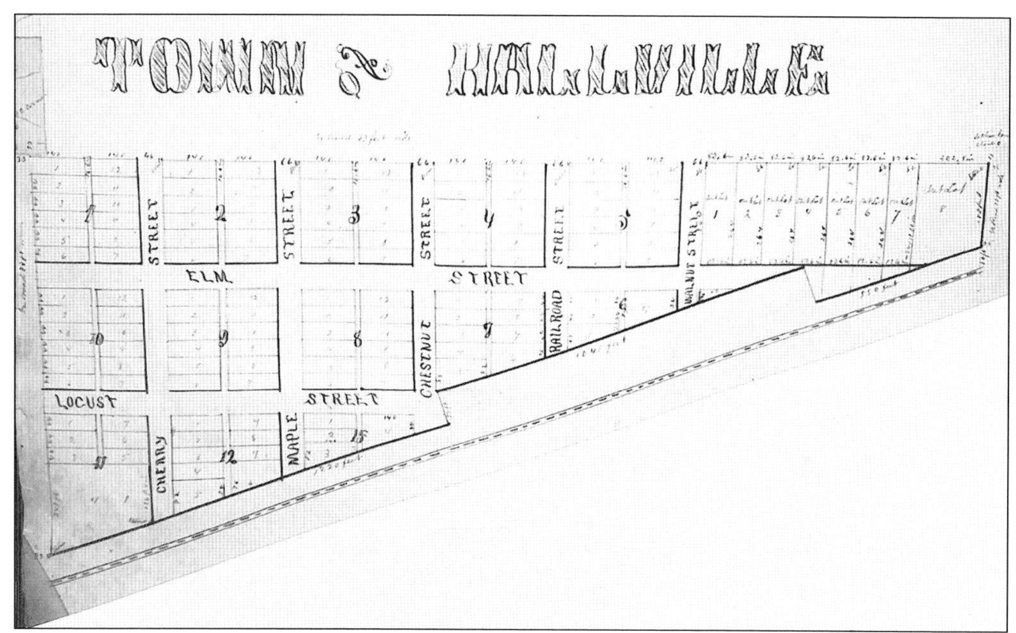

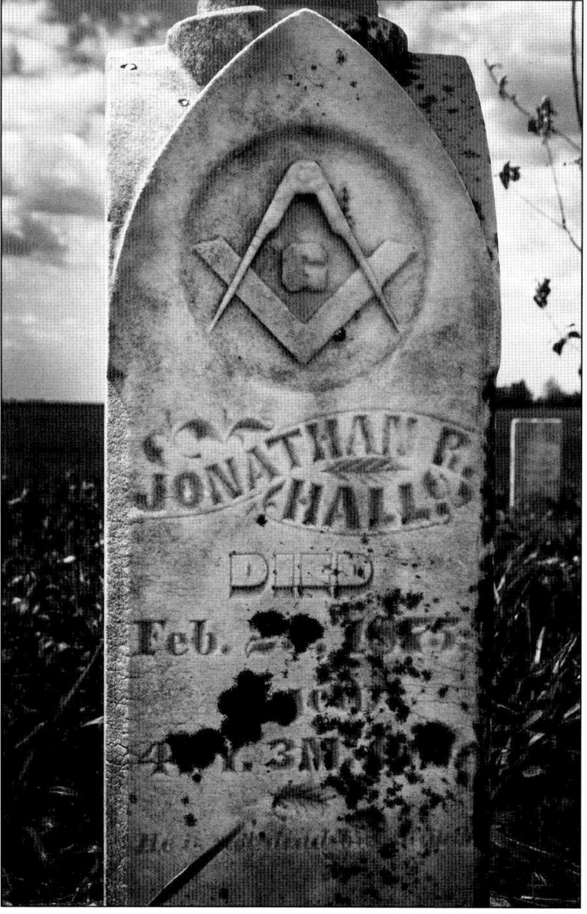

The plat for the town of Hallsville, an unincorporated area in Barnett Township, was entered by Jonathan R. and Eliza E. Hall on June 20, 1873. Some sources say the original name of the town was Dunham, but the plat was entered as Hallville, with the *s* to make it Hallsville appearing in the plat narrative. Many Halls are buried in Hall Cemetery. (DCGS.)

Jonathan R. Hall (1827–1875), son of Mahlon and Hannah Hall, befriended Abraham Lincoln during Lincoln's time as a circuit lawyer, frequently offering the future president a place to stay. From 1869 until 1873, Hall was a DeWitt County judge. In 1871, during his time as judge, he laid out the town of Hallsville. He is buried in Hall Cemetery. (AC.)

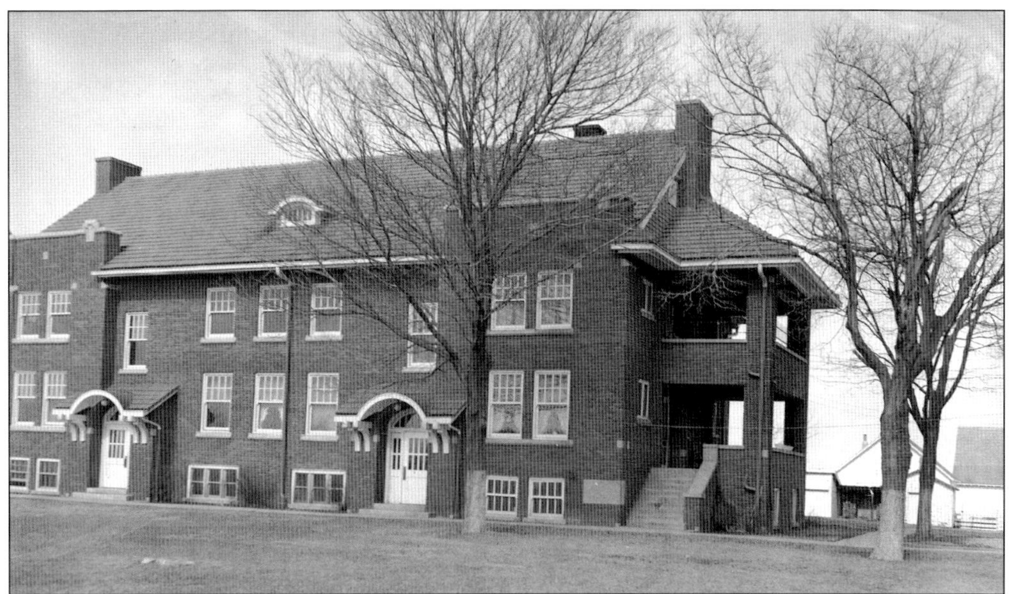

This 1937 photograph shows the two-story brick dormitory that replaced Hallsville's earlier county poor farm. Completed in 1915, the dormitory was located on the north side of Route 10 near Hallsville Road. Its cornerstone stands at the intersection of Route 10 and McClimans Road. In 1946, the enterprise became a nursing home with a maximum of 42 patients who, in 1961, were charged approximately $128 per month. (MCMH.)

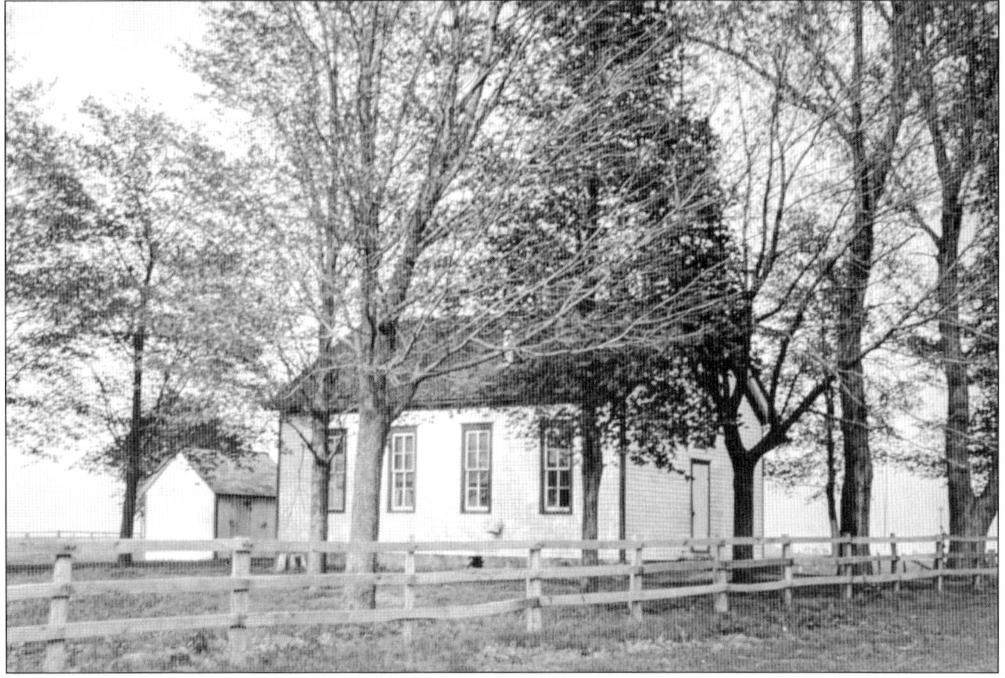

An unusual theft occurred in 1937 when the lightning rods were stolen from Hallsville's Central School. Five years later, Tunbridge Township announced that Central and Vance Schools would not open that year. In 1949, area newcomers Paul and Vera Lecouris purchased the former Central School and one-acre property. They had the building remodeled into a five-room bungalow. (DCM.)

Discover Thousands of Local History Books Featuring Millions of Vintage Images

Arcadia Publishing, the leading local history publisher in the United States, is committed to making history accessible and meaningful through publishing books that celebrate and preserve the heritage of America's people and places.

Find more books like this at
www.arcadiapublishing.com

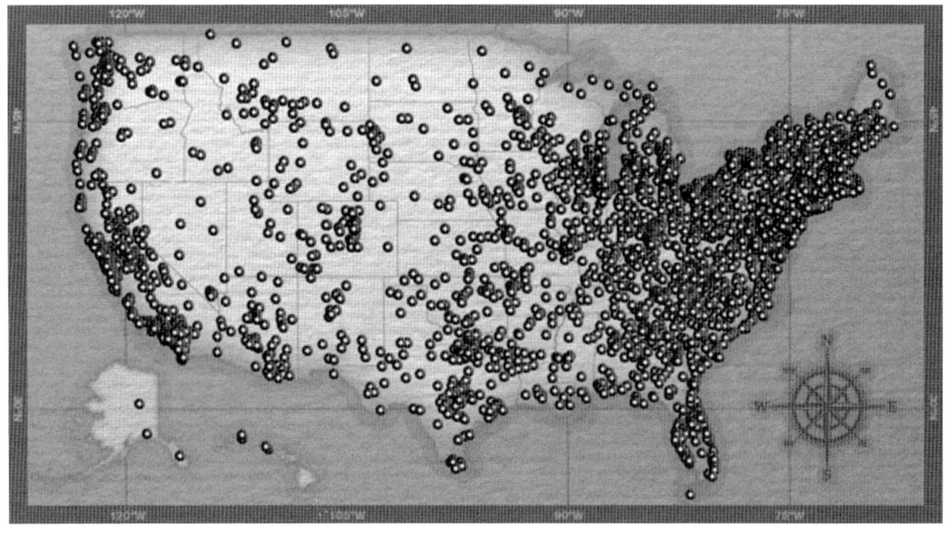

Search for your hometown history, your old stomping grounds, and even your favorite sports team.

Consistent with our mission to preserve history on a local level, this book was printed in South Carolina on American-made paper and manufactured entirely in the United States. Products carrying the accredited Forest Stewardship Council (FSC) label are printed on 100 percent FSC-certified paper.

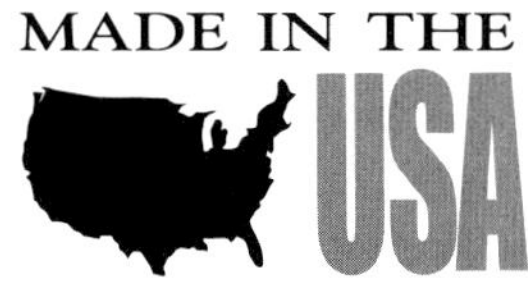